The Future of Philanthropy

Economics, Ethics, and Management

SUSAN U. RAYMOND, Ph.D.

WILEY

John Wiley & Sons, Inc.

Copyright © 2004 by John Wiley & Sons, Inc. All rights reserved.

Published by John Wiley & Sons, Inc., Hoboken, New Jersey
Published simultaneously in Canada

For general information on our other products and services, or technical support, please contact our Customer Care Department within the United States at 800-762-2974, outside the United States at 317-572-3993 or fax 317-572-4002.

Wiley also publishes its books in a variety of electronic formats. Some content that appears in print may not be available in electronic books.

For more information about Wiley products, visit our web site at www.wiley.com.

Library of Congress Cataloging-in-Publication Data:
Raymond, Susan Ueber.
  The future of philanthropy : economics, ethics, and management / Susan U. Raymond.
    p. cm.
  ISBN 0-471-63855-2 (cloth : alk. paper)
  1. Nonprofit organizations. I. Title.
HD2769.15 .R39 2004
362.7—dc22
                                    2003021759

Printed in the United States of America.

10 9 8 7 6 5 4 3 2 1

For Rich,
whose patience with this process was endless;
Jenny,
whose fact-checking and red pen were irreplaceable;
and Colin, Nate, and Becca.

About the Author

Susan Raymond is Managing Director of Research, Evaluation, and Strategic Planning for Changing Our World, Inc. She has extensive experience in research, analysis, and planning, most recently with the prestigious New York Academy of Sciences. Prior to this, Dr. Raymond was a project officer at the World Bank and a consultant to the U.S. State Department and to various private organizations, including the Carnegie Corporation, specializing in healthcare and international economic research. Dr. Raymond serves as Chief Analyst for OnPhilanthropy.com, Changing Our World's media division and a global resource for nonprofit professionals. She writes regularly for CW's e-publications, including *Observations in Philanthropy* and *Inside Corporate Philanthropy*. She has written for many publications, particularly in the areas of economics, healthcare, and corporate responsibility, including: "Foreign Assistance in an Aging World," *Foreign Affairs,* March 2003; *Medical Education Meets the Marketplace* (editor and contributor), New York Academy of Sciences, 2002; "Global Cooperation in Science, Engineering and Medicine: An Overview of the Issues," *Technology in Society,* 1997; *Corporate Voluntarism: Private Support for Social Policy, Economic Reform Today,* 1996; *Life Sciences and Health Challenges* (editor), New York Academy of Sciences, 1998. Dr. Raymond earned her BA from Macalester College and her MA and Ph.D. from The Johns Hopkins University School of Advanced International Studies. Her substantive focus was in the field of health and medical economics and in international public health.

Contents

LIST OF EXHIBITS   VIII

FOREWORD   XI

SECTION ONE   Philanthropy and the Economy   I
Introduction to the Issues   1
Measuring the Economic Importance of Nonprofits:
   What Happens When Methods Change   3
Size Counts in the Foundation World: The Dilemma
   of Absorptive Capacity   7
What You Know or Who You Know? Relationships Matter   11
Foundation Endowments: How Big? How Vulnerable?   15
Does Philanthropy Interfere with Markets?   21
Venture Philanthropy: Two Sides of the Coin   25
Wages in the Nonprofit Sector: Poor Cousin or Twin Sister?   33
Diversity and Governance: The Not-Good News   37
Minority Philanthropy: The Future Has Arrived   41
Will There Be a Nonprofit Shakeout? Comparing
   Nonprofits to Small Business Trends   47
The Growing Demand for Philanthropic Accountability:
   Will There Be Room for Risk?   51
Managing through the Market: Responding to
   Severe Economic Cycles   55
The Philanthropic Instinct: Government Walks the Talk   59
Does Wall Street Matter? The Unknowns about Elasticities   63

SECTION TWO   Ethics and Accountability   67
Introduction to the Issues   67
How Shall We Govern Ourselves?   71
The Mission Meets the Numbers: Is It Okay to Lie?   77
A Privilege and an Obligation: Why Stewardship Matters
   and Competition Is a Good Thing   83
Are Organizational Hybrids Nonprofits?
   The Problem of Fairness   87

Have We Learned Nothing? Practical Applications
   of Lessons from Corporate Scandal   91
Great Expectations Collide: The Consequences
   of Assumptions   95

SECTION THREE   Nonprofit Management Dilemmas   **101**
Introduction to the Issues   101
Organizational Benchmarking:
   Management Solution or Performance Petard?   105
The Illusion of Knowing Something:
   The Diversity of Nonprofit Definitions   111
Philanthropy and the Nonprofit Budget Cycle:
   No Silver Bullet   117
State Budget Deficits: Why Red Ink Today
   Will Plague Management Tomorrow   121
Drilling Down: Deeper Revenue Sources for Nonprofits   125
Nonprofit Compensation: Charitable Managers and
   Their Tax-Exempt Colleagues   131
To: Nonprofit Human Resources Managers;
   From: Washington; Subject: Watch Your Back   135
Estate Taxes and Giving: Crepe Armbands versus
   Thinking Caps   139
The Growth of the Nonprofit Sector: Is It Really Real?   145
When Philanthropy Demands Evidence and Results:
   Developing a Compelling Rationale for Funding   147
What History Teaches about the Root Systems
   That Nourish Philanthropy   151

SECTION FOUR   Philanthropy and Healthcare   **155**
Introduction to the Issues   155
Healthcare in the Twenty-First Century:
   Why the Charity Gap Will Grow   159
Hospital Philanthropy: David versus Goliath   163
Fighting Disease with Philanthropy: Who Gets the Funds?   167
Picking Targets: Healthcare Philanthropy's Unenviable Task   173
Philanthropy and the Academic Medical System:
   Cavalry to the Rescue? Or, Hope Springs Eternal?   179
Mental Illness: Major Health Burden;
   But Is It a Philanthropic Priority?   183

SECTION FIVE   Philanthropy and Education   **187**
Introduction to the Issues   187
With College Costs Rising Quickly,
   Can Philanthropy Close the Gap?   191

Scholarship Grants: You Can't Always Get
    What You Need   195
University Foundations: Memo to the Dean:
    After the Faculty Meeting, Check the Dow   199
Philanthropy in K-12 Education:
    A Minor Player Missing a Major Opportunity   203
Learning to Be Charitable: Is It a Girl Thing?   209
Philanthropy and National Academic Research Funding   213

SECTION SIX   U.S. Philanthropy in an International
               Context   217
Introduction to the Issues   217
America's International Giving: Search Elsewhere
    for Scrooge   221
The International Scope of the Nonprofit Sector   229
The Globalization of Education:
    How Important Is Philanthropy?   233
Indigenous Philanthropy: Poorer Nations Also Give   237
North of the Border: Canada-United States Philanthropic
    Comparisons   241
Is Europe Poised for a Golden Age
    of Community Philanthropy?   245
Evidence of Philanthropic Impact: A De Novo Case
    from Poland and the Lessons It Teaches   249
Learning from International Conflict: Philanthropic
    Strategy Is as Important as Sympathy   253

SECTION SEVEN   Corporate Philanthropy   259
Introduction to the Issues   259
Corporate Giving: A Workhorse in Small States   261
Gifts in Kind: The Good of Goods   265
Corporate Giving and Tax Policy: Let's Do the Math   269
Global Health and Corporate Philanthropy:
    Fickle Funder or Lasting Partner?   273

SECTION EIGHT   Reflections on
                 September 11, 2001   279
Introduction to the Issues   279
Philanthropy Put to the Test   281
U.S. Diversity Creates Philanthropic Opportunity...
    and Risk   287
Did September 11 Change Philanthropy Forever?   291

INDEX   295

List of Exhibits

SECTION ONE Philanthropy and the Economy |
1.1	Percent Private Industry Output from Nonprofits, 1997	4
1.2	Nonprofit Current Receipts	5
1.3	Percent Foundations by Asset Size, 1999	8
1.4	Percentage of Foundations Preselecting Grantees	12
1.5	Inflation-Adjusted Foundation Asset Growth, 1975–2000	16
1.6	Hewlett-Packard Stock Performance, July 2001–April 2003	17
1.7	Foundation Board Composition by Profession	38
1.8	Foundation Board Composition—Percent Female by Region	38
1.9	Lower-Income Limit of Top 5 Percent of Households (1999 Constant Dollars)	42
1.10	Number of Households with Income in Top 5 Percent of Minority Households Rises 25 Percent	43
1.11	Foreign-Born Individuals Living in the United States	44
1.12	Sources of Nonprofit Revenue, 1999, by Asset Size	64

SECTION TWO Ethics and Accountability **67**
| 2.1 | Individual Giving, 1962–2002 | 97 |

SECTION THREE Nonprofit Management Dilemmas **101**
| 3.1 | Number of Nonprofit Organizations, 1982–2000 | 102 |
| 3.2 | U.S. Tax-Exempt Organization Types | 113 |

3.3   Percent of Nonprofit Organizations by Type, 1998   114
3.4   Distribution of Foundation Grants by Purpose
       (Percent Dollars)   118
3.5   U.S.Volunteer Behavior by Age   119
3.6   Philanthropy Rankings for Largest State Deficits   122
3.7   Nonprofit Revenue Composition, 1998   126
3.8   501(c)(3) Expenditure Distribution, 1999   132
3.9   Percent Government Workforce Retiring by 2007   136
3.10   Estate Tax Returns as Percent of Adult Deaths,
       1934–1993   141

SECTION FOUR   Philanthropy and Healthcare   **155**
4.1   Source of Healthcare Funds, 2000   156
4.2   Health and the U.S. Economy: Average Annual
       Percent Change from Previous Year Shown,
       1990–2002   160
4.3   Growth in U.S. Elderly Population by Age Group   161
4.4   Falling U.S. Hospital Margins, 1997–2000   164
4.5   U.S. Hospital Bond Trends, 1997–2001   164
4.6   Percent Surveyed Total Funding by Selected Diseases 169
4.7   Percent Surveyed Foundations Making Grants
       to Selected Diseases   170
4.8   Distribution of U.S. Healthcare Expenditures, 2001 174
4.9   Percent Specialty Services Located at Teaching
       Hospitals, 2000   180
4.10   Disease Burden in Industrialized Nations:
       Percent DALYs   184

SECTION FIVE   Philanthropy and Education   **187**
5.1   U.S. Educational Enrollment, 1949 and 2000   188
5.2   Average Annual Tuition, Room, Board,
       and Fees per FTE Undergraduate, 1976–2003   192
5.3   Average Grant per Dependent Student by Family
       Income Level, 1999–2000   196
5.4   Average Student Aid Grant, 1995–1996   197
5.5   Annual Income Level of Redundant
       Postsecondary School Foundations, 2001   201
5.6   Distribution of the K-12 Public Educational
       Dollar, 2000   204
5.7   K-12 Parents Volunteering at School   205
5.8   National Academic R&D Expenditures   214
5.9   Support for Academic R&D by Sector   215

SECTION SIX   U.S. Philanthropy in an International
Context   **217**
6.1   Foreign Students in the United States 1954–2002   218
6.2   U.S. Giving for International Affairs 1988–2001   218
6.3   Globalization of International Aid: United States
        as Percent of Official Development Assistance   222
6.4   U.S. Resource Transfers to Developing Countries,
        2000   225
6.5   Growth in International Nongovernment
        Organizations, 1909–1996   230
6.6   Source of Foreign Student Funds, 2002   235
6.7   Five-State Dominance of Public Charity Revenue   242
6.8   Population Decline in European Nations   246

SECTION SEVEN   Corporate Philanthropy   **259**
7.1   1997–1999 Corporate Presence Relative
        to State Household Income   262
7.2   Noncash Corporate Giving by Industry, 2000   266
7.3   Value of Noncash Corporate Contributions,
        1990–2000   267
7.4   Corporate Giving as Percent of U.S. Pretax
        Income, 1970–2001   270
7.5   Profits and Income for Industrial Sample, 2002   271

SECTION EIGHT   Reflections on
September 11, 2001   **279**
8.1   September 11 Philanthropy by Source   280
8.2   Immigrants as Percent of U.S. Population,
        1850–2000   288

Foreword

There are many misconceptions about philanthropy, even in places as bonded to philanthropic endeavor as these United States. Misconceptions lead to missteps, for philanthropists and nonprofits alike. The most common misconceptions include:

"If you build it, they will come." They will not; mere existence is no longer a rationale that attracts philanthropic attention.

"We do good works." Perhaps, but so does everyone else. Philanthropy will not flow merely because a nonprofit is admirable.

"There is so much money out there." True, but the vast majority of it is already spoken for.

"If everyone just gave a dollar..." If wishes were horses, beggars would ride.

As in any endeavor, when misconceptions are rife, information and insight are at a premium. The value of this book of essays rests in those two intersecting dimensions: the nature of philanthropic change and the nature of societal expectations.

Philanthropy in the United States is nearly a third of a trillion-dollar endeavor. It is much more than an emotional or ethical element of the nation's soul; it is an economic driver. Yet little is known about philanthropy's true scope. Much giving is individual, informal, even unrecorded. Much nonprofit work is voluntary, informal, and often unrecorded. Yet $300 billion is not loose change out of the nation's sock drawer. It represents a significant pool of resources by any measure.

This book attempts to look more deeply into that pool, to plumb its depth, to span its breadth, and to compare its size and nature with other elements of the social and economic makeup of the nation. These empirical comparisons—not simply of philanthropy itself, but between philanthropy and indicators of economic and social change—comprise a critical and unique step forward for philanthropic analysis.

The second dimension of these essays is equally important. The growth and visibility of philanthropy and its nonprofit outlets in the last two decades have raised serious questions about its role in the nation's future, in the marketplace, and in the systems of institutional accountability that rest at the heart of free societies. We cannot simply go forward willy-nilly, with a ballooning stock of wealth and a growing flow of philanthropy, then neglect to ask about implications. More of a good thing is not always a good idea. The size of the philanthropic endeavor and the pervasiveness of nonprofit patterns woven throughout the nation's social and economic fabric both argue for careful consideration of the impact of these trends on how we as a society are organized. They demand that we ask questions, both about what we as a society will expect from these resources and what we wish to (or can realistically) demand in relationship to the larger societal commons.

There are no easy answers to the questions that these essays raise about those deeper issues. Nevertheless, the essays provide insight and, perhaps more importantly, raise yeasty, questions about our assumptions on that commons. They are questions that, I am sure, will provoke heated debate. In the years that I have worked with, and developed tremendous respect for, Dr. Raymond, I have never known her to shy from such debate. This book displays that spirit.

Philanthropy will continue to play a major role in the American economy. It will continue to attract voluntary leadership, from the nation's towering corporate boardrooms to its tree-shaded living rooms. The analyses and insights contained in these essays provide illustrations of the careful search for productive paths forward that should occupy everyone engaged in the philanthropic and non-profit worlds.

Michael P. Hoffman, President, CEO, Chairman
Changing Our World, Inc., New York, NY
August 2003

Philanthropy
and the Economy

INTRODUCTION TO THE ISSUES

Knowledge, it is said, can be dangerous. Illusory knowledge is more dangerous still. Thinking we know something basic when, in fact, we do not can lead to errors of assumption and of conclusion. Such errors then give rise to failures of judgment about everything from national policy to local accountability.

The philanthropic sector is a case in point. Much philanthropy is formal, emanating from concrete organizations like foundations and corporations. Much, however, is informal, emanating spontaneously from our collective wallets. The former can be measured, at least in theory. The latter often cannot.

If we ignore context, this failure of empiricism is not troubling. A free and independent people acting as they wish with their own resources is certainly no cause for concern. But there is context. Historically, America has always been a believer in the power of individual effort. Alexis de Tocqueville remarked on that penchant repeatedly nearly 170 years ago. America is a nation of doers, of believers, of joiners in common private effort for the common good. Over the last decade or so, the nation has turned ever more toward harnessing the power of philanthropy to resolve long-standing societal and economic problems, from healthcare to education to

I

poverty. The coming global and security demands on public budgets will likely reinforce the need to turn to private solutions.

> "[Americans] have all a lively faith in the perfectability of man, they judge that the diffusion of knowledge must necessarily be advantageous, and the consequences of ignorance fatal; they all consider society as a body in a state of improvement, humanity as a changing scene, in which nothing is, or ought to be, permanent; and they admit that what appears to them today to be good may be superseded by something better tomorrow."
> —Alexis de Tocqueville, 1835

If this is so, then knowing more about philanthropy, its size, directions, motivations, and—importantly—effectiveness, is critical. This is not an academic matter. Illusory knowledge will be dangerous. Confidence about the ways in which philanthropy can (and perhaps cannot) hit the targets placed before it will be essential to determining whether philanthropy is effective relative to national priorities.

There are difficult questions that must be asked. They must be asked with rigor. The answers must be faced without qualm. If there is improvement needed, then it must be demanded. The nation's philanthropic institutions, and the nonprofits they fund, from the largest to the very smallest, can no longer consider themselves part of a cottage industry, an informal network focused only on their own local activities. The game is now much bigger than that. Reliable data and empirical analysis will be critical to decision making about the allocation of limited public and private resources to limitless needs.

The essays in this section address a variety of issues and questions about the linkage between future directions of philanthropy and the nation's nonprofit infrastructure and larger economic trends.

Measuring the Economic Importance of Nonprofits: What Happens When Methods Change

Given the diversity of categories comprising the nonprofit sector, it has been difficult to reliably assess the importance of nonprofits to the U.S. economy In April 2003, the Bureau of Economic Analysis of the U.S. Department of Commerce published a paper ("Income and Outlays of Households and of Nonprofit Institutions Serving Households") that set out a new analytic framework for this assessment. The results of the preliminary analysis are striking, and may become more so as the methods are used in the future.

In essence, the paper argues that nonprofits engage in two broad types of transactions: those that intersect with households (e.g., museums) and those that intersect with business (e.g., chambers of commerce). Any given nonprofit may engage in both types of transactions (e.g., the museum that sells holiday gifts for business giving), but, generally, nonprofits can be categorized in these two ways. Educational institutions, hospitals, welfare organizations, and the like provide service value to households. In turn, they receive portions of the personal and household incomes of the nation, not only via charitable contributions, but also via the payment for services.

The paper then proceeds to combine what it terms "nonprofit institutions serving households" (NPISH) with personal income data to form a total picture of household income behavior. Several remarkable results ensue.

First, the nonprofit sector is nearly coterminous with four industrial sectors when viewed through the lens of the North American Industrial Classification System. NPISHs produce 83.1 percent of the private industry output of educational services in the nation, 85 percent of the hospital output, and 89 percent of the private industrial output of institutions such as museums. No surprise there. However, although discussions of nonprofits in the economy usually remark on the concentration of nonprofit output in healthcare, only 11.1 percent of the ambulatory healthcare services, and only 38 percent of nursing and residential care services output, comes from household-directed nonprofits. So it would appear that casting broad nets (such as healthcare) into the nonprofit data waters may produce a misleading catch.

Second, viewing nonprofits as part of the household economy also results in a role for the nonprofit sector that is larger than previously estimated. Nonprofit current receipts, including transfer

EXHIBIT 1.1   PERCENT PRIVATE INDUSTRY OUTPUT FROM NONPROFITS, 1997

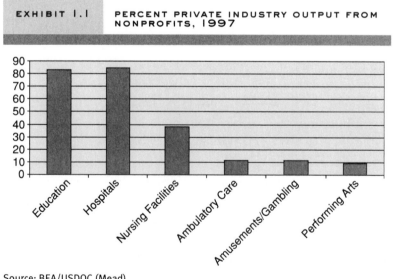

Source: BEA/USDOC (Mead)

EXHIBIT I.2   NONPROFIT CURRENT RECEIPTS

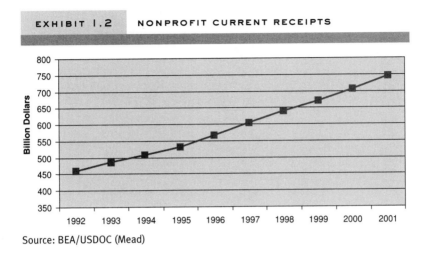

Source: BEA/USDOC (Mead)

payments to nonprofit institutions from business, government, and households, totaled $743 billion in 2001, approximately a 60 percent increase in the 1990s. Based on operating expenses, household service nonprofits alone represent nearly 10 percent of personal consumption expenditures.

Third, the savings behavior of nonprofits is also important to the economy. Between 1992 and 1998, households accounted for the decline in personal savings. Thereafter, however, the gap between nonprofit expenses and sales grew to nearly $170 billion and began to play an important role in overall national savings declines.

These very different methods for looking at the nonprofit sector may become standard procedure at the Department of Commerce. If they do, they will cast a clearer light on the role of nonprofits in the economy and make distinctions among nonprofit types that have long been needed. Like all novelties, of course, they will muck up historical comparisons. So, analysts beware.

SOURCE

Mead, C.I., C.P. McCully, and M.C. Reinsdorf. "Income and Outlays of Households and of Nonprofit Institutions Serving Households," Survey of Current Business, April 2003.

Size Counts in the Foundation World: The Dilemma of Absorptive Capacity

In this bold new world where electrons are both process and content, organizations are increasingly small and/or decentralized. Innovation comes from lean, flexible organizations, centered around clients with instant communications to respond to changing needs and changing product and service opportunities. Decentralization of knowledge and action is the key to success. Indeed, three-quarters of American firms have no employee payroll at all! They are self-employed persons operating unincorporated businesses.

Speed and decentralization are everywhere. E-commerce now affects 30 percent of the entire U.S. economy. Over half of all American households are connected to the World Wide Web. Three-quarters of all Web content originates in the United States. Less than a third of working Americans are employed in companies with more than 5,000 employees. Indeed, three-quarters of all U.S. firms with payroll have fewer than 20 employees.

Viewed in terms of proliferation, the foundation world seems to mirror these trends of diversity. There are well over 40,000 foundations in the United States, more than half of which have been formed since 1980. This might imply a yeasty mix, generating organizational change with close and diverse community links, but the totals mask the extraordinary concentration of resources in the foundation world.

Independent foundations with assets over $100 million represent only 3.5 percent of all U.S. foundations, but they account for 67 percent of assets and 56 percent of total giving. Those with assets of $5 million or less represent over half of all independent foundations, but account for only 4.7 percent of assets and only 3.4 percent of total giving.

The picture is much more balanced on the corporate side of the foundation street. Although there are 13 behemoths of over $100 million in assets, these represent only 1.4 percent of total corporate foundations and only 9 percent of total corporate foundation giving. In contrast, those with assets of $5 million or less represent 60 percent of corporate foundations and 32 percent of giving. This is perhaps not surprising in that, as noted previously, most U.S. business is no longer "big business" in the traditional sense.

It is striking that the portrait of concentration depicted by independent foundations is replicated in community foundations. Community foundations are created to pool the philanthropy of individuals in a community so as to grow total resources and relieve

EXHIBIT 1.3   PERCENT FOUNDATIONS BY ASSET SIZE, 1999

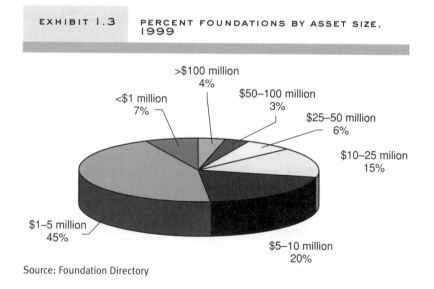

Source: Foundation Directory

the overhead of operating very small philanthropic foundations. They represent one of the fastest-growing types of foundations both in the United States, and in Europe. In the United States, the $100-million-plus asset foundations represent 13.4 percent of all community foundations but 69 percent of giving, while those with $5 million or less are 22 percent of the total and account for only 1.6 percent of giving.

While there is increasing diversity in the foundation world, only a few of the new entrants play in the philanthropic major leagues. Does that matter?

In a way, it doesn't. The philanthropic dollars supporting nonprofit efforts are all the same color of green, whether they come from tycoons or the retired couple down the block. It would be a short list indeed of groups that refuse grants on the basis of the size of the philanthropist.

In another way, however, perhaps it does matter. The best, most successful innovation at the community level comes from contact with the community, whether that community is a church, a neighborhood, a hospital, or a school. It is possible that there is a sizing problem with foundation resources in this sense. The biggest institutions with the greatest resources must spend equally large sums to comply with tax law. Efficiency calls for moving such sums in large financial pieces, and that, in turn, results in programs that address major problems at relatively high levels of generality.

Community innovation, however, rarely comes in big chunks of high generality. Community innovation comes block by block, child by child. It may have neither the size nor the visibility to attract the attention or interest of large organizations. Even where it does, community-level innovators may not have the professional systems or organizational infrastructure to satisfy the efficiency and accountability structures that large organizations do (and must) put in place to police the efficiency and effectiveness of their resource flows.

So, when the structure of size does not match the structure of problems, opportunities for small-scale innovation at the community level may go begging. Can that be prevented? Are there ways for the 50 percent to 60 percent of giving from 3 percent of foundations to better flow to small units of community innovation? And can that be done in ways that maintain the level of intellectual rigor, promise of replicability, and strict accountability that is the burden that accompanies the privilege of husbanding huge pools of resources?

Certainly there are. This is a problem that is common in the international development community. When the World Bank or the U.S. Agency for International Development has tens of millions of dollars to allocate to a problem (e.g., gender equity) that is ill suited to absorb such levels of funding, they create community pools of funds. These pools then are supervised at the community level, and granted on in smaller amounts for appropriate activities (e.g., small business development). The World Bank cannot lend at the $5,000 level; women in Costa Rica cannot absorb at the $50-million level. Hence, the marriage between the two is made through disaggregating the total funding into smaller community pieces, giving communities input into the on-lending (or on-granting) of that amount. Large amounts of money, then, can be moved in appropriately small pieces.

The size mismatch problem between huge philanthropies and local community needs can be resolved. But doing so will require creativity in project design, on the part of the funders, and organizational entrepreneurship, on the part of the communities.

■ SOURCES

The Foundation Directory, 1999.
Salamon, Lester. America's Non-Profit Sector, NY: Foundation Center, 1999.
U.S. Bureau of the Census, Economic Census, Enterprise Statistics, 2000.
"Gigabytes Behind: Europe Can't Match US," *Washington Post*, January 15, 2000, Section A, p. 1.

What You Know or Who You Know? Relationships Matter

There is often great debate over whether what you know matters more than who you know. But, whatever the universal answer, in the world of philanthropy who you know matters a lot.

Some 70 percent of all giving in the nation is from individuals. So networks are a critical part of success for those organizations seeking charitable support. Reaching out to individuals is the key to philanthropic success.

What is not generally recognized is how important "who you know" can be in the world of organized philanthropy, specifically in the world of foundations. There are more than 40,000 registered foundations in the United States. But the sum does not reflect the nature of its parts. The foundation world is highly segmented, with the vast majority of foundations serving only organizations in specific geographic regions or localities. This is well-recognized.

That said, the foundation world can also be impenetrable to nonprofits even within geographic confines. On average, 17 percent of foundations preselect their grant recipients.[1] That is, they do not accept unsolicited proposals, even within the geographic or substantive areas of their concern. So who you know can be

---

[1] Percentages in this essay are derived from the foundation sample contained in the Taft Group's Prospector's Choice. The sample includes both private and corporate foundations. Regional subgroupings and associated data were developed by the author.

EXHIBIT 1.4   PERCENTAGE OF FOUNDATIONS
PRESELECTING GRANTEES

Region	Percentage
New England	17%
Mid-Atlantic	23%
Southeast	11%
South	14%
Midwest	16%
Plains States	9%
Mountain States	12%
West/Southwest	20%

quite important indeed. In fact, the actual percentage is probably much higher. The sample used includes corporate foundations, most of which allow, and even encourage, applications from a wide range of groups in the communities they serve. Netting out corporate philanthropy would reduce the denominator to private independent foundations but not decrease the preselect numerator, hence the preselect numerator, hence the preselect rate would rise.

The national pattern differs by geographic region. Only 9 percent of foundations in the Plains States preselect recipients, while the Mid-Atlantic States lead the nation with 23 percent preselecting. The prize for exclusivity goes to New York State, where nearly a third (32 percent) of all foundations do not accept unsolicited proposals. Rhode Island comes in second, with a 29 percent preselection rate, followed by California at 25 percent.

Furthermore, preselection is more characteristic of cities than of nonurban philanthropy. A full 36 percent of New York City's foundations do not accept unsolicited proposals, followed by Los Angeles at 26 percent and San Francisco at 25 percent. In terms of the difference between statewide and city preselection rates, however, the prize goes to Seattle, where 22 percent of foundations preselect compared to 11 percent elsewhere in Washington state, with second place to Boston, where 24 percent preselect, compared to 15 percent elsewhere in Massachusetts.

So, nonprofits would be well served to take a page from the real estate industry. In real estate, what matters is location, location, location. In philanthropy, it appears that what matters is networking, networking, networking. Or, to the reader interested less in commerce than in philanthropy and the arts, heed the pen of William Shakespeare: "Those friends thou hast, and their adoption tried, grapple them to thy soul with hoops of steel." (*Hamlet*, I, iii, 61)

Foundation Endowments: How Big, How Vulnerable?

With the ups and downs of the stock market, much has been written about fluctuations in the size of foundation endowments and their (theoretical) moral might in the marketplace. As in many other areas, the conclusions to be drawn depend on where you begin.

The Foundation Center estimates a total U.S. philanthropic endowment base of something on the order of $480 billion in current dollars in 2000 (about $152 billion in inflation-adjusted 1975 dollars). This represents a fivefold increase since 1975 in real terms. After lackluster performance into the mid-1980s, assets experienced double-digit real growth in the 1995–1999 period. Of this total, about 6.7 percent ($30 billion) is held by community foundations and 3.3 percent ($15 billion) underpins corporate foundations. The remaining 90 percent represents the capital assets of private, independent foundations.

This is almost certainly an underestimate. By the center's own admission, it does not include many small foundations. But four other categories are also missing, or at least undercounted.

First, the estimate does not (and perhaps cannot) keep pace with market changes in the private sector. For example, the merger of the nonprofit USA Group with Sallie Mae in 2000 immediately kicked $700 million into the USA Group Foundation. The endowment of the Annie E. Casey Foundation (created by UPS) nearly

EXHIBIT 1.5   INFLATION-ADJUSTED FOUNDATION ASSET
GROWTH, 1975–2000

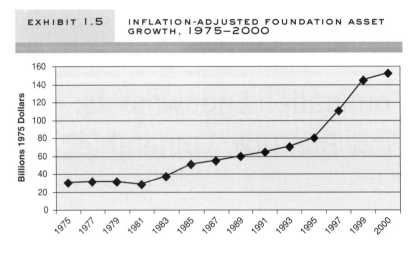

Source: Foundation Yearbook, 2002

doubled overnight (from $1.7 billion to $3.3 billion) when UPS went public. But being beholden to a single stock also has its disadvantages. When Hewlett-Packard stock lost 50 percent of its value between July and October 2001, the fortunes of the Hewlett-Packard Foundation, whose assets were tied to stock, plummeted as well. A snapshot at any point in time will miss the fluidity of values over time, hence may risk misrepresenting the state of overall foundation capacity.

Second, the estimate probably does not include most association foundations—that is, independent foundations created by professional, avocation, or industry associations. There is no comprehensive census of these foundations; but a rough assessment based on association directories indicates that as many as 700 associations have created affiliated foundations. Some are exceedingly small (e.g., the Pot Bellied Pig Association Foundation), but some are significant (e.g., those affiliated with major medical specialties or national voluntary health associations). In aggregate, such foundations probably raise hundreds of millions of dollars annually, and support not insignificant amounts of research and public education.

Third, the estimate does not include all foundations that house and manage university endowments. Nearly a third of all giving to

universities goes for endowments. As an example, the University of
Florida Foundation alone holds nearly a billion dollars in assets.

Finally, the estimate does not include the controversial new entrants into philanthropy—the donor-advised funds of Wall Street's
money management firms. The philanthropy windows of Fidelity,
Schwab, and Vanguard alone have total assets of over $2.4 billion,
and Merrill Lynch has now set its sights on knocking Fidelity from
the top of the donor-advised fund heap.

So let's assume that $360 billion is an underestimate. Let's further
speculate that it is off significantly, say by 50 percent. How big is
the resultant half a trillion dollars of capital?

In fact, it is not so big. U.S. nonprofits control about $1.9 trillion
in assets (although admittedly this includes state pension funds,
but no longer includes TIAA/CREF, which has been stripped of
its nonprofit status). Thus, foundations would represent less than
a third of this total. But beyond the nonprofit world, the U.S.
financial markets include $16 trillion in professionally managed

**EXHIBIT 1.6   HEWLETT-PACKARD STOCK PERFORMANCE,
JULY 2001–APRIL 2003**

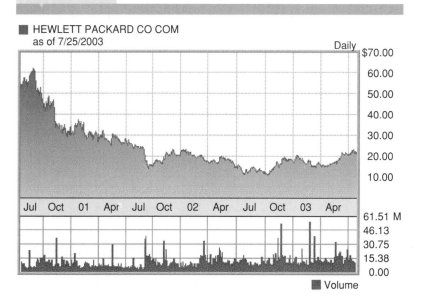

capital. At even $500 billion, foundation endowments would be only about 3 percent of that total!

While it is true that $500 billion is hardly loose change out of the top drawer, why is it not more? Why are there not more endowed foundations, and why are those endowments not larger? The answer is certainly not that foundations are giving away their asset base. Most do not exceed the IRS requirement that they give away 5 percent of their base. With market gains in the double digits, assets have been growing, even when recent downturns are factored in. It is also almost certainly not that foundations are settling for smaller investment returns because they choose to trap their assets in socially responsible investment funds. Most foundations do not use social issues as investment criteria.

Moreover, socially responsible investment funds are now often outperforming the overall market. Hence, for those foundations that do tear down the wall between the social issues that drive their grants and return on endowment capital, investment yields continue to be impressive.

So, is the issue not the growth of endowments that exist but the growth in the number of endowments? There may be at least three factors at work.

First, decision making about resources. A foundation with an independent board may not behave in accordance with the wishes of the founding organization. Many of the classic examples come from the academic world. The nearly decade-long feud between the University of South Alabama and the University of South Alabama Foundation is a case in point. Philanthropic structures that retain assets within the recipient organization without benefit of a parallel foundation may be seen as simpler means for ensuring management control.

Second, the complexity of establishing and managing a foundation is not trivial. The rule of thumb is that $1 million is the minimal "opening bid" for establishing an independent foundation. Many individuals and families have the option of annual giving or giving via the new donor-advised funds just noted. In fact, in inflation-adjusted dollars, new capital received usually represents less than 5 percent of total foundation assets. Even in the go-go 1990s, record levels of new gifts still only accounted for, at most, 9 percent of foundation asset growth. And even these record gift years were skewed by the multibillion dollar endowment of the Gates Foundation. Clearly, establishing a foundation or growing an existing foundation is not the engine behind philanthropic growth.

Third, most people committed to giving are also committed to impact. There may be a tendency to see endowments as less productive relative to impact than direct and immediate giving to the nonprofit in need. The foundation model might be seen as an unnecessary "middleman" in a giving strategy.

Fourth, new, big pools of money are not immediately attracted to the foundation model. Conversion of community health institutions to for-profit status over the last 15 years has resulted in over $14 billion in community charitable foundation endowments. There is a growing concern in the newest category of private sector conversions, community banks, that this approach has more risk than reward. Some banks have used part of their new stock to endow associated foundations; some have not. A 1999 analysis of the annualized return on capital of thrift institutions would seem to support that caution. The study compared community thrifts that created foundations with stock donations upon privatization with those that did not. Of the 55 community thrifts that went public between January 1998 and December 1999, those with new foundations (30) had an annualized return of 2.73 percent. Those without foundations enjoyed a return of 8.86 percent, 225 percent higher. For these conversions, the newest question is how to respond to their community roots without compromising working capital.

▓ SOURCES

Abelson, Reed. "Charities' Investing: Left Hand, Meet Right," *New York Times,* June 11, 2000, Section 3, p. 1, col. 1.

Basinger, Juliana. "Trustees of South Alabama Sue to Dissolve the University's Foundation," *Chronicle of Higher Education,* July 9, 1999, p. 38.

Caffrey, Andrew. "Some Investors Say 'Bah Humbug' to Converted Thrifts' Foundations," *Wall Street Journal*, December 15, 1999, NE 2.

"Coming of Age: Findings from the 1998 Survey of Foundations Created by Health Care Conversions," Grantmakers in Health, 1999.

Egodigwe, Laura Saunders. "Sweet Charity: Top Firms Follow Fidelity's Lead in Offering Funds Acting as Charitable Accounts," *Wall Street Journal*, May 5, 2000, c 1, c 19.

Foundation Yearbook: Facts and Figures. Foundation Center, 2002.

Korn, Donald Jay. "Winning the Giveaway Game: Their Long-Term Approach and Tax Advantages Are Making Donor-Advised Funds Increasingly Popular," *Financial Planning*, April 1, 2000, pp. 85–90.

Does Philanthropy Interfere with Markets?

In the next several decades, as much as $38 trillion will change hands from members of the boomer generation to their progeny and, to some extent, America's charities.[1] And the ranks of those charities have grown enormously. In 1940, the nation had 15,000 nonprofits; today there are an estimated 1.6 million, of which about 700,000 are providers of services to households.

> "To give away money is an easy matter and in any man's power. But to decide to whom to give it, and how large and when, and for what purpose and how, is neither in every man's power nor an easy matter."
>
> —Aristotle

By any measure, these are not trival numbers. Beyond their eye-popping magnitude, however, such numbers raise a variety of interesting questions about how these expanded resources and growing institutions will map onto the larger economy. Let's begin with a basic economic parameter: Will the new money value efficiency?

---

[1]The exact amount of the transfer is, of course, dependent on assumptions about markets. As of January 2003, the range of $38–$41 trillion was still considered valid, despite the three-year economic downturn.

In an open marketplace, resources flow to efficient organizations. Assuming that product or service demand can be expressed in the market (efficiency was of little importance in Soviet systems, for example), efficiency drives down costs and boosts productivity, attracting both demand and investment and spurring competition. That is the beauty of markets.

Does efficiency matter to philanthropy? Perhaps more troubling, does philanthropy actually impede efficiency? As to the first question, the answer would appear to be no, or at least, not much. Research from 2001 by P. Frumkin and M.T. Kim examined philanthropic flows to a sample of nonprofits over 11 years. Efficient organizations (defined in terms of administrative costs) fared no better than inefficient ones in attracting individual, corporate, or foundation philanthropic resources.

These are sobering findings. They imply that the philanthropic dollar (or 38 trillion philanthropic dollars) does not reward efficiency and, where it attempts to do so, faces difficulty instigating or improving efficiency measurably. The further implication is that society (which is voluntarily forgoing tax income on those dollars) accepts (or will need to accept) the degree of waste that accompanies inefficiency.

The second question—does philanthropy impede markets— rests equally uneasily on the shoulders of the future. Of course, for many philanthropic targets, markets are not an issue. There is no market for soup kitchens or for homeless shelters, for example. But for others, markets do operate, and they operate with increasing public acceptance. Healthcare is a prime (but far from the sole) example. A hypothetical example will illustrate the difficulties inherent in the tension between philanthropy and the market.

Assume there are two teaching hospitals within a one-mile radius in a city that all analysts acknowledge has too many hospital beds relative to efficient medical management and cost structures. They both are affiliated with large medical schools, have comparable world-class research, and regularly vie for "best hospital" in national rankings. Neither, however, can fill more than 60 percent of its beds; each has at least one empty floor.

Though access to primary and preventive care may be problematic in the city, there is no evidence of unmet demand for the type of tertiary care provided by teaching hospitals. Given their cost structures and reimbursement rates, negotiated in competition with other hospitals in the city, both hospitals have run operating deficits for the past three years. Both have powerful boards and are initiating multiyear fundraising campaigns to cover deficits and build yet more buildings. Egos are at stake, and the philanthropic betting says that both will achieve their fundraising goals.

The product is the same. The quality is the same. The proximity to market is the same. Underutilization is similar. Financial vulnerability is shared. Nevertheless, philanthropy allows both to exist; left to its own devices, the market would drive toward efficiency either by scaling both back, shutting one completely, or merging both. Two added difficulties compound the problem.

First, the healthcare industry is not the cement industry. Life and death are matters of deep importance to most individuals. Institutions that hold life and death in their hands are, therefore, intimately bound up in community expectations that extend beyond market performance.

Second, nonphilanthropic healthcare dollars are dear. Scarce resources (public and private) must regularly be spread across competing life-and-death needs. These decisions affect patients and the communities these healthcare institutions serve. So, by enabling the continued existence of inefficient providers, does not philanthropy's role raise questions of distributive justice for the allocation of scarce funds (public, payor, and consumer) that have both a market and a societal purpose?

Of course, health is not a perfect market. Clearly there are values on the public commons that justify less-than-perfect efficiency in the location, size, and operation of healthcare facilities. But the hypothetical illustration just presented is not very far removed from the overbedding reality in many urban areas of the nation. In large cities, hospital service duplication and overbedding, hence inefficiency and cost escalation, can be maintained in part because of community demands and in part because philanthropic financial leadership allows institutions to escape the effects of supply and demand.

The healthcare market does, in fact, operate in the United States. Whether or not it has produced better medicine is a matter of debate. But it has certainly increased the efficiency with which healthcare resources have been applied to provision.

Is philanthropy fuel for using every scarce dollar wisely? Or is it a brake on efficiency? The influx of trillions of philanthropic dollars into systems that operate with scarce resources in market conditions suggests that the question is not academic. If a significant presence of philanthropy in an economic sector impedes the continued achievement of efficiency and productivity in that sector, then the overall economic commons may, in fact, suffer rather than benefit.

■ SOURCES

Cobbs, L.S., P.A. Clark and M. Brusa. "The Million-Dollar Question," The Hastings Center Report, September/October 2000, pp. 24–26.

Colvin, G. "The Gift of Arrogance," *Fortune*, December 24, 2001, pp. 50–51.

Frumkin, P. and M. T. Kim. "Strategic Positioning and the Financing of Nonprofit Organizations: Is Efficiency Rewarded in the Contributions Marketplace," *Public Administration Review*, May/June 2001, pp. 266–275.

Karatnycky, A. "The Merits of the Market, the Perils of 'Market Fundamentalism'," *Wall Street Journal*, January 2, 2001, A20.

"Why the $41 Trillion Wealth Transfer Is Still Valid: A Review of Challenges and Questions," *The Journal of Gift Planning*, 7:1, 1st Quarter, 2003, pp. 11–15, 47–50.

Venture Philanthropy: Two Sides of the Coin

AN IDEA WHOSE TIME HAS COME

Charitable giving—of time and money—is an acknowledged pillar of American culture. A recent study by Johns Hopkins University estimated that 49 percent of Americans volunteer their time for civic activities, compared to 13 percent of Germans and 19 percent of French. Similarly, nearly three-quarters of Americans make financial contributions to charity, compared to 44 percent of Germans and 43 percent of French. Indeed, U.S. charitable giving garners nearly a third of a trillion dollars per year, about one-third the total of the entire U.S. government domestic budget.

But, as with any large and complex endeavor, major change does not come easily. The Queen Mary does not turn on a dime. Neither does America's approach to philanthropy.

The philanthropic "buzz" over the last several years has been the rise of *venture philanthropy*, an approach that takes the principles of entrepreneurial business financing and applies them to charitable giving. Yet only an estimated 5 percent of giving falls in this category. What is venture philanthropy and is it so different?

In effect, venture philanthropy attempts to break what, in other work, I have called the greatest tragedy of post-World War II society—the donor-recipient relationship. By conceiving of and treating individuals (or organizations or even entire nations) as "recipients," we should not be surprised that this is how they begin to think of themselves. Hence, creating self-reliance is predictably difficult. The recipient receives from the donor. Therein lies the tragedy. The very approach creates dependency. Venture philanthropy is different from traditional philanthropy in at least four ways.

> "The dignity of the individual demands that he not be reduced to vassalage by the largess of others."
> —Antoine Saint-Exupery

First, it supports a relationship between investor and "investee." Far from that between a donor who gives and a recipient who receives, this relationship is more akin to a partnership, in which all parties have a mutual interest in success. The relationship is built on equality, not on dependency.

Second, the partnership is not merely about money; the investor also proffers human assets—professional time and skills—and, often, scarce goods (technology) to ensure that the investee is building the organizational capacity to pursue the investment over the long term. Venture philanthropy is not a matter of writing checks for good works; it is a personal and organizational commitment between partners.

Third, accountability for performance is the "bottom line." The venture philanthropist, and by definition the organization in which he/she is investing, is interested not in charity but in solutions. Systems for aggregating evidence of performance against which the investment will be held accountable are critical.

Finally, it drives toward sustainability. Just as no entrepreneur works 70 hours each week in order to create something that cannot last, so the venture philanthropist seeks sustainable initiatives, seeks to support programs and organizations that demonstrate their own commitment to survival without philanthropy. The venture philanthropist, in effect, seeks to invest such that, ultimately, philanthropy goes out of business.

This venture philanthropy movement has most widely been identified with the new wealth generated by the electronics and telecommunications economy. This remains the core. But, here and there, the nondot-com philanthropic world has begun to change as well.

A (perhaps startling) case in point is the Innovation Fund created by the Franciscan Sisters of the Poor Foundation.[1] With the divestment of their healthcare facilities, the Sisters and the foundation reexamined the directions of their philanthropy within the Sisters' core religious and social mission to serve the poor. The Innovation Fund is an effort to support a variety of social service sectors, but with a rigorous demand that the initiatives be clearly innovative relative to other approaches, quantitatively demonstrate impact, and build sustainability into the initiative from its very inception. Proposals are considered only after an initial brief letter has been submitted to document both the need and the innovation of the approach. The Grants Committee of the foundation board is intimately involved in monitoring development of a full proposal and in subsequent site evaluations. Finally, although innovative approaches to complex problems take time, the foundation's multiple-year commitment to any organization will be withdrawn if services do not begin to flow to the needy population within one year of start-up. Theory must become reality, not a dissertation.

This is but one example. There are others in the nondot-com world. Too few, perhaps, but the recognition of the need for innovation, accountability, and sustainability is growing. But how different is this, really? Certainly, venture philanthropy differs from many approaches to "charity" of the last several decades. It has broken forcefully with the tendency of philanthropy to ask few questions and demand few answers. Yet it is not so different from the early approaches to philanthropy of major American foundations. Andrew Carnegie's effort to build lasting libraries in every community strove for sustainability and impact at the fundamental level of community learning. The early Rockefeller Foundation's

---

[1]The author served as a member of the board of the foundation and as chair of the Grants Committee, as well as having designed the Innovation Fund.

push to eradicate yellow fever, and the subsequent support of major U.S. philanthropies in the global campaign to eradicate smallpox, all were clear examples of early approaches that carefully selected problems, targeted the best minds and best technologies at them, and then drove toward a full and complete solution.

So, in a way, venture philanthropy is not so much a new phenomenon as a return to the roots of U.S. philanthropy. It may become a reaffirmation that investing in terrific ideas carried out by powerfully capable people and organizations targeting critical societal needs can bear lasting, meaningful results.

> "As I study wealthy men I can see but one way in which they can secure a real equivalent for money spent, and that is to cultivate a taste for giving where the money can produce an effect which will be a lasting gratification."
>
> —John D. Rockefeller

. . . OR JUST A BAD IDEA?

In sum, venture philanthropy seeks to hold social action and nonprofits to the same standards of performance that the new philanthropists themselves had to meet to attract market venture capital and build the new burgeoning economy.

The central problem, of course, is that the societal problems addressed by much of the nation's nonprofit infrastructure differ elementally from market opportunities. For some problems, root causes are not even clear, hence strategic action with measurable results is difficult to design. If you do not know, fundamentally, why Johnny cannot read or why Jane hates or why Joe chooses the street over a safe shelter or why Jean knowingly risks disease and death, then we will have difficulty crafting an effective intervention. Core societal flaws—fault lines created by human weakness, historical events, cultural mandates, and the like—give rise to significant dilemmas in any nation. The foundation for responding to such problems consists of 10 percent knowledge and 90 percent risk—and even the 10 percent is often imperfect.

For such problems, investments that demand strategic interventions and measurable results over the short term (for example, perhaps, in less than a generation) may demand too much. The risk factor is simply too high. For philanthropy, the question is clear: Is there not a floor to problem selection? Is there not a set of problems that are so complex, so poorly understood, so fundamentally entwined in societal structure that, at least for now, they call for a purely charitable approach? Is not charity—pure-and-simple giving because shared human destiny and common human respect demand a moral response—a socially appropriate and intellectually defensible response?

> **"In charity there is no excess."**
> —Sir Francis Bacon

But even short of these fundamental, generational problems, venture philanthropy, in turn, poses a series of questions for the nonprofit community. These questions are not imponderables, but they will require the expenditure of considerable energy from between the ears of nonprofit leaders.

How do we measure results in ways acceptable to philanthropists who are used to starkly clear market indicators like price per share? What should be measured? Outcome (clients served, food distributed, classes given) or impact (change of behavior)? And if it is impact that investors seek (a fairly sure bet, it would appear), then how can program intervention into complex problems with multiple causes be shown to have sufficient social return? And what is "sufficient?"

Is a venture philanthropy approach scalable? Perhaps, with insight, hard work, and even a bit of luck, programmatic intervention in a neighborhood can be demonstrated to have investment return on social measures. Perhaps it will even be sustainable in the community. But such initiatives will need to build in significant efforts in communication across the nation to achieve broader results. Nonprofits will need to explore whether a successful venture philanthropy approach to a problem on a limited scale can be applied more broadly (to a larger place, or more complex population).

What is the time frame? Over what period does the investor expect results? And is that time period reasonable from the viewpoint of the nonprofit and from the viewpoint of the investor? Let us be frank: There is a tension here. To the extent that venture philanthropy is impact-oriented, to the extent that it seeks sustainable solutions in reasonable time frames, it may work to the organizational disadvantage of the nonprofit. Under these conditions, philanthropy ceases to be a reliable income flow to nonprofits to meet general operating costs of their core organizations over time. Instead, when philanthropy seeks impacts and solutions for investments made at a particular point in time, it clearly implies that the philanthropist assumes an exit strategy. In that context, no time frame for impact may be organizationally comfortable for the nonprofit, because success means the investor exits. Hence, the nonprofit and the philanthropist have quite different assumptions about the task at hand. One wants a specific return on investment in a clear time frame, the other wants operating support indefinitely.

Finally, is the nonprofit sector up to the task? Are most (or even many) nonprofits staffed to develop the types of specific, efficient, goal-disciplined, output-oriented, measurement-intense organizations implied by a venture philanthropy approach? Do nonprofits—community groups, social service agencies, religious communities, welfare advocates—have the horses on the track to run this race? Currently, probably not. A change in philanthropic approach, if it spreads widely, will require aggressive and rigorous leadership in the nonprofit community to ensure that organizational capacity adjusts.

In the past decade, there has been a 40 percent increase in the number of nonprofits in the United States. In the end, it is leadership that will matter. Nonprofits will need to meet venture philanthropy on its own terms, with the skills, responsiveness, and creativity that a new generation of philanthropists are used to seeing in the marketplace. As in any market, the money will follow the combination of great ideas and creative management. And, as in any market, organizations without great ideas and creative management will find their future in doubt.

■ SOURCES

Calhoun, Alexander. "Holding Charities to a Higher Standard," *Christian Science Monitor*, December 6, 1999, p. 16.

Cannon, Carl M., "Policy: Charity for Profit," *National Journal*, June 17, 2000, pp. 1898–1904.

Cook, W. Bruce "The Psychology of Investing," *Fund Raising Management*, March 1998, pp. 13–18.

Delaney, Dennis. "Client Strategies: Venture Philanthropists," *Financial Planning*, June 1, 2000, pp. 93–95.

De Marco, Donna. "New Organizations in Business of Giving: Venture Philanthropy Idea Taking Root," *Washington Times*, March 9, 2000, p. B9.

Fryes B., "Gazillionaires Give Back," *Upside*, May 2000, pp. 248–258.

Greenfield, Karl Taro, "The New Philanthropy: A New Way of Giving," *Time*, July 24, 2000, pp. 48+.

Verhovek, Sam Howe. "From Web Fortunes, Innovative Philanthropy," *Minneapolis Star Tribune*, April 9, 2000, 4–E.

Wages in the Nonprofit Sector: Poor Cousin or Twin Sister?

Conventional wisdom holds that compensation in the nonprofit world is a poor cousin to pay scales in the for-profit world. If you want to "follow the money," the street signs all point to corporate America. Moreover, if that is so, wisdom continues, overtures by nonprofits to the workforce are most likely to be successful when pitching cause rather than cash.

But, as with all conventional wisdom, the truth appears to be more complex. In 1999, top executives in nonprofits received median pay increases of 6.2 percent, more than the 4.2 percent recorded in the private, for-profit sector. The median compensation for surveyed CEOs was $225,924, perhaps not equivalent to the corporate stratosphere, but certainly better than, for example, a U.S. Cabinet secretary's annual take of $150,000. The highest-paid nonprofit CEOs are to be found in the health sector, where CEO pay can exceed $450,000 per year.

The more interesting question is how compensation compares for the larger workforce. The story here appears to have at least three layers.

For some categories of nonprofit industries (e.g., healthcare and nursing facilities), pay levels are comparable to those in the for-profit sector. Certainly, part of this trend is due to the effects of organized labor in some sectors. In part, it is also a function of the ways in which services are compensated. Insurers pay for health services on fairly fixed schedules, irrespective of the market status of the provider. Hence, the drive toward cost containment is equal for the for-profit and the nonprofit healthcare provider.

For highly trained personnel (information systems managers, lawyers, financial managers), the for-profit marketplace probably does offer higher compensation. Hence, finding the trained personnel to bring nonprofits (especially small ones) into the age of electronic communication and the Internet does represent a challenge for nonprofits. This is particularly true because, irrespective of cash compensation, the siren song of stock options has (until the NASDAQ's implosion) been clear and sweet.

For the majority of workers, however, the compensation gap between for-profit and nonprofit is much smaller than expected. The National Bureau of Economic Research (NBER) found that, over time, workers who move from the for-profit to the nonprofit sector only experience a wage penalty of between 2 and 4 percent. Indeed, looking at the New York area, comparison of overall compensation levels for such positions as public relations, sales management, and clerical positions indicates little difference between nonprofit pay levels and the region's average.

There is one outstanding question, however: What happens as people get older? How do the compensation levels for young workers in the for-profit and nonprofit sector compare to similar levels for those who have been on the job for several decades? This is a critical question, because it might reveal the potential vulnerability of professional experience in nonprofits. The lesson from the teaching profession provides a sobering warning.

The wage gap between teachers and all other workers with a similar education varies tremendously across the nation, from a high of 60 percent in places like Texas to 18 percent in places like Connecticut. As a national average and taken as a whole, teachers experience only a $7,000 difference in compensation relative to equivalent workers from other economic sectors. However, by age 45, teacher compensation is on average $24,000 less per year. Over time, workers in other sectors and professions grow their compensation packages much more rapidly than do teachers. The result: an experience drain out of the teaching profession.

An interesting (and important) research question would be whether the same phenomenon happens in the nonprofit workforce. Does the NBER's 2 to 4 percent penalty grow greater as workers age? If so, is it possible that the experience drain that plagues education will come to bay at the heels of nonprofits as the American population ages?

▓ SOURCES

Abbott, Langer and Associates, "Compensation in Nonprofit Organizations," September 1999.

"An Apple for the Teacher: Regional Teacher Training and Pay Compares Well with U.S.," *Tri-State Trends*. New York Academy of Sciences, July 2000.

Libman, Harvey, "Pay for Leaders at Biggest Charities Rises 6.2%," *The Chronicle of Philanthropy,* September 21, 2000, p. 38.

Ruhm, Christopher and Carey Borkoski. "Compensation in the Nonprofit Sector," NBER Working Paper No. W7562, February 2000.

"S&T Occupation Compensation: It Pays to Be a Techie, and It Pays More to Manage Them," *Tri-State Trends,* S. Raymond Senior Editor, New York Academy of Sciences, May 1999.

Diversity and Governance: The Not-Good News

The issues of diversity and inclusion in governance—whether for nation states or private organizations—justifiably belong on the top ten list of concerns of private and public organizations everywhere.

Philanthropy is no exception. Grantmakers seek to affect societal dilemmas. Arguably, they would make the most insightful decisions about how to do that if their decision-making structures (as represented by their governing bodies) reflected a broad swath of society. So, to paraphrase the Big Apple's former mayor, Ed Koch, "How're we doin'?"

If the limited data available are any indication, the answer would seem to be, not too well.

Using the Taft Corporation's index, Prospector's Choice, a random sample of 142 private, independent foundations in 47 states was selected. The sample did not include Montana, Maine, or Idaho because board of directors data for foundations in those states did not include sufficient information to characterize the backgrounds of board members. The total board member sample for these foundations was 846 individuals. Board size ranged from a high of 19 to a low of 2. Within this sample, the backgrounds of about 75 percent of the board members could be determined. Of course, racial or ethnic makeup was not traceable. Still, there was a surprising homogeneity to the sample. Nearly three-quarters of board members (72 percent) were male. Nearly half (47 percent)

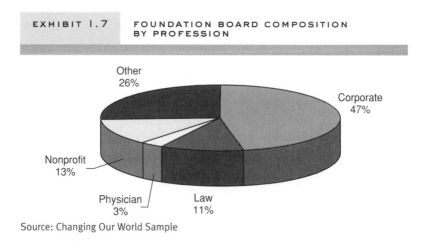

EXHIBIT I.7   FOUNDATION BOARD COMPOSITION BY PROFESSION

Source: Changing Our World Sample

had current primary employment in the corporate world. Another 11 percent were practicing lawyers. In the "doctor, lawyer, merchant chief" troika, doctors were definitely also-rans. Only 3 percent of foundation board members were physicians. Another 13 percent were currently employed in the nonprofit sector, including educators and religious leadership.

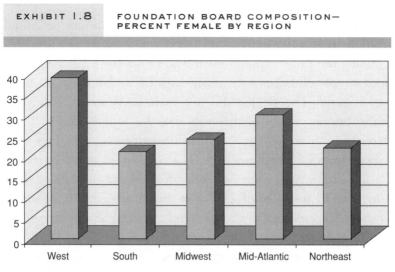

EXHIBIT I.8   FOUNDATION BOARD COMPOSITION— PERCENT FEMALE BY REGION

Source: Changing Our World Sample

Between 25 percent and 33 percent of the board members, irrespective of professional background, also held governance seats on other foundations or nonprofits. This interlocking board rate can be seen as a plus in the sense that board members are experienced in issues related to nonprofit management. But it can also be seen as a negative in the sense that it measures how narrow the absolute pool of board participants really is.

Most striking was the gender gap in philanthropic governance. Furthermore, that gap seems to narrow significantly only on the West Coast. Foundations in the Northeast, Midwest, and South trail significantly behind, and the Northeast is head-to-head with the South for dead last in board gender balance.

Obviously, these observations do not a dissertation make. The sample may be biased, although excluding Montana probably did not skew the analysis. Questions of the correlation of diversity with other factors such as foundation size are relevant. But the depth of the concentration of board leadership, measured by either gender or current employment, raises at least the suspicion that even further analysis would not significantly change the conclusion.

Does it matter? Perhaps not. There is no research that supports a reliable correlation between gender and wisdom or between profession and acumen. Smart people come to the party wearing many cloaks. Equally, there is no correlation between competence and chromosomal makeup.

Still, to the extent that, as a nation, we seek to ensure that decisions about resources targeted at societal problems reflect the perspectives of those involved, it would appear that philanthropies may have some housekeeping of their own to do.

■ **SOURCE**

Data from the Taft Corporation, Prospector's Choice.

Minority Philanthropy: The Future Has Arrived

The longest period of economic growth in the nation's history has lifted many boats. And, increasingly, modern philanthropy is not just about the mega-rich. It is also about Americans from all walks of life. The number of small family and community foundations has doubled since 1980. Among the significant actors in the growth of current and future U.S. philanthropy are America's minorities. By the end of 2000, 28.7 percent of the U.S. population was nonwhite (79.13 million people) compared to 12 percent a century ago. By 2015, that portion is expected to rise to 30 percent.

Let us pause, however. It is important to acknowledge that the economic good times have not resolved the nation's poverty problem. Indeed, poverty rates for full-time workers have stayed constant in the last two decades, and wealth concentration in the uppermost tiers of income levels has increased. Moreover, the economic elevator goes both up and down. Three-quarters of Americans can expect to see their annual income rise or fall by 5 percent in any given year.

Still, it is important to recognize that economics is creating new philanthropic leadership in American minority communities. In the African American community, the philanthropic spirit is not, admittedly, a "new new thing." Charitable giving in the black community dates from at least the late 1700s, when Richard Allen and Absalom Jones founded societies of free men to support poor

EXHIBIT I.9   LOWER-INCOME LIMIT OF TOP 5 PERCENT OF
HOUSEHOLDS (1999 CONSTANT DOLLARS)

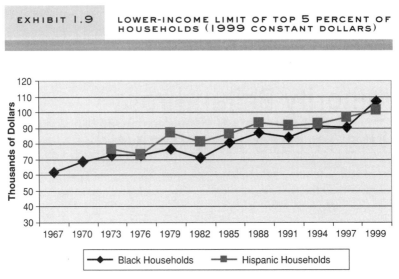

Source: U.S. Bureau of the Census

widows and orphans. Indeed, the Underground Railroad of 1804 certainly qualifies as a black philanthropic effort, with a social return on investment that would satisfy even the most hard-nosed of today's venture philanthropists! Economics is further enabling this history. In metropolitan Boston, with the fastest-growing urban black population in the nation, household incomes among blacks rose 40.2 percent in the 1990s. This change is striking in comparison to the overall Massachusetts increase of only 16 percent and the national increase of 11 percent. Nationally, 25 percent of African American households are in the top two quintiles (top 40 percent) of income. In the black community, 53 percent of households made charitable donations in 1997, up from 51 percent in 1993. This contrasts with a decline in the national average from 73 percent to 69 percent in the same period. Some 60 percent of African American giving flows through church communities.

In the Hispanic community, poverty rates have dropped to their lowest levels since the late 1970s. Less than a quarter (23 percent) of Hispanic households are below the poverty level, and median income rose 6 percent between 1998 and 1999. Latino business leadership is also stepping into the front lines of philanthropy. The

New America Alliance has been formed by Latino entrepreneurs interested in addressing deep-rooted problems within their own community, as well as in creating greater opportunities for Latino entrepreneurs.

Immigrant minorities are also major philanthropic players. In recent years, the United States has received more than 1 million immigrants annually, 660,000 legally and an estimated 300,000 without documents. The United States is now home to nearly 30 million foreign-born residents. More than 25,000 high-tech émigrés from India have settled in the United States to lead the technology explosion. They now run more than 750 technology companies in Silicon Valley alone. Immigrant giving is global. Beneficiaries are not just communities in which immigrants live and succeed, but also those back home. In 2002, the United States recorded $32 billion in remittances to Latin America alone from foreign-born workers sending money to their home countries. Nearly 23 percent of all international remittances originate in the United States.

In the United States, minority leadership in philanthropy tends to focus resources on deep and historically intractable social problems, seeking to work creatively at the community level. Minority

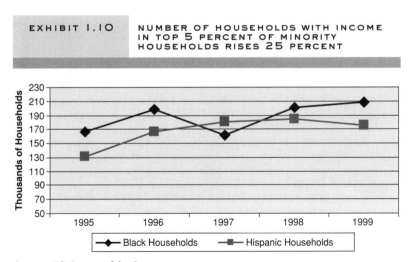

EXHIBIT 1.10   NUMBER OF HOUSEHOLDS WITH INCOME IN TOP 5 PERCENT OF MINORITY HOUSEHOLDS RISES 25 PERCENT

Source: U.S. Bureau of the Census

EXHIBIT 1.11   FOREIGN-BORN INDIVIDUALS LIVING IN
THE UNITED STATES

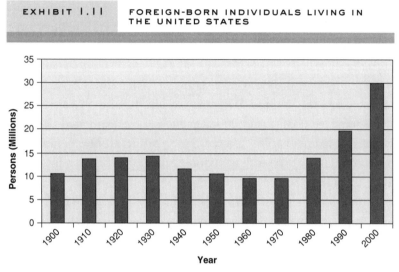

Source: U.S. Bureau of the Census

resources also focus on opening up market opportunities for their communities, so that progress on the educational and social fronts will lead to progress and stability economically. While the "new philanthropy" that generates eight-figure donations to academic centers may grab the headlines, it is quieter, less-flashy minority philanthropy that may be making the most creative investments in street-level solutions to the nation's enduring social and educational inequities.

The longer America can preserve and extend economic growth, the more new entrants to philanthropic leadership will come from America's minorities—and the more robust and creative will be the philanthropic landscape.

■ SOURCES

"Black Philanthropy Conference Taps into the Collective Wealth of the Black Middle Class in New England," *Business Wire,* May 22, 2000, p. 1.

Dugger, Celia. "Return Passage to India: Émigrés Pay Back," *New York Times,* February 29, 2000, Section A, p. 1, col. 2.

Hernandez, D. "With Fewer Dollars to Go Around, More Are Going Around the World," *New York Times,* July 14, 2003, Section B, p. 1, col. 2.

"Latino Leaders Form Philanthropic Alliance," *Los Angeles Times,* January 12, 2000, p. 6.

Meredith, Denise. "Black Philanthropy Will Continue to Be a Strong Force," *The Business Journal (Phoenix),* 20:29, April 21, 2000, p. 18.

Migration News, 7:11 November 2000, Web newsletter published by University of California at Davis.

U.S. Bureau of the Census, Detailed Income Tabulaitons, Census 2000.

Will There Be a Nonprofit Shakeout? Comparing Nonprofits to Small Business Trends

The vast majority of U.S. nonprofits are extremely small (with less than $25,000 in annual income), with limited capacity to support major investments in technology or management. They are close to their community need, and dominantly run by volunteers. These are organizational assets. But, they are likely not well positioned to take advantage of the $38 trillion intergenerational transfer of wealth. What will happen? Two trends provide food for thought, one from small business and one from the nonprofit sector in New York City.

Small business is similar in structure to the nonprofit sector. Fully 20 percent of America's 5.8 million small business establishments have annual revenue of less than $100,000. Nearly 50 percent have revenues of less than $250,000. Only 6 percent have sales of over $1 billion. Just as in the nonprofit sector, the base of the business pyramid is very broad; the top is very narrow.

But, in contrast to nonprofits, in the small business model, "business death" is a common, and indeed healthy, phenomenon. Annually in the United States, between 550,000 and 600,000 small businesses are born each year; only about 50,000 more than the number of small firms that die. However, the overall numbers are misleading. In 2000, in 31 of 50 states, the rate of termination of small business exceeded the rate of small business formation. In 31 states (but not necessarily the same 31), the number of termina-tions in 2000 exceeded those in 1999. Such turnover is an indicator of economic growth, as new firms replace outmoded ones. Even with the churn of birth and death, small business employment has risen by nearly 11 percent in the last decade, wage and salary income has risen 71 percent, and nonfarm proprietors' income has nearly doubled.

Change is indeed good. And the change is not all due to busi-ness "failure" as measured by bankruptcies. Annual small business bankruptcies have declined by nearly half in the last decade. The birth-and-death cycle is driven by closures (for whatever reason) of firms in which entrepreneurs pursue other opportunities, or by mergers. Small business mergers totaled $12 billion at the end of the 1990s. And the merger phenomenon characterizes the bottom of the pyramid as much as it does the top. In the mid-1990s, more than 1,000 mergers took place for which the transaction was worth $50 million or less.

Could the dominance of small nonprofits within an environment of huge wealth transfers lead to similar results? Might the nonprofit sector begin to see a death cycle, as new opportunities are created by growing firms at the mid- and large-sized levels, and as small nonprofit founders and managers pursue these new opportunities? Will that wealth transfer also create an urge to merge? Will small nonprofits, seeing the cycle begin, actively pursue mergers so as to better position themselves to access the wealth transfer?

If change is good for business, might it not also be good for nonprofits? There may be some evidence from the nonprofit sector itself that these patterns are on the horizon.

The May 2002 report on New York City's Nonprofit Sector, published by the Nonprofit Coordinating Committee of New York, indicated that nearly a quarter (24 percent) of surveyed nonprofits in New York City pursued joint venture or merger efforts with other nonprofit or for-profit organizations in an effort to increase revenues. The motivation for the "urge to merge" is

WILL THERE BE A NONPROFIT SHAKEOUT?   49

more striking when the survey data are combined with data in a later section of the report. According to the report's scenario analysis, 29 percent of New York's public charities had deficits in 2000. If total revenues were to decline by 15 percent, that portion would rise to 71 percent. In that case, the total net income of public charities in New York would shift from a $4 billion surplus to a $2.5 billion deficit.

That is an amazing finding. When a 15 percent decline in revenue more than doubles the number of nonprofits with deficits and results in a loss of $6.5 billion in net income, then something is very seriously wrong. If true, nonprofits in New York appear to be living on a financial knife's edge. The merger or consolidation option would appear to be much more than academic.

> "Deals often look more exciting from the outside. We had a story about this back in Iowa. A man found that his horse was ailing. So he took the horse to the vet and asked, 'Can you help me? Sometimes my horse walks fine. But other times, he limps.' The vet looked at the horse and said, 'Yes, I think I can help you. When he's walking fine, sell him.' That's a good thing to remember in the merger market. The buyer must always beware."
>
> —James D. Ericson,
> Chairman and CEO, Northwestern Mutual

For New York's nonprofits, change may be more than good. It may be the stuff from which survival itself is made.

■ SOURCES

Seley, J.E. and J. Wolpert. "New York City's Nonprofit Sector," Nonprofit Coordinating Committee of New York, May 2002.

Small Business Economic Indicators 2000. U.S. Small Business Administration, 2001.

Stone A., D. Leonhardt, and W. Zellner. "You Don't Have to Be Ted Turner to Merge," *Business Week*, March 18, 1996, ENT6.

U.S. Bureau of the Census, "Statistics About Business Size," 2001.

The Growing Demand for Philanthropic Accountability: Will There Be Room for Risk?

With growth in philanthropic roles in American society, and with greater media awareness of instances of philanthropic mismanagement, there is growing demand for organizational accountability within the philanthropic sector. In turn, there is an expectation that funders be as cognizant of the need to produce both efficiency and impact as their nonprofit grant recipients.

This is not news. Numerous observers have pointed out that foundation accountability is problematic. Beyond their board members, foundations are not subject to the scrutiny of either the market place or public regulation. There is no market measure determining whether they spend their money well or ill. As a consequence, there has been a growing call for the functional equivalent of benchmarking among foundations. Led in part by the W.K. Kellogg Foundation and the David and Lucile Packard Foundation, this effort has attempted to achieve consensus among foundation leadership that measuring effectiveness is important and that unanimity be reached on the methods to be used for such measurement.

"Great deeds are usually wrought at great risk."
—Herodotus

The 2002 conference of Grantmakers for Effective Organizations devoted considerable attention to the impact and accountability issues, including the application of performance measures to foundations. The conference report makes for an interesting read. Although "effectiveness" often does not equate with impact, certainly, the ideas of effectiveness and accountability receive applause.

Two issues remain troubling, however. One emerges from observations that are in the report, one from an issue omitted.

Grantmakers at the conference were asked to rank "current reality" and "desired future" along a spectrum for a series of 13 issues. Understandably, grantmakers' average scores for the desired future diverged from their assessment of current reality. But the two issues on which grantmakers felt that current reality was closest to optimal were "regulatory requirements for philanthropy" (understandably, since few industries of any type seek to be more aggressively regulated) and "results-based accountability." Grantmakers on average portrayed the current importance of results-based accountability as being almost the desired importance. This does not seem to reflect a burning desire to explore new worlds of benchmarking among the philanthropic rank-and-file. There would appear to be a difference of perspective between the enthusiastic comments of leaders in the report and the views of those who would follow.

The more difficult question posed by the application of benchmarking or performance measurement to philanthropy however, does not appear in the report. I am a firm believer in rigorous accountability and merciless evaluation, but, when applied to foundations, what happens to risk?

"There are risks and costs to a program of action. But they are far less than the long-range risks and costs of comfortable inaction."
—John F. Kennedy

In part because they are endowed and independent, philanthropies have the capability to explore new frontiers. They have the capability to identify promising innovations, untested approaches, and blasphemous theories, and to place bets (well-educated bets, hopefully) on these novel solutions. They have the capability to be society's risk-takers. Where private enterprise must minimize risk to ensure return, and where government must beware of risk in its role as the guardian of the taxpayers' purse, foundations can seize risk. The daycare provider with the novel approach to reaching undocumented workers, the laboratory with the preclinical insight that is too early for National Institutes of Health (NIH) consideration, the teacher with the caution-to-the-wind inspiration about how biology really ought to be taught—none of these will find funding through conventional public sources, nor through market-sensitive private enterprise.

Yet, because they are untested and therefore risky, such opportunities are also likely to suffer a higher rate of failure than conventional approaches. If a foundation's role (at least in part) is to explore the novel, then it must also be expected to fail. Indeed, there is a case to be made that any foundation grant portfolio without a healthy proportion of failures is not taking enough risk; it is simply substituting philanthropic money for government or market money, hence is not fulfilling its societal role.

But, if we are to apply performance and effectiveness standards to foundations, what shall we do with risk? There is no "reward" to risk in philanthropy comparable to the market reward that provides incentives to risk. The reward is only in the consistency with the larger mission of foundations. So, if there is not reward, and if risk is avoided in the interests of performance, who (except the MacArthur Foundation's "genius" grants) will fund the blasphemers, the innovators, the revolutionaries?

Further, will the coming transfer of wealth and the growing reliance on philanthropy for the funding of basic services add propulsion to the evaluation-sensitive, risk-averse momentum of foundations? Where resources are increasingly consumed by grants for basic services, and where the needs of such services exponentially

exceed the resources available, will innovation, insight, inspiration—
hence, risk—be further avoided?

As ardent abolitionist and Fireside Poet James Russell Lowell
put it, "Not failure, but low aim, is the crime."

▧ SOURCES

"Capacity-Building for Impact: The Future of Effectiveness for Nonprofits and
Foundations," Grantmakers for Effective Organizations, in partnership with
Forum of Regional Associations of Grantmakers and Grantmakers Evalu-
ation Network, 2002.

Cohen, Todd. "Taking Stock: The Value of Evaluation," *Philanthropy Journal,*
November 15, 2001.

"Toward a Common Language: Listening to Foundation CEOs and Other
Experts Talk about Performance Measurement in Philanthropy," The Center
for Effective Philanthropy, 2002.

Managing through the Market: Responding to Severe Economic Cycles

The October 11, 2002 edition of the *New York Times* made quite an issue of the effect of Wall Street's "Blue Period" on philanthropic capacity, and the hard times that the philanthropic response promises for nonprofits. Gloom and doom is the bread and butter of the news business, so one should not be surprised that the article found bits of the sky scattered about the landscape. But, skeptic that I am, let's look more closely at the numbers and their implications.

> "Wall Street indexes predicted nine out of the last five recessions."
>
> —Paul A. Samuelson, 1966

First of all, from the point of view of the nonprofits. It is certainly true that a rise in the number of nonprofits and an inflation-adjusted decline in charitable dollars has constrained the total resource base for nonprofit funding (more on this later). And, of course, that is particularly true for any nonprofit that bet the ranch on one or two frisky technology thoroughbreds whose legs gave way in the back stretch. All betting entails risk, and, often, risk wins.

But, by and large, U.S. nonprofits are smarter than the *Times* gives them credit for being. Nonprofits do diversify their revenue streams. A 2002 report by the New York City Nonprofits Project of the Nonprofit Coordinating Committee of New York indicates that foundation and corporate grants accounted for only 5 percent of the revenue sources of New York City nonprofits. In comparison, 25 percent came from government grants and 37 percent from service fees and sales. Of course, there are differences by sector, with the arts overwhelmingly more dependent on grants. Still, even there, grants accounted for only 23 percent of receipts; when individual donations were added, the total was 40 percent, making that sector notably vulnerable. But human services organizations relied on individual donations and foundation grants for only 13 percent of their revenue. The point is, if the sky is falling, it is falling only selectively.

How about from the point of view of foundations? It is absolutely true that many foundations have seen endowments erode. How much is a function of their investment strategy over the last (at least) three years. Then again, the erosion and its link to investing choices is not unique to the world of philanthropy. Most Americans with Individual Retirement Accounts have experienced little financial joy in the last several years.

The endowment erosion of foundation assets raises management issues. How does one manage around the realities of business cycles? The article provided two examples, but did not "do the math" that illuminated their implications. By doing that math (arithmetic, really), the effects of management choices become clear. Doing the math reveals two alternative approaches to market-driven change. One foundation saw its assets erode by 80 percent, the other by 36 percent. Neither, to its credit, reduced its grantmaking at a pace equal to its assets. That is where the similarity ends.

The foundation with 80 percent erosion reduced its grant level by 20 percent and its staff by 50 percent. The result was a net increase in grant resources allocated per staff member. In turn, this implies a decrease in the cost of doing business and an increase in productivity. The second, with 36 percent erosion, reduced its total grant resources by 9 percent, but cut its staff by only 3 percent. The result was a net decrease in grant output per staff member—implying, in turn, an increase in the cost of doing business and a decrease in productivity. Further, in the 80 percent case, with an increase in money moved per staff member, the absolute level of grant dollars per staff member ($2.5 million) was over three times that of the foundation with 36 percent erosion (just over $800,000).

These simple calculations probably understate the differences in impact on the cost of doing business between the two examples. In the 36 percent erosion case, 74 percent of the eliminated positions were in the developing world. If at least part were local salaried personnel, then reduction in costs was not parallel with an equivalent impact on reducing U.S.-level compensation.

So the more interesting questions about severe market cycles and philanthropy are about the management strategies that maximize the money flowing from the foundation spigot.

SOURCES

Giving USA, *American Association of Fund Raising Counsel*, 2002.

Seley, J.E. and J. Wolpert. "*New York City's Nonprofit Sector,*" The New York City Nonprofits Project, May 2002.

Strom, S. "Cultural Groups and Charities Are Feeling Each Bump on Wall Street," *New York Times*, October 11, 2002, Section A, p. 27, col. 1.

The Philanthropic Instinct: Government Walks the Talk

The close relationship between government and the nonprofit sector is neither new nor news. At its most basic level, the growth of the nonprofit community is, at least in part, a product of government policy, especially tax policy. In addition, however, government is a major source of nonprofit revenue. Grants, contracts, and reimbursements from public agencies provide the nonprofit sector with 36 percent of its revenue. For civic affairs organizations, that portion rises to 51 percent and for healthcare, 41 percent.

Although government funding has had its ups and downs over the decades, since the late 1970s government support for nonprofits has risen an average of 6 percent per year.

The success of the nonprofit sector, and the concomitant growth in private philanthropy supporting that sector, however, have not been lost on government agencies. The government itself has recently entered the philanthropic world, and entered it at its heart—as a fundraiser for its own programs!

For years, of course, local public agencies, notably fire departments and sheriff's offices, have established independent foundations for community donations to support public safety services. In a few instances, local or county public service agencies have also established foundations to raise supplemental funds for their programs. For example, the Craven County Health Department Foundation in New Bern, North Carolina, reported just over $51,000 in income to support county public health programs.

But the urge to fundraise has leapt across the equivalent of governmental species. The federal government now shares the philanthropic itch. Taking a page from its local public and voluntary agencies, and banking on the success of private philanthropy in the go-go 1990s, the federal government has now begun to encourage private fundraising to pursue its agenda. Foundations and other funds affiliated with federal agencies and quasi-agencies are pursuing philanthropic donations from individuals, corporations, and foundations. The Centers for Disease Control (CDC) Foundation, for example, was founded in 1994 to "champion . . . initiatives" of the Centers for Disease Control and Prevention of the U.S. Department of Health and Human Services. For the fiscal year ended June 2000, the CDC Foundation reported nearly $5 million in revenue and $12 million in net assets.

The National Academy of Engineering (NAE) Fund, established to supplement the work of the NAE (which carries out scientific and technical analyses for the Congress and executive agencies) reported $10.4 million in operating revenue for 2000, of which about $8 million was from private contributions and $2.35 million was from income on its $58.4-million asset base of investments and securities.

Of course, the federal fundraising granddaddy of them all is the Library of Congress, which, after a specific act of Congress, was permitted to receive its first private monetary gift in 1909. The Library of Congress Trust Fund was created in 1925, with authority to accept and invest gifts. With the opening of its development office in 1987, and a fundraising Web site in 1998, the trust fund is setting new precedents for its federal philanthropic counterparts.

There are, perhaps, two ways to look at this trend. Raised eyebrows is certainly one option. These are, after all, public institutions, accountable to the public, via democratically elected representatives, for their policies and programs. If the electoral process results in an expression of public support for (or lack of support for) particular efforts or directions, then the financial expression of that view is meted out in the budgetary process allocating public funds. Diversification of programs into areas of private interest and/or

supplementation of public funding with privately interested resources might give the purist pause.

That caution would be deepened for those in the nonprofit
world who might see such fundraising as competition for finite
philanthropic dollars. How can a local health nonprofit compete for
donations for prevention programs, when the private fundraising competition is the federal government?

Conversely, a hearty "bravo" is the second analytic option.
Taking the easiest criticism first, there are no data that portray philanthropy as a zero-sum game. What one nonprofit gains does not
equal a loss for another. Rather, the consistent growth in philanthropy would indicate that philanthropy is a positive-sum game
(i.e., every fundraising gain has the potential to increase the total
philanthropic pie by encouraging additional new giving from elsewhere). In that sense, the power of a major player (e.g., the federal
government) in the philanthropic marketplace might increase
awareness of prevention needs, hence motivate local philanthropy
to become more supportive of local efforts.

That said, is private philanthropic fundraising by public agencies
appropriate? It is true that one can think of scenarios in which
raised eyebrows would be justified. Money talks. There is as much
opportunity for horse-trading of dollars and programs in the nonprofit world as in the corporate boardroom. The risk is always
troubling, and it is doubly troubling where the public trust is an
organization's raison d'etre.

The answer to that concern, of course, is not prohibition, but
transparency. It is key that private fundraising organizations dedi-
cated to supplementing the resources of public agencies be transparent. Fortunately, the quintessential American combination of
the Internal Revenue Service, energetic national watchdog organizations, and a lively press corps give hope that transparency will
prevail. Indeed, transparency will be more likely for these agency-
support foundations than anywhere else in the nonprofit world.
After all, they shadow federal agency efforts, and those agencies
answer to the electorate. Where the electorate is to be found, there
also will Congress be found. Nothing encourages the straight and

narrow like the potential for being called before the House or Senate.

Besides, it's a free country. One of the first philanthropic donations in America at its infancy was from Benjamin Franklin in 1789. He handed his money not to some nonprofit, but to the City of Philadelphia. If Joe and Jane Taxpayer are fond enough of the work of the government that they want to supplement their tax bill with an additional donation, then caveat emptor.

SOURCES

Boris, Elizabeth, and Eugene Steuerle, "What Charities Cannot Do," *Christian Science Monitor*, October 1, 1999, p. 11.

Government foundation data from Centers for Disease Control, National Academy of Engineering, Library of Congress, Web sites.

Philanthropy data from Guidestar 2002 and The Foundation Center, 2002.

Does Wall Street Matter? The Unknowns about Elasticities

Nonprofit private charities are, it is said, so heavily dependent on revenues from the private sector that the dip in the Dow equates to a Maalox moment for nonprofit budgets. How true is that? There are three ways to look at the problem.

First, and most directly, there is the question of the direct relationship between the revenues of charitable nonprofits and their assets. An IRS sample of 162,559 charitable nonprofits' balance sheets illuminates the issue. Overall, revenue from investments, sales of securities, and sales of other assets (including rent) amounted to just 4.1 percent of revenue. For nonprofits with assets under $1 million (two-thirds of the sample), it accounted for under 1 percent. So, for all but the largest charitable nonprofits swings in the Dow have little direct bearing on the balance sheet. Even for the largest nonprofits—those with assets of greater than $50 million each—income from investments and assets rarely exceeds 4 percent of total institutional revenue.

Second, the two most important sources of nonprofit income are government grants and service revenues. Together, these account for over three-quarters of the income that funds nonprofit budgets. The effect is more pronounced for extremely large charities (with assets of over $50 million) for which nearly 80 percent of revenue is attributable to service sales and government. In the smallest charities, however, these two sources also account for over 50 percent of revenues. So, to the extent that the Dow reflects a

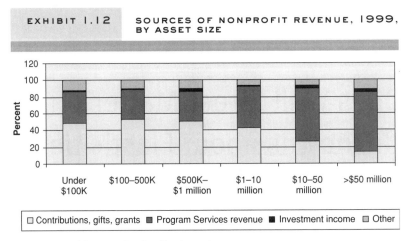

EXHIBIT 1.12   SOURCES OF NONPROFIT REVENUE, 1999, BY ASSET SIZE

Source: Internal Revenue Service (Arnsberger)

broader economic downturn (which is not always the case), then it matters not so much in terms of the market value lost in the dip, but the reduced tax support for government budgets and the purchasing power of consumers. That means for the heart of the nonprofit charity's budget capacity, it is not the Dow that matters but the economy. The tax take in Washington matters more than the price-to-earnings ratio on Wall Street.

Third, it may also be true that contributions by the public to nonprofits are affected by the Dow, but only insofar as contributions are made out of gains from assets represented by the Dow. Foundations make such contributions because they give from endowment earnings, but foundations are only 10 percent of all philanthropic giving in the nation. Individual behavior is more important. Do individuals give out of assets or out of income? If the former, then the Dow clearly matters. But most quotidian giving is not a result of the sale of assets, so the value of those assets is not a driving force.

"We make a living by what we get, but we make a life by what we give."

—Winston Churchill

If giving is out of income, then, again, it is the economy that matters. And, as with the market for sale of services by nonprofits, the issue for contributions behavior relative to income is akin to what economists call elasticity. This is an interesting question about which little has been written. Elasticity measures the relationship between price and demand or price and supply. If demand does not respond to changes in price, then it is said to be inelastic. The question, then, is how to measure the elasticity of individual giving.

If the economy stumbles and incomes decline (or people perceive that their income declines), how much decline must occur before giving also declines? Alternatively, for every dollar of decline (or perceived decline), how many cents of giving are withheld? Does income level matter? Does place matter? Does age matter?

"Medical science has developed two ways of actually determining insanity. One is if the patient cuts out paper dolls, and the other is if the patient says: 'I will tell you what this economic business really means.'"
—Will Rogers

This metric is important for two reasons. First, of course, it is important because it allows organizations to plan. Having some sense of elasticities would allow charities to anticipate revenue constriction in advance, and plan accordingly. In turn, planning prevents unnecessary handwringing through economic cycles, and, in turn, unnecessary public expressions of alarm over giving levels.

Understanding elasticities is also important because it would provide a more accurate and realistic picture of the American philanthropic impulse. Most research treats philanthropy as a stock. It measures amounts given annually just the way a warehouse measures widget inventory: "$300 billion of goodwill delivered in 2001." But philanthropy is not a stock; it is a flow. It is not widgets; it is finance. Giving is the monetized value of a stream of behavior by individuals. That stream has a course and a depth, and it flows with currents and eddies whose physics are determined by the obstacles in its path. Thinking about philanthropy as a flow rather than a stock would lead to a better understanding of all of those factors—and, in turn, a better understanding of and ability to predict future trends.

Why bother? Because the more the nation relies on individual initiative and behavior to resolve societal problems, the more the understanding of that behavior will be important. If we are to turn to individual giving and volunteering as a solution, we must forge strategies from accurate information, not from common wisdoms.

■ SOURCE

Arnsberger, Paul. "Charities and Other Tax-Exempt Organizations, 1998," Special Studies Special Projects Section, Internal Revenue Service. In *IRS Statistics of Income Bulletin*, Fall 2002, Publication 1136.

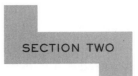

Ethics and Accountability

INTRODUCTION TO THE ISSUES

Standards for behavior—for individuals or for institutions—should not shift just because the microscope of the media is suddenly trained on a particular event or leader. What is wrong is wrong, irrespective of who's looking.

Still, the more prominent the organization or the more powerful its role in society, the more concerns about behavior seem to find their way to page one of the morning papers, hence center stage in the public and regulatory consciousness. If institutions are not prepared for the emergence of questions about their behavior before those questions are raised, if they have not set in place and taken seriously the systems to ensure transparent and accountable governance and finance before the media lens turns to them, then all times afterward will be "too late."

The regulatory and legal structure and process that govern the commercial marketplace have long provided the for-profit sector with strict parameters for and standards of financial and gover-nance behavior. These are complemented by voluntary standards set by business professions and whole industries, standards intended to prevent wrongdoing as well as build public trust.

In the commercial sector, both legal and voluntary standards are oft times violated. When they are, the judicial trigger is pulled, a price is paid, and the parameters and standards themselves are tightened. There is an expectation in the commercial sector that this will be so. Hence, there may be debate about the validity of public or regulatory accusations of malfeasance, and long legal battles over enforcement, but commercial institutions are rarely surprised that judicial action ensues.

As the nonprofit sector has become a larger portion of the national economy, the public lens has turned more readily to its financial and governance structure and behavior. The greater the power of nonprofits, the more evident their economic and social importance, the more probing the scrutiny. Over the past several years, it has become clear that many nonprofit institutions, executives, and members of boards of directors have not been prepared for that scrutiny. Indeed, surprise has been the most common reaction. That the public (or government) should expect greater care in the management of financial resources, greater transparency in philanthropic process, greater efficiency in program administration has evoked startled responses from nonprofit and philanthropic leaders.

> "We have, I fear, confused power with greatness."
> —Steward L. Udall
> Commencement address to Dartmouth College, June 13, 1965

This is surprising on two counts. First, high standards of behavior and strict discipline in the stewardship of resources should be expected, irrespective of media attention. What is right is not a function of who is looking. Second, that people care about those standards and disciplines as the power of nonprofits grows should not be remarkable. Power generates expectations.

That there is some resistance to deep questioning on these dimensions is, in some senses, understandable. The nonprofit and philanthropic worlds do much good, both at home and abroad. There is, perhaps, justifiable frustration at being questioned. But, "doing good" is not the standard against which accountable organizations hold themselves. And accountability—even new and more rigorous definitions of accountability—is what the future will be about. It is useless to fulminate about the rise of those definitions and expectations. They reflect public concern and, by virtue of their existence, must be the standards adopted by organizations that rely on public acquiescence (and the privilege of tax-free status) for their existence.

> "The mind likes a strange idea as little as the body likes a strange protein, and resists it with a similar energy. It would not perhaps be too fanciful to say that a new idea is the most quickly acting antigen known to science. If we watch ourselves honestly, we shall often find that we have begun to argue against a new idea even before it has been completely stated."
> —Wilfred Batten Lewis Trotter, MD
> *The Lancet,* 1939

The essays in this section address the issues associated with growing public expectations about nonprofit and philanthropic transparency, accountability, and efficiency. These issues are not merely matters for academic debate. Their increasingly widespread discussion will gradually bring these issues before legislative and regulatory bodies. Indeed, that process has begun. Mastering the issues and seizing the initiative for reform may prove fundamental determinants of the future evolution of the nonprofit sector.

How Shall We Govern Ourselves?

It did not take the Enron Corporation debacle to create the logic for careful board structure, but it certainly helped to jolt awake any executive who was nodding off. Boards of directors are (or ought to be) where the buck stops. Final responsibility rests with the board. The simplicity of the rule, however, masks the complexity of its implications. The board role is not an easy one. Board members must be at once cheerleaders and cops, public promoters and private overseers. They have vested interests (often financial, always psychological) in success, but are ultimately accountable for ensuring that success is achieved validly and that failure, when it occurs, is public.

The question of governance is not only a persistent problem for corporations. It also increasingly dogs the waking hours of non-profits and philanthropies. The nonprofit sector is a significant part of the national economy. It now accounts for 7 percent of the American economy and employs 10 percent of the work-force. In the last three decades of the twentieth century, paid employment in nonprofits rose at nearly twice the rate of national employment. Increasingly, the nation turns to nonprofits for the delivery of significant amounts of social services. Many non-profits are as large as major commercial firms. Some nonprofits even compete with commercial enterprises for the provision of goods and services in the marketplace. Expansion of expectations about nonprofit boards of directors has evolved apace with these changes.

Given the importance of the sector and the complexity of the board role, then, it is curious that nonprofit guidelines for boards of directors seem less serious than those taught in business schools for commercial corporate governance. Examine, for example, the standards for governance of charitable organizations developed and promulgated by the New York Philanthropic Advisory Service (NYPAS). The examination will not take long. There are only three rules. That's right, three.

First, the board has to be "active," defined as meeting three times a year, with a majority present. It has to be "independent," with compensated members constituting no more than 20 percent of the voting membership. Finally, board members should not be engaged in business transactions in which they have "material conflicting interests." The NYPAS takes no position on board knowledge, education, or access to information. More troubling, it provides no benchmarks for board function. It does not, for example, offer standards for roles in ensuring that financial filings are correct or for ensuring compliance with the law. With nonprofit growth and complexity, both would appear to be fundamental to resource stewardship.

Contrast this skeletal advice with the standards and guidelines bounding the behavior of commercial enterprises. For example, the "Principles of Corporate Governance" published by the Organization for Economic Cooperation and Development (OECD), reflect the general commercial practices of industrialized nations. As a median, they are not even the most strict or rigorous within the industrialized world. The principles are organized into six sections, with the function section comprising seven items. Most of these items are included (and many are expanded upon) in the "Best Practices Roadmap for Excellence in Corporate Governance" of the Business Roundtable in New York.

The board roles and responsibilities these principles outline extend beyond showing up three times a year. In the OECD's corporate governance framework, boards of market enterprises are to:

- Set corporate strategy, performance objectives, and major expenditures.
- Select, compensate, monitor and replace key executives, and oversee succession planning.
- Set and review remuneration.
- Make a clear distinction in board participation in matters of audit and compensation, allowing only independent members to sit on these committees.
- Ensure the integrity of financial accounting and reporting systems.
- Ensure compliance with the law.
- Oversee and ensure disclosure of all items material to corporate performance.
- Have access to accurate, relevant, and timely information to accomplish these functions.

Why is there such a difference between the nonprofit expectations of the NYPAS and the enterprise expectations of the OECD? And, whatever the reason, is the difference to be commended or condemned?

At one level, nonprofits argue that charities as sources and producers of "social goods" are not part of the market. Hence, they should not be required to have boards that hold fiduciary responsibility for performance and, therefore, boards that must have a central role in information and decision making. But, with the expansion of the concept of "markets" in which nonprofits do everything from sell used cars to pharmaceuticals, the for profit/not-for-profit distinction is losing its meaning. As the government pays nonprofits to provide more and more services, and as they acquire more economic and social power, this distinction will further blur.

> "Nearly all men can stand adversity, but if you want to test a man's character, give him power."
>
> —Abraham Lincoln

Nonprofits also argue that, in the nonprofit world, there are no stockholders and no return on investment. Those who govern and manage nonprofits, therefore, do not have a fiduciary responsibility to some large group of owners, hence do not need the legal strictures that rigorous board structure and regulation requires.

This argument fails on two counts. First, in fact, board members of nonprofits are increasingly being sued for breach of fiduciary responsibility. Whether more careful and comprehensive development of board function would have mitigated these suits is unclear, but the existence of litigation argues for greater care in governance. It also argues for greater care in choosing and training nonprofit trustees. If lawsuits loom, no rational leader will agree to serve on a board that does not set forth clear and careful criteria for board selection and institute careful preparation of board members for their responsibilities.

Second, the rationale for rigorous board management is not just litigation prevention. Well-educated and informed boards, whose functions reach deeply into the financial and management aspects of an organization, bring huge operational expertise and benefits to the planning and execution of an organization's mission. Attracting and taking advantage of this expertise requires that nonprofits take their own boards very seriously and communicate that seriousness of purpose to every leader they encounter.

Charities take (or make) money to deliver a socially valued good or service. The bigger they become, and the more central they are to the nation's progress, the more board governance will be looked to as a measure of their credibility. Moreover, the more central nonprofits become to the nation's social and economic fabric, the more board governance will matter in ensuring the transparency and accountability of the financial base and management structure of nonprofits. Nonprofit boards cannot escape the evolution of their role in ensuring rigorous financial management and public accountability.

We would do well to look frankly in the mirror and measure nonprofit board governance using the same metric as for our corporate brethren.

▓ SOURCES

Business Roundtable, 2002 Principles for Corporate Governance, May 2002.

"Governance and Accountability," *Board Member,* March 1999. Published by the National Center for Nonprofit Boards.

"Make Change, Not Money: More Like Big Business." Minnesota Public Radio broadcast of 9/3/98 archived by American Radioworks, September 3, 1998.

New York Philanthropic Advisory Service Standards, Educational Research Foundation of the Better Business Bureau of Metropolitan New York, 1998.

The Mission Meets
the Numbers:
Is It Okay to Lie?

$\mathbf{A}$n extraordinary article in the *New York Times* "Week in
Review," August 18, 2002, raised to the surface a long-submerged
issue for nonprofits. The article, "African Numbers, Problems
and Number Problems," reviewed the often glaring discrepancy
between what is known (and largely not known) about African
population, health, and economic development levels and what
advocates and international organizations say. Often, even the total
population of countries is in dispute, as is the degree of, for example, disease incidence and the importance of various diseases on
actual death rates. Death rates themselves, parenthetically, are also
empirically unknown.

Absent precision, advocate organizations select, or calculate, or
estimate the worst case universally from narrow survey data. They
then use those numbers as fact, and muster them to argue their particular missions. They do so knowing that the numbers are wrong,
hence that the empirical basis for their normative mission is at least
in question and perhaps in error. But commitment to mission in the
service of a perceived larger need is viewed as justified in overriding
the empirical truth.

"A lie which is all a lie may be met and fought with outright.
But a lie which is part of a truth is a harder matter to fight."
—Alfred, Lord Tennyson in "The Grandmother," 1864

This is not a matter of semantics, of what we mean by "is." Clearly, it is at least a matter of misrepresentation, and perhaps a matter of untruth. Should that bother us? Should the nonprofit feel compelled to tell the truth?

First, let's compare the nonprofit situation to that of the commercial world. People misrepresent, hide, or skirt the truth in commerce every day—as they do in families, relationships, and often self-knowledge. In business, however, the truth ultimately will come out. It will do so because (a) the SEC and the Justice Department are watching; (b) shareholders and investment analysts are watching; (c) lawyers are watching; and (d) the business media are watching and licking their collective chops for a shot at newsstand sales and cable TV audience share. The marriage of market and regulatory structure ultimately will find the truth about the relationship between what a company says and what is true. And when truth and reality diverge, consequences will ensue. Handcuffs fit all-sized wrists.

Moreover, whether what is true in a particular company is at odds with what is said, or whether truth is a matter of statistical interpretation, the mission of the industry is seldom compromised. Enron traded energy futures (and a bunch of other stuff). Although statistical truth was mispresented, and lies appear to have been told, the legitimacy of futures trading is not necessarily at risk. Pork belly futures on the Chicago exchange traded hands calmly even as Enron executives faced congressional committees.

"Facts are stubborn things; and whatever may be our wishes,
our inclinations, or the dictates of our passions, they cannot
alter the state of facts and evidence"
—John Adams, "Argument in Defense of the Soldiers
in the Boston Massacre Trials," December 1770

How does this map to the mission-meets-numbers conundrum for nonprofits? Let's look at the problem from three perspectives, two of which have commercial parallels and one of which perhaps does not.

First, where is the arbiter? For commerce, it is the market, the stockholder, and the public and private overseers. Even for the least honest, the motivator for truth is the certainty of financial and legal consequences. Unless there is fraud, however, nonprofits face no such consequences. If I do not know how many babies die of malaria, but neither do you, then I can say "10 million," knowing that I do not know; and I don't have to admit that I do not know, because I cannot be proved wrong. Indeed, I can even cite important international organizations (which also do not know) to bolster my claim, and, again, not have to admit that they do not know either. There is no legal consequence for me.

Moreover, there is no required due diligence on my claims as a prerequisite to getting money to fund my mission. This is true not only for accessing private philanthropy, but also for obtaining federal funding. Indeed, the financial consequence is positive not negative. The larger I can make the problem, the more attention I draw to it, hence to my organization whose mission is to address the problem.

The example is not trapped in the tragedies of Africa. The temptation is present in many areas of nonprofit advocacy and service provision in the United States. "Don't bother me with the numbers, my mission is just" is an approach that can be found lurking under the surface of many debates about societal needs. It can be found in organizations advocating environmental causes, as well at those addressing food safety, public health, poverty, and a wide range of other issues. With no legal oversight on the validity of claims about problems, the nonprofit world is governed internally by a combination of voluntary organizational integrity, and caveat emptor for financers. Is this enough? Does the public trust held by nonprofits require more structure to ensure the equivalent of "truth in advertising?"

Second, the divergence of empirical truth from articulated mission drives to the core of nonprofit credibility in ways that corporate accounting vagaries do not. Misrepresentation about the very justification for organizational existence can generate skepticism, not about organizational management, but about both nonprofits and the very real societal problem under scrutiny. The credibility price of untruth unmasked is paid by the nonprofit involved. It is also paid by the entire category of nonprofits working in related areas of endeavor. But, perhaps more importantly, it is paid by those affected by the problem.

Let us return to our overly simplistic example and examine the consequences of untruth. Debunking an unsupported claim of malaria deaths not only tars the nonprofit making the claim but also other nonprofits in global health. By creating skepticism, however, it also endangers resources for the babies (however many there are) who are, in fact, dying of malaria. The consequences of untruth about the relationship between numbers and mission reach deeply into the societal justification and need for nonprofits themselves. There are few parallels in the commercial world.

Third, societal problems and needs build political followings. Politics, in turn, can give life to nonprofit missions even where experts widely agree that empirical justification is ambiguous. The more attractive the political benefits of alliance with a societal problem, the greater the adhesion between political support and the mission and existence of nonprofits serving that problem. The more visibility and momentum the problem and mission gain, the more powerful the alliance becomes. When numbers raise technical doubts, the cost of acknowledging them is exacted both for the mission-driven nonprofit and for its political supporters. In those circumstances, speaking truth to power is not only difficult, it is often futile. So truth is never spoken.

These are extremely serious questions that are not simple to answer. These are not problems of measuring nonprofit *performance*; these are problems of measuring and verifying the bases for *core missions*.

As nonprofits compete for a slice of the philanthropic wealth being apportioned in the coming decades, the pressure to justify their existence will only grow stronger. Greater pressure to compete for resources from ever larger pools of resources will tempt truth. Blurring the edges of the empirical, "pitching" the problem, marketing the basic need so that it appeals to major funders, surrounding program results with shadows—all will be temptations.

What is the standard of truth that should be applied to nonprofits? Who should apply it? And who should ensure consequences? These are not trivial issues. In self-interest, however, there is also a temptation for nonprofits to portray these questions as exceedingly complex—and to allow the claim of complexity to stand as an excuse for inaction. Perhaps, however, the questions do not merit a complex response.

Upon entering the United States Military Academy at West Point, a freshly shorn 18-year-old plebe accepts a straightforward standard of honor. Violation of that standard results in an internal Honor Board hearing, and consequences include permanent separation from the United States Corps of Cadets. That private standard of honor is this: "A cadet will not lie, cheat, steal, or tolerate those who do." Holding the public trust as nonprofits, is it not reasonable to expect from ourselves what we as a nation demand from an 18-year-old plebe?

A Privilege and an Obligation: Why Stewardship Matters and Competition Is a Good Thing

No doubt, there are many nonprofit boards of directors that are models for commercial enterprises. But in the last several years, the nonprofit sector and the public have been reminded that nonprofit boards can be plagued with the same self-dealing as one sees in that substrata of corporate America under siege for accounting and oversight shortcomings. Failure to ask performance questions, failure to attend to agenda issues, failure to hold management to benchmarked standards—these are board failures that span organizational type. They are failures of both people and systems.

The problem is not who should emulate who. The problem is that board failure to police performance (and organizational failure even to document performance) is more insidious when it occurs in nonprofit organizations than in their commercial counterparts. This is because the reason that nonprofits exist rests not with stockholder self-interest, but with societal value. Corporate America answers to private stockholders and is policed by a plethora of government regulatory entities to ensure that private stockholder rights are upheld. In the end, the right to exist as a corporation ensues from the trust of individual private stockholders, a trust that (as Wall Street can testify) is easily withdrawn. The price of board and performance failure in corporate America is clear: Not only do you cease to exist, you also end up in court.

> **"The price of greatness is responsibility."**
> —Winston Churchill

Nonprofits derive their right to exist from the common will of the people. The privilege of being excused from paying taxes (hence imposing your tax share on everyone else) brings with it the obligation to produce social value in at least as great a measure as the taxes forgone. Being a nonprofit is a privilege granted by the people. Failure to measure and document performance, and board failure to insist on performance and to hold management to performance, eats at the heart of that societal obligation. Hence, it violates the will of the people, which is, in my view, as egregious a wrong as it is possible to commit in a democracy. That makes performance and evidence a much more sacred trust for nonprofit boards than—at least in my observation and board experience—most nonprofit boards recognize.

Which brings us to competition. Would that everyone strove for excellence and settled for nothing less than outstanding performance simply because doing so was right and just. But in a world of human frailty and limited resources, competition is both inevitable and good. Indeed, given human frailty, thank goodness we have limited resources. The best ideas will rise when it is clear that only the best will succeed. The accountability of nonprofits to the will of the people makes excellence an obligation, hence competition is an important mechanism to ensure that obligation.

It is true that competition is common when the subject is financial resources. It is less common when the subject is services. That is because there is no market for free soup. But nonprofits do, in fact, compete in the service marketplace, even where only other nonprofits exist. Education (especially in the brave new world of vouchers) and healthcare are prime examples. Whether it be community hospitals competing among themselves for patients, or academic medical centers in New York City vying with Memorial Sloan Kettering, evidence abounds. And, as reported by the *New York Times* on July 26, 2002, improper incursions by Princeton's admissions director into a confidential Web site for Yale applicants seem to reflect the fierce competition for top students, what one testing official called "an arms race in which each side tries to one-up the other."

Moreover, where for-profit service providers exist in the marketplace, nonprofits must compete with them as well. That was the most distressing finding of the recent study of the healthcare marketplace by the Leonard Davis Institute, which is an interdisciplinary research institute that sits between the Wharton School of Business and the Medical School of the University of Pennsylvania. Where nonreimbursed service was the measure of performance relative to the untaxed social good, the nonprofit healthcare community performed *less* well than its for-profit counterparts. For-profit healthcare systems provided *more* social value than did nonprofit systems. Moreover, nonprofit hospitals provided uncompensated care at a value *less* than the value of the tax dollars they were allowed to forgo.

The good news of the Wharton study, however, is that it was the marketplace that allowed us to know about the relative performance of nonprofit systems. Competition for resources raised questions of efficiency and claims about social roles. Competition led to the analysis, and competition revealed this central failure of societal obligation. Hence it is competition that ought to be thanked.

▓ SOURCES

Arenson, K.W. "Princeton Pries into Web Site for Yale Applicants," *New York Times*, July 26, 2002, Section A, p. 1, col. 3.

Nicholson, S. and M.V. Pauly. "Community Benefits: How Do For-Profit and Nonprofit Hospitals Measure Up?" Issue Brief, Leonard Davis Institute of Health Economics, 6:4, December 2000/January 2001.

Are Organizational Hybrids Nonprofits? The Problem of Fairness

Things used to be fairly clear.Private corporations sold things in the marketplace. Governments protected the national security, made the rules that governed the nation, and caught and punished those who broke the rules. Charities took care of society's poor and its orphans and widows. Individuals and families took care of pretty much everything else.

Today, very little is clear, at least by yesterday's metric. Nonprofits compete with corporations in the marketplace for everything from used cars to healthcare. Government agencies are setting up charitable foundations. Private entrepreneurs are taking the principles of the marketplace into social service provision via venture philanthropy. Commercial corporations are educating the nation's children, dissecting its genes, and managing its prisons.

Identity crisis? Or further proof of evolutionary theory? Either way, the mixing of institutional forms and functions poses serious questions about the impact of a multitrillion-dollar transfer of assets into the "nonprofit" world in the coming decades.

To begin, how will the principles of market fairness be affected? What will it really mean to be "nonprofit"? If a mission to serve a noble, needy cause allows competitive pricing advantage because the organization does not need to add tax-paying to its unit cost, and the nonprofit thereby gains market advantage, is that a good thing, at least in economic terms? Whether it is good or bad, is it a fair thing?

Benefiting from growth via the next two decades' wealth transfer, many nonprofits (even those that are currently large) can be expected to grow larger. Moreover, small nonprofits will be motivated to merge. A full 71 percent of the nonprofits registered with Guidestar have less than $25,000 in annual income. The investment needed to make these nonprofits market viable will be significant.

Information technology (IT) provides an example. IT is surely one of the most important investments to be made in a drive toward administrative efficiency. If nonprofits' administrative overhead is reimbursed by philanthropy at 12 percent of granted funds, then where will the investment money come from? Twelve percent of $25,000 is $3,000. Even if all humans in the nonprofit's administration were volunteers, if payroll was zero, and if candles replaced electric lights, a full $3,000 allocation to an IT budget would not buy much technological power. Meeting the market test of efficiency will require that small nonprofits join forces.

If nonprofits grow larger (whether through organic growth or merger), the question of fairness vis-à-vis the private sector becomes even more important. When does a nonprofit selling used cars, the revenues from which at least partially fund its operations, become the same species as Bob's A-1 Used Cars down the block? And if it is like Bob's in all but core mission (after all, the mission of the car lots is the same: sell cars), then should its market position be put on equal footing with Bob's? Is it only fair that nonprofits should pay taxes? As the trillions change hands, these will become frothy questions for markets and economic policy.

"What the people want is simple. They want an America that is as good as its promise."

—Barbara Jordan,
Harvard University Commencement Address, June 16, 1977

What about governments? The multitrillion-dollar sword will cut two ways. On the one hand, Federal, state, and local government agencies are now (and, presumably, will increasingly be) establishing philanthropic entities and quasi-governmental nonprofits to pursue their agendas. These exist apart from legislative appropriations, yet they serve public agency interests with private resources. But those resources are not accountable to the voting public to which the agency answers. Is it fair for a government function to be financed apart from the oversight of voters? Is it fair for voters to be paying taxes to support agencies that pursue their self-determined programs with private resources?

Finally, what about corporations? Apart from the market implications noted, significantly expanded assets held in the nonprofit sector provide (of course) huge opportunities for financial management companies. But, again, the sword cuts two ways.

Assuming that nonprofits (educational institutions, foundations, service organizations, etc.) do not spend these assets as they are received, they will be held in some form. To the extent that they are held, the role of nonprofits as institutional investors grows. To some extent, this is irrelevant. The market motive of nonprofit capital managers is the same as that of Warren Buffett: Grow the asset. Or it ought to be the same—although a 2003 *Harvard Business Review* study indicated that the asset management track record of nonprofits had been sufficiently poor that billions of dollars in return had been forgone.

The fairness problem for the management of large slices of capital by mission-driven nonprofits is that (presumably) their nonprofit mission also carries into their stockholding behavior—they can exert their stockholder prerogative in all manner of corporate decisions. This has been a periodic problem for corporations. It introduces decision-making criteria into asset management that exist apart from the economic role of those assets. From the market point of view, this can be suboptimal. From the nonprofit point of view, this can represent the concurrence of mission and money.

On the other hand, when nonprofits become stakeholders in economic growth, will they be tempted to compromise their missions in the interests of a better return on investment? Is that fair to the philanthropist who donated funds precisely because of that mission? Should the abandonment of mission in the interests of asset return be transparent to the philanthropist? If so, is philanthropy an investment in mission rather than a gift? If that is the case, what rules should apply to the relationship between funder and grantee?

Hybridization creates exciting and potentially robust organizational models for nonprofits. The fairness implications, however, are real but too poorly understood. America prides itself on the value of a level playing field, with rules that are transparent and apply to everyone vested in the game. On a level playing field, the prize goes to the most competent player. The problem is that organizational hybridization can tilt the field. The question for America then becomes how much do we value fairness?

▨ SOURCES

Abzug, R. and N.J. Webb. "Relationships between Nonprofit and For-Profit Organizations: A Stakeholder Perspective," *Nonprofit and Voluntary Sector Quarterly*, December 1999, pp. 416–431.

Bradley, B., P. Jansen, and L. Silverman. "The Nonprofit Sector's $100-Billion Opportunity," *Harvard Business Review*, 81:5 May 2003, pp. 94–103.

Iglehart, J.K. "Business and Government: Striking New Balances," *Health Affairs*, January/February 2002, pp. 7–8.

Moe, R.C. "The Emerging Federal Quasi-Government: Issues of Management and Accountability," *Public Administration Review*, May/June, 2001, pp. 290–312.

Salamon, L.M. "An 'Associational' Revolution," *UNESCO Courier*, Paris, June 2001, pp. 36–37.

Have We Learned Nothing? Practical Applications of Lessons from Corporate Scandal

It is getting to the point at which more than one cup of coffee is needed before opening the *New York Times* in the morning. Take Tuesday, November 19, 2002, for example. Above the fold on the front page, right under the picture of President Bush and former President Carter, was yet another accounting scandal exposé.

But, wait! This one was not about Wall Street. It was about "Our Street," a major thoroughfare in the philanthropic community. One of the largest nonprofits in America was facing questions about how money was counted, possible revenue inflation, cost and expense misrepresentation, even double-counting of donations.

How could this be?

It is possible that the reporting was not fully accurate. It is also true that accounting rules are difficult to decipher. Indeed, accounting rules often seem to be composed less of "rules" than of advisories on the making of Swiss cheese. Certainly, they provide full employment for the accounting profession. Be that as it may, had the previous six months of corporate America's "death by a thousand cuts" taught us nothing?

To this pained observer, the lesson of our times seems very simple: Nothing will suffice short of the straight and narrow, and an honest admission of the resulting bottom line. It is not good enough to be in technical accounting compliance. Nor is it good enough to argue that the holes in the cheese were put there for the express purpose of permitting multiple points of entry into basic arithmetic. It does not matter whether smoothing the edges of numbers about revenue or costs (at best) or straight-out fudging them (at worst) can be defended by some accounting rule. The post-Enron, post-WorldCom reality is that even the appearance of skating on the edge—whether or not it is true—will be assumed to be worse than whatever the truth is.

There is no safety in the shadows. Excuses provide no shield. No comfort can be taken in sleight of hand. The truth will out, and it is truth that provides the only legally or publicly acceptable standard of organizational management. This is the basic lesson of the last year of corporate America's coming of age. It is a lesson that must be learned quickly in the nonprofit and philanthropic sectors.

And those sectors must go one step further. Honesty is more than a preventive measure to avoid scandal or financial embarrassment. Hedging and obfuscation should be rejected not because they are dangerous and risk poor press. They should be rejected because they are wrong. They betray the public trust.

Nonprofits of all types exist on the societal commons. They are banking and spending someone else's hard-earned money. This is a fundamental principle that should underpin every decision, every action, every day and every night of every nonprofit. Harry and Maude in Dubuque did not just give their donation to a nonprofit solicitation. They gave up to give. For the vast majority of Americans, philanthropic support for those who labor on the societal commons is not a matter of putting one less tank of gas in the Porsche. It is a matter of putting one less hamburger on the grill. Harry and Maude's money should be sacrosanct. Nonprofits and philanthropies are honor-bound to the people. And, so, they are honor bound to the truth.

With that responsibility comes the potential for unpleasantness. The straight and narrow may have less than the preferred results for individual nonprofits or for the philanthropic sector overall. I have long argued that the national data on philanthropy are abysmal.

They are incomplete, often unverifiable, and mostly unreliable. Reading the *New York Times* of November 19, 2002, I concluded that perhaps they are more abysmal than I thought. If there was double-counting, perhaps the national philanthropic sector is not valued at nearly $300 billion. Perhaps it is less. Perhaps it is much less.

But failure to be transparent and precise exacts a price steeper than the embarrassment of a particular organization, or even the communal embarrassment of a sector overall. It exacts a price in public trust. It betrays Harry and Maude, and encourages them to toss that extra hamburger on the grill. And who can blame them if they do?

What is to be done? A first step would be to conduct an honest, searching assessment among philanthropic and nonprofit leaders about the state of their own houses, their finances, their accountability, their systems of oversight, their goals. Do they understand what Harry and Maude truly intend? The second step would be to implement a set of national standards covering revenue accounting, cost accounting, financial oversight, board independence, and fiduciary responsibility. The third step would be to invoke a national pledge based on those standards, which every nonprofit and philanthropic board chair and organizational president, CEO, and CFO would sign and post in every publication, electronic and paper, of every signatory organization. That signed pledge would provide concrete evidence of an organization's commitment to those standards.

"The undiscover'd country, from whose bourn
No traveler returns, puzzles the will,
And makes us rather bear those ills we have
Than fly to others that we know not of,
Thus conscience does make cowards of us all,
And thus the native hue of resolution
Is sicklied o're with the pale case of thought,
And enterprises of great pitch and moment
With this regard their currents turn awry
And lose the name of action."
—William Shakespeare
Hamlet, Act III, Scene 1

There would also be an essential fourth step. The fourth step would take a page from the continuing legal education required of lawyers who wish to continue to practice at the Bar. Every nonprofit or philanthropic executive and board chair would be required to resign that pledge every three years, but could do so only after certifying 10 hours of participation in a continuing education series related to these issues, perhaps offered by the Independent Sector, the Council on Foundations, and major university philanthropic research centers.

Some would say such a plan is overkill, an overreaction to technically acceptable accounting and management practices. The status quo is good enough, others would say. Perhaps. Let's put it to the test. Let's take the *New York Times* front page, fly to Dubuque, and ask Harry and Maude how they feel about it.

■ **SOURCE**

Strom, S. "Question Arise on Accounting at United Way," *New York Times,* Nov. 19, 2002, Section A, p. 1, col. 1.

Great Expectations Collide: The Consequences of Assumptions

In September 1861, the *Atlantic Monthly* reviewed Charles Dickens' *Great Expectations* after it had appeared in a series of installments in the magazine. The hero, Pip, the reviewer commented, was the fulcrum for both the form and the color of the narrative, and Pip himself was "amiable, apprehensive, aspiring, inefficient, the subject and the victim of *Great Expectations*."

Expectations govern all of life. And expectations are deep and abiding in the world of charitable giving. But there appears to be a growing conflict of expectations, many of them even great expectations, between nonprofits and philanthropy. Like Pip, those involved are both subject and victim, at times amiable and apprehensive, always aspiring, and quite often inefficient. And just as with Pip, great expectations are playing themselves out in an era of social and economic change, when the rules that governed genteel philanthropic tradition are giving way to fine print guarded by phalanxes of lawyers and accountants.

Let's start with nonprofits. Society has increasingly expressed great expectations of nonprofits. The decentralization and privatization of social services has transferred the burden of service provision from the shoulders of government to those of the nonprofit sector. The expectation of society is that nonprofits will step up to shoulder that burden and bear it at least as well as, and hopefully better and more efficiently than, government has done in the past. Whether non-profits are the victims of social expectations or merely the subject of expectations they helped to create is a matter of debate.

But expectations run in both directions, and nonprofits have great expectations of their own. The nonprofit expectation has long been that one central equation holds true:

$$just \; cause + clear \; need = philanthropic \; income$$

That equation lies at the core of much nonprofit philosophy. Arguably, it must rest at the core, because much of what non-profits do is, by definition, soft and malleable. It requires flexibility in the face of deep social problems, experimentation where risk is great, attention to the shifting needs and conditions of those served, and acknowledgment that reliable service provision to society's needy requires sustained financial support.

In the last decade, nonprofit expectations have become great indeed. As philanthropic inflation-adjusted dollars have grown from $100 billion in 1981 to over $200 billion in 2001, the expectation that cause, need, and inflow would grow apace has often proved true. Now it appears that, despite the economic downturn, U.S. foundations are, by and large, maintaining their levels of grant expenditures. While there is constraint at the margins, at the core, philanthropy is continuing apace. For nonprofits, this reaffirms an expectation of financial support that grows to match organizational needs.

But measuring monetary prospects by cash value trends may, in fact, make nonprofits the victims of their expectations. The giving environment has changed, and nonprofits now face changed ex-pectations of philanthropists, for whom the measure of future pros-pects is not cash but intent and impact.

It once was (and still is in many quarters) sufficient to write a check, attend a ball, bid on a weekend in Paris, and go home feeling warm and meaningful. These genteel days of giving—with philan-thropists as the preoccupied but always-proper Miss Havesham trusting that effort and good intentions would be sufficient to guarantee at least the veneer of results—are fading. For philan-

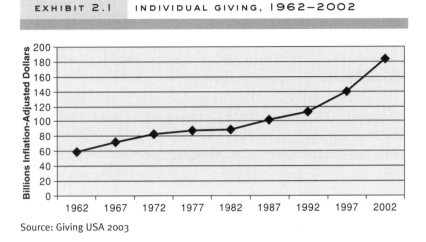

EXHIBIT 2.1   INDIVIDUAL GIVING, 1962–2002

Source: Giving USA 2003

thropy, pushed and pulled by a combination of entrepreneurial money and public scrutiny, that traditional genteel equation is no longer valid. Cause and need do not necessarily equate to funding.

> "For it is mutual trust, more even than mutual interest, that holds human associations together."
>
> —H.L. Mencken

As evidence, a commentary in the March 29, 2003, *New York Times* stated that a recent tendency for philanthropists to demand measurable outcomes and impact in exchange for support is evolving further. The philanthropy dollar is not just expecting outcomes, it is expecting to be spent exactly and precisely as the giver intends and specifies. The great expectations of philanthropy are no longer for warm feelings about causes, but for precise results and resource allocations that conform to exact donor specifications embedded in contractual agreements.

Those contracts are likely to become subjects for litigation. A case in point is the July 2003 suit against the New York Metropolitan Opera for allegedly failing to heed the artistic wishes of a deceased benefactor. The plaintiffs, representatives of the heiress, do not simply wish the artistic direction changed, they want their money back. Millions of dollars of it.

In effect, philanthropic cash is no longer a gift; it is a contract. And in the world of contracts, heartfelt causes and amiable goodwill are often left on the cutting-room floor.

If these trends are true, what is to be done? If the channels that guide philanthropic dollars are becoming more rigid, even as the flow itself deepens, and if those channels are ill-suited to the non-profits' continued need for nimbleness and flexibility, is a crisis upon us? Do we have here the makings of a breakdown in trust between those who give and those who request? If trust is lost, on what standard of expectation will philanthropy be built? Can it be built on anything but trust?

Perhaps what is happening is akin to the core experiences of Dickens' young Pip, a movement from childhood to adulthood, a movement from simple equations and aspiring expectations to deeper understandings of the fundamentals of relationships. This is not a bad thing. When charity between giver and receiver is replaced by partnerships of mutual interest, the result might be both greater stability of relationships and greater, not weaker, trust. When each of two organizations understands and accepts the great expectations of the other, paths of action are smoother. Communication is served by openness and transparency. Trust can be built not on assumptions but on clear and mutually agreed-upon facts. And trust, built on those terms, is arguably made more resilient.

How to get from here to there? How to overcome nonprofit resentments over philanthropy's increasing expectations for specificity and impact and philanthropy's increasing resentment over nonprofits' expectations of funding for good intentions?

A dangerous downward spiral yawns. How do we step back from it? What is alarming about the *New York Times* description of the trend toward litigation and contractual arrangements in philanthropy is the degree to which everyone interviewed seemed surprised. Grantees seemed surprised that philanthropists expected concrete results. Philanthropists seemed surprised that grantees did not deliver (or maintain in perpetuity) expected outcomes.

It is up to leadership on both sides of the table, nonprofits and philanthropies, to sit down together and put clear expectations on the table. This is true at the macro-level of national associations and conferences, where agendas should include clear dialogue between funders and grantees about changing expectations. Every annual meeting of every nonprofit or philanthropic organization for the next two years ought to include a panel of major organizational leaders, donor and grantee, to explicitly state changing expectations and to grapple with consequences.

This also applies at the micro-level of campaigns and gift solicitations. Expectations should be explicit and accepted. Wallpapering over true expectations will only lead to surprise. And the victim of surprise is trust.

■ SOURCES

Giving USA, 2003, AAFRC Trust for Philanthropy.

"Great Expectations, by Charles Dickens," *Atlantic Monthly,* 8:47, September 1861, pp. 380–382.

Pogrebin, R. "Donor's Estate Sues Metropolitan Opera," *New York Times,* July 24, 2003, Section B, p. 3, col. 4.

Strom, S. " Donors Add Watchdog Role to Relations with Charities," *New York Times,* March 29, 2003, Section A, p. 8, col. 1.

———, "Foundations' 2002 Giving Held Steady, Report Finds," *New York Times,* March 31, 2003, Section A, p. 8, col. 5.

Nonprofit Management Dilemmas

INTRODUCTION TO THE ISSUES

In a simple world with abundant resources, universal goodwill, and the luxury of a leisurely pace, it may be that there is little premium to be placed on organizational efficiency and management performance. But such a simple world, if it ever existed for nonprofits, is currently nowhere to be seen.

The number of tax-exempt organizations registered with the Internal Revenue Service in the United States has increased by 38 percent over the last two decades. More telling, the number of organizations registered as tax-exempt 501(c)(3) charities, a subset of all nonprofits, has increased by 128 percent in the same time period. In that period, the total income of tax-exempt organizations, including the value of volunteer time, has more than doubled. Within the tax-exempt sector, the income of 501(c)(3) charities has nearly tripled. As a result, the nonprofit sector is increasingly composed of a greater number of charities that compete for tax-deductible philanthropic contributions.

The expectations of philanthropists have begun to approximate those of commercial investors. The government is looking increasingly askance at loose accounting. Resources continue to grow, but at a slower pace. Every dollar is more dear and its expenditure more carefully scrutinized under the microscope of the media.

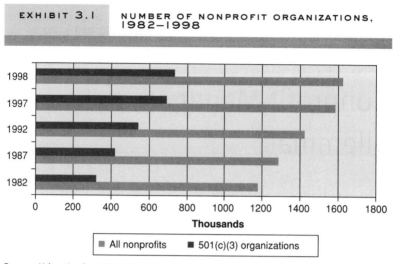

EXHIBIT 3.1   NUMBER OF NONPROFIT ORGANIZATIONS, 1982–1998

Source: Urban Institute Center on Nonprofits and Philanthropy

Public trust of nonprofit institutions now turns as much on demonstrated effectiveness as it does on affinity for social causes.

When the nonprofit world begins to approximate the world of commerce, the metrics of management become equivalently important. This management change poses difficult dilemmas for the world of philanthropy. Personnel are not necessarily skilled in management innovation, nor does the structure of rewards and upward mobility in nonprofits approximate that of commercial organizations. In nonprofits, empathy, dedication, and belief in the cause take the place of sales charts and profit margins. But the former are less well aligned to management skills than the latter.

Technology and its application are also less widespread and, where present, less deeply integrated into operations. But technology is increasingly recognized as the source of a significant amount of the recent massive gains in productivity in the U.S. economy. Hence, it is intimately tied into management strategies to achieve efficiency. Methods for measuring impact are not widely understood among nonprofits. Boards are not steeped in traditions of accountability. Revenue sources are often not flexible enough to allow nimble management responses to financial changes. This list could go on.

The realities of management problems are even more severe given the size of most nonprofits. Only 3 percent of nonprofits have expenses of over $10 million; 43.2 percent have assets of under $100,000. Size can impede management depth and responsiveness. But the problems do not obviate the realities. The public, and donors, increasingly expect sophistication of process and clarity of results. Excuses and explanations will not be greeted with quiet murmurs of sympathy. The management challenges that nonprofits face require leadership and creativity.

The essays in this section address a number of these management challenges. Of necessity there is overlap with topics such as economics and ethics. What is economically possible for, and what is ethically incumbent upon, a nonprofit organization affects its management options, contributes to management problems, and determines management opportunities.

SOURCE

Data from The National Center for Charitable Statistics of The Urban Institute, 2001, and Giving and Volunteering in the United States, 2001, Washington DC: Independent sector.

Organizational Benchmarking: Management Solution or Performance Petard?

The pace of change and the market's demand for performance have long driven corporations and economic analysts to apply "best practices" as the yardstick for assessing organizational merit. This process, known as *benchmarking,* compares the performance of similar organizations (whether in terms of products, services, size, or scope) over time. The resulting analysis is used to identify failings and to motivate management to improve performance and maintain competitive advantage. Because everyone is always compared to the "best," the performance bar constantly moves upward.

Raising expectations for efficiency and effectiveness among nonprofits has opened a discussion of the utility of benchmarking as a management tool in the nonprofit sector as well. Many nonprofits resist the application of benchmarking because of the purported uniqueness of the sector's organizational nature and the social objectives of its performance. Despite the problems associated with the nature of the nonprofit sector, however, the actual application of benchmarking hints at deeper concerns about nonprofits operating in the marketplace.

First, the problems. Benchmarking is about relative performance. Performance is best measured where metrics for success or efficiency are common across organizations and can be objectively judged. Comparisons are only fair if the same things are being compared.

> "No legacy is as rich as honesty."
> —William Shakespeare
> *All's Well That Ends Well*, III, v

For nonprofits, there is no commonly shared or mutually perceived market measure of performance. Nonprofits tend to think of their performance in terms of their own organizational goals (number of grants made, number of species saved, number of soup bowls filled), rather than relative to a general best practices standard derived from a larger organizational universe. Perceived uniqueness of product or service impairs comparison. In effect, then, benchmarking leaves a nonprofit comparing itself to itself. The method then bears much in common with Snow White's Queen. Asking the mirror, "Who's the fairest in the land?" likely elicits a predictable answer. And the answer will be about as useful to the nonprofit as it was to the queen.

The second problem is with determining "similar organizations." Industry is fortunate to have industrial codes and other commonly accepted ways to classify product and service production. We can then compare the performance of all producers in the cement industry or all manufacturers of wing nuts. We know what cement is, and we can touch wing nuts.

Nonprofits do not have such neat categories. Nor do they have markets that will motivate the evolution of easy groupings for purposes of financial analysis. Some soup kitchens counsel about family violence. Some also give out clothing. Some also distribute bags of food. Some also provide after-school snacks at the YMCA. They are all soup kitchens, but they are different in fundamental ways. The "similar organizations" proviso is the ultimate bailout for resistance to external comparisons; staff can simply say that no other organizations are truly similar. Who will object? And if objection is raised, what market will mandate that a comparison be made anyway?

> "All systems either of preference or of restraint, therefore, being thus completely taken away, the obvious and simple system of natural liberty establishes itself of its own accord. Every man, so long as he does not violate the laws of justice, is left perfectly free to pursue his own interest his own way, and to bring both his industry and his capital into competition with those of any other man or order of men."
>
> —Adam Smith
> *An Inquiry into the Nature and Causes*
> *of the Wealth of Nations,* 1776

Third, how will benchmarking motivate management? There are no stockholders, no quarterly conference calls with Wall Street analysts poking holes in earnings statements, no stock options to be withdrawn if performance falls below industry standards, no CNBC with embarrassing charts of share prices broadcast for all the world to see. True, boards of nonprofits should perform the same fiduciary roles as corporate boards on these matters. But they often do not, with little price exacted. Some have said that nonprofit executive skills must be equivalent to those in business, hence executive salaries should be benchmarked to business. If that is so, then presumably executive performance should be equally benchmarked. And that would motivate management. But if in fact performance cannot be benchmarked, then how do you derive such fundamentals as compensation and budget?

Finally, what does "competitive advantage" mean in the nonprofit sector? There are some who think it does and should mean a great deal. Competition should be embraced by nonprofits as good and wholesome because it provides a prod to push "good" to become "best," and to keep "best" from getting complacent. Instead, however, competition is often decried as a mechanism that pits organizations against one another, pressures organizational changes that are harmful to social missions, and thereby destroys the nonprofit spirit of universal good on the global commons. If competition itself is viewed as bad, then measures used to motivate and gain competitive advantage will not be popular.

Beyond these problems of the nature of the nonprofit sector, however, lies a much larger issue. Many of the problems associated with the application of benchmarking to nonprofit institutions are rooted in the organizational characteristics that distinguish the non-profit sector from commercial institutions. These distinctions qualify the results of nearly all benchmarking exercises of nonprofits.

But what if the claim to uniqueness fails in the marketplace? Even if nonprofits accept benchmarking in its most rigorous terms and as a mechanism to judge and force organizational improvement, will economic realities hoist nonprofits on their own claimed petard of individuality? It is an interesting and very new question, and one that finds its best illustration in the healthcare sector. While healthcare, admittedly, is more of a market than soup kitchens, the trend toward nonprofit provision of services akin to those provided in the commercial sector is growing. Hence, it is an illustration that foreshadows other economic sectors in the years to come.

In a recent study, the Leonard Davis Institute of Health Economics at the University of Pennsylvania's Wharton School of Business asked an intriguing question: Do nonprofit hospitals provide community benefits in excess of those provided by for-profit hospitals? Both nonprofit and proprietary hospitals provide comparable services; both are reimbursed by the same payments mechanisms; both are subject to the same market forces. The non-profit claim to uniqueness rests in its purported provision of greater community value in the form of uncompensated care. If they do not provide greater value, Wharton asked, should tax exemption provide them with an unfair competitive advantage over their proprietary colleagues?

The study is long and technical, but the upshot is that, in fact, for-profits provide as much or more "community benefits" value than do nonprofits. Further, the value of community benefits provided by nonprofit hospitals did not even equal the taxes forgone by society in exchange for their nonprofit status.

In fact, acknowledging claimed uniqueness and then comparing the provision of that unique service with supposedly not-unique commercial enterprises revealed that, as businesses, for-profits and nonprofits are more alike than they are different. As nonprofits engage in commercial activity, that may become more and more true. So, if that is true, then benchmarking can compare "similar organizations."

The specter may perplex nonprofit leadership, but it ought not. The opportunity for change that drives toward excellence makes the challenge of meeting or exceeding for-profit best practices exciting. The process might entail an upheaval in organizational culture, and widespread staff angst. The price may be high; most things that are exciting come with significant price tags.

As all tennis players know, you can't get better unless you play against someone better than you. And in the future, as the intergenerational trillions change hands, the game may go to whoever is best.

■ SOURCES

2001 RIMS Benchmark Survey, Ernst & Young, and the Risk and Insurance Management Society, Inc.

Becker, M.M. "Nonprofit Benchmark Study 1999," Community Foundation of Silicon Valley, 2000.

Coplin, W.D. and C. Dwyer, "Common Sense for Performance Measurement," ASPA Online, September 28, 2001.

Nicholson, S. and M.V. Pauly, "Community Benefits: How Do For-Profit and Nonprofit Hospitals Measure Up?" Issue Brief, Leonard Davis Institute of Health Economics, 6:4, December 2000/January 2001.

Ueda, Dwight. "Salary Comparison: Nonprofits," Salary.com, 2000.

The Illusion of Knowing
Something: The Diversity
of Nonprofit Definitions

The number of U.S. private nonprofit entities of all types increased by 29 percent between 1982 and 1998, the last year for which detailed data are available, from 1.18 million to 1.63 million. The conventional wisdom is that this leap is a measure of increased competition for philanthropy in the nonprofit community. But, like many numbers, the overall trend tells us very little that is meaningful. Distinctions are important in identifying true trends, hence management issues.

There are actually many types of nonprofits caught up in the 1.63 million organizational net. In the tax-code category 501(c) there are actually 27 types of tax-exempt organizations (see Exhibit 3.2). These range from charities, which the public usually associates with the term *nonprofit* to (very profitable) insurance companies to recreation clubs. The annual number of organizations seeking designation in one of the categories grew from 40,000 in 1990 to 87,000 in 2001. The resulting impact of organizational diversity on underlying data is not necessarily trivial. Indeed, it can matter very much.

In 1997, the tax-exempt status of the Teachers Insurance Annuity Association and the College Retirement Equities Fund (known as TIAA/CREF) was revoked by the IRS. For the first time, then, TIAA/CREF data was not included in nonprofit trend data. But these insurance funds are huge;TIAA/CREF now ranks eightieth on the Fortune 500. As a result of this one change, between 1997 and 1998, the assets of nonprofits declined by 6 percent. Netting out the TIAA/CREF change results in an increase of 6 percent in nonprofit assets.

The point is, overall trend statements should be taken with caution. Furthermore, their implications for philanthropy should also be judged carefully. Why? Because within the 501(c) categorization, only 9 of the 27 subcategories can receive tax-exempt donations; 18 cannot. So, their behavior (organizational growth, revenue changes, etc.) does not have philanthropic impact.

How important is the philanthropic subset of nonprofits within the nonprofit universe? The answer, of course, depends on what we measure and where we get the data. IRS longitudinal data do not include tax-exempt organizations with receipts of less than $25,000 per year. Yet the number of these organizations is significant, representing about 70 percent of the charities listed by Guidestar. Nor do the data include most churches and certain other religious organizations, most of which do not report to the IRS in ways comparable to other nonprofit organizations.

Still, if the question is how trends in the organizational universe impact philanthropy for tax-exempt fund recipients, these exclusions actually serve to underestimate the size of the recipient subcomponent, since most such organizations have 501(c)(3) designation. There are actually more 501(c)(3) organizations competing for funds than the IRS data would lead the analyst to believe.

With that caveat, what do the data teach? Let us put aside tax-exempt categories for things like mutual ditch or irrigation companies, cemetery companies, and mutual insurance companies, organizations that are large but not relevant to philanthropy. Focusing only on the categories 501(c)(3) through 501(c)(9) in the IRS sample data, the importance of the 501(c)(3) category becomes clear.

These organizations represent about 75 percent of all private nonprofit organizations. That said, quantity and significance do not necessarily track together. Among larger organizations sampled by

EXHIBIT 3.2   U.S. TAX-EXEMPT ORGANIZATION TYPES

Tax Code Section	Description of Organization
501(c)(1)	Corporations organized under act of Congress, including federal credit unions
501(c)(2)	Title-holding corporations for nonprofits
501(c)(3)	Religious, educational, charitable, scientific, literary, public safety, amateur sports competition, prevention of cruelty to animals or children
501(c)(4)	Civic leagues, social welfare organizations, associations of employees
501(c)(5)	Labor, agricultural, horticultural organizations
501(c)(6)	Business leagues, chambers of commerce, real estate boards
501(c)(7)	Social and recreational clubs
501(c)(8)	Fraternal societies
501(c)(9)	Voluntary employees' beneficiary associations
501(c)(10)	Domestic fraternal societies
501(c)(11)	Teachers' retirement funds
501(c)(12)	Benevolent life insurance associations, mutual ditch or irrigation companies, mutual or cooperative telephone companies, and so on
501(c)(13)	Cemetary companies
501(c)(14)	State-charterd credit unions, mutual reserve funds
501(c)(15)	Mutual insurance companies or associations
501(c)(16)	Cooperative organizations to finance crop operations
501(c)(17)	Supplemental unemployment benefit trusts
501(c)(18)	Employee-funded pension trust (created before June 25, 1959)
501(c)(19)	Post or organization of past or present members of the armed forces
501(c)(20)	Group legal services plan organizations
501(c)(21)	Black lung benefit trusts
501(c)(22)	Withdrawal liability payment fund
501(c)(23)	Veterans organizations (created before 1880)
501(c)(25)	Title-holding corporations or trusts with mutiple parents
501(c)(26)	State-sponsored organizations providing health coverage for high-risk individuals
501(c)(27)	State-sponsored workers' compensation reinsurance organizations
501(d)	Religious and apostolic associations
501(e)	Cooperative hospital service organizations
501(f)	Cooperative service organizations operating educational organizations
501(k)	Childcare organizations
501(n)	Charitable risk pools
521(a)	Farmers' cooperative associations

EXHIBIT 3.3   PERCENT OF NONPROFIT ORGANIZATIONS
BY TYPE, 1998

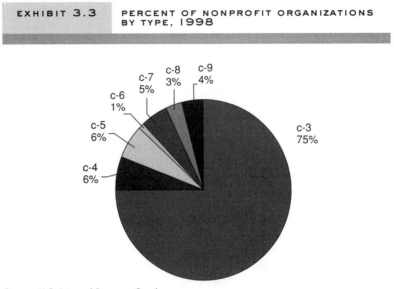

Source: U.S. Internal Revenue Service

the IRS from 1998 tax returns, the most recent date for which complete information is available, 501(c)(3)s represent 82 percent of assets. However, the average asset base of the 501(c)(3) was only $8.2 million, compared to, for example, $12.2 million for the 501(c)(9), voluntary employee benefits associations. The classic charitable organizations may be more numerous, but they are not always as large.

What if we control for size? How do small charities compare to their small tax-exempt counterparts in other categories? Again, using the IRS sample, differences can be discerned. Among small nonprofits, 501(c)(3)s represent 55 percent of total assets, but their average asset size is $40,000, compared to, for example, $58,000 among recreational clubs.

The point, of course, is not the weight of any particular number. The point is that sweeping statements about nonprofits, and implications of those statements for the philanthropic marketplace, need to be carefully qualified to account for the diversity within the nonprofit sector. Simply generalizing about trends in the nonprofit sector of the economy, and extrapolating that to trends in philanthropy, sweeps over the extreme differences among non-profits, whether in terms of size or mission. Simple generalizations oversimplify reality. The U.S. nonprofit sector is extremely diverse—more diverse perhaps than anywhere else in the world. That diversity should be reflected in analytics as well as in the law.

■ SOURCES

Arnsberger, P. "Charities and Other Tax-Exempt Organizations, 1998," Special Studies Special Projects Section, U.S. Internal Revenue Service.

Overall nonprofit entities estimates from The Urban Institute Center on Non-profits and Philanthropy, 2001.

"Report to the IRS," Advisory Committee on Tax-Exempt and Government Ethics, June 21, 2002.

Philanthropy and the Nonprofit Budget Cycle: No Silver Bullet

The assumption that private philanthropy and nonprofit budgets are one and the same is frustratingly false. The problem lies not so much in the structure of the nonprofit budget but in the structure of philanthropic giving. What money is given for does not match what money is needed for.

The core costs of any service organization are people. Meeting payroll is the constant budget challenge for any manager. And payroll cannot always be efficiently disaggregated to allocate personnel time and costs against particular project activities. Techniques, and even software, have long been available to do this. Most nonprofits, however, have not evolved the management systems to think about and manage human resources on an hours-by-task basis.

Without such a granular approach to human resources and payroll, the central challenge for budget managers in nonprofits is to acquire unrestricted support for operations. What managers seek is money for the core, unallocated costs of existing. The problem is that, increasingly, philanthropy does not consider mere existence to be a compelling rationale for giving.

In 1998, the last year for which detailed data are available, only 13.7 percent of all grant dollars flowed to proposals for support of unrestricted operations. This represents a considerable erosion over

EXHIBIT 3.4   DISTRIBUTION OF FOUNDATION GRANTS
BY PURPOSE (PERCENT DOLLARS)

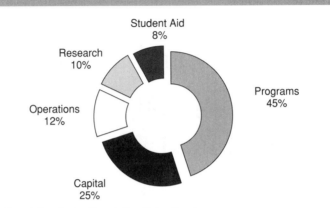

Student Aid
8%

Research
10%

Operations
12%

Programs
45%

Capital
25%

Source: Foundation Center, Foundation Giving Trends 2000

the decade of the 1990s. In contrast, 50 percent of grant dollars flowed to programs' support—that is, to specific projects or initiatives. The dollar value of program grants increased by nearly 50 percent in the 1990s.

Interestingly, although the conventional wisdom is that it is difficult to attract foundation support for bricks and mortar, capital support represented nearly a quarter of all foundation grant dollars in 1998. This was the second largest area of grant support after programs.

Unrestricted grants also face a distinct bias when viewed in terms of grant size. The average unrestricted grant in 1998 was $83,772, compared to $91,700 in 1994, an 8.6 percent deterioration in size. In contrast, program grants averaged just under $120,000 per grant, up from $108,000 in 1994. This represented an 11 percent increase in average grant size.

The real winner in the 1990s, however, was capital support, with an average grant size of $200,000. The total value of grants for building and renovation increased by 75 percent between 1994 and 1998. Monies for computer systems and technology nearly doubled.

Funders tend to differ in their propensity to provide nonprofits with funds for various categories of operations. For example, 26.6

percent of independent foundation funds were awarded to capital projects, compared to only 8.6 percent of corporate funds. Program support attracted 46.2 percent of independent foundation funds and approximately 25 percent of corporate philanthropic funds. But for *no* funding source was unrestricted giving an attractive option. Unrestricted grants represented only 13.7 percent of independent foundation resources, 14 percent of corporate resources, and 10.4 percent of resources from community foundations.

What is the lesson? The management choices are narrow. Either managers must learn to load core costs into project and program operations, and master the methods and technologies that allow both the costing and the capture of real accounting data on that basis, or they must continue to find nongrant options for meeting their operating budgets.

There is a third way, of course. Core operations could be turned over to cost-free volunteers. But that option has management conundrums of its own. Core operations (front-office management, accounting, communications, external affairs, human resources) need reliable, consistent execution. The vicissitudes of volunteers match poorly to such requirements.

Moreover, the American population is aging. In 2000, the life expectancy of an American at birth was 78 years, and 6 percent of

EXHIBIT 3.5   U.S. VOLUNTEER BEHAVIOR BY AGE

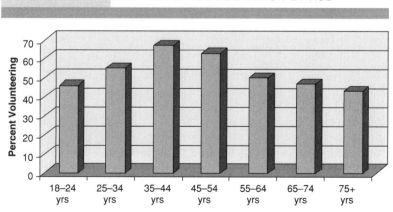

Source: Independent Sector 1999

the population was over 75 years of age. By 2040, average life expectancy will be 82.5 years, and 13 percent will be over 75. The fastest-growing group of elderly will be those aged 85 and over. Voluntarism tends to drop off with age, a victim of health and mobility. Relying on volunteers to solve core operational cost problems may be a losing proposition.

The message is fairly clear: Either master cost-loading techniques, or turn elsewhere than to philanthropy for budget support.

■ SOURCES

Age projections from 2003 World Development Indicators, World Bank.

Data derived from S. Lawrence, C. Camposeco, and J. Kendzior, "Foundation Giving Trends: Update on Funding Priorities," The Foundation Center 2000. Proportions are calculated for that percentage of grant activity that can be allocated to specific purposes. This represents about 87 percent of grant dollar value in independent foundations, 51 percent in corporate foundations, and 64 percent in community foundations.

State Budget Deficits: Why Red Ink Today Will Plague Management Tomorrow

Given all the diversity and divergence in this nation, it is a wonder sometimes that the Union still stands. But, on occasion, all states and communities share a common experience that does truly make us one. Unfortunately, that current experience appears to be budgetary deficits.

Nearly every state of the Union, with the apparent exception of Wyoming, faces a yawning gap between expected revenues and desired expenditures. For some, that gap is a chasm. California, for example, may face a deficit that is a third as large as its budget. New York faces a deficit that is equal to 25 percent of its budget. Along with budget-paring knives, the political long knives are out in many states.

The question that ensues is whether philanthropy has the depth to make up any of the difference. The paring knives will almost certainly begin to carve away at finances for services. If history teaches well, the services affected will include those for community programs focused on social support. With a federal deficit also spiraling upward, the communities and nonprofits affected will turn instinctively to private philanthropy. Assessing state philanthropic patterns, rather than national sources, is important, since so much of U.S. philanthropy is tied to the communities in which the givers (be they individuals or foundations) live or are headquartered. National resources are a poor measure of local availability.

How does the pattern of state budget deficits match up with the pattern of philanthropy among states? Sadly, not well.

Among the top 10 states in terms of projected budget deficits for 2004, only one, New York, ranks in the top 10 of state philanthropy as measured by the average contribution per tax return and philanthropic contributions as a percent of gross income. The philanthropic options for New York organizations may not ease all the budgetary pain, but they are certainly robust.

Not so elsewhere. Alaska has the dubious honor of placing first in terms of its budget deficit, near the bottom of the pack in terms of philanthropic depth. Maine is in similar straits. Many of the top 10 deficit states do not even rank in the top half among states on philanthropic measures.

EXHIBIT 3.6   PHILANTHROPY RANKING FOR LARGEST STATE DEFICITS

State	Deficit Rank	Average Contribution/ Tax Return Rank	Contribution as Percent Gross Income Rank
AK	1	46	48
CA	2	9	17
NY	3	4	8
OR	4	24	18
TX	5	35	39
WI	6	31	28
ME	7	49	47
AZ	8	26	23
SC	9	18	6
WA	10	20	34

Furthermore, only in New York and South Carolina does philanthropy as a portion of gross income better national giving rates. In 2002, philanthropy represented 2.3 percent of gross domestic product (GDP). In New York and South Carolina, contributions were 2.4 percent of gross income. The rest of the top 10 states saw philanthropy come in at lower levels. Again, Maine and Alaska are at the bottom of this measure, with 1.5 percent of gross income going to philanthropic contributions. Surprisingly, given its "new economy" status, Washington State is not much better, with 1.8 percent.

What can we conclude? At least three consequences are likely.

First, philanthropies and philanthropists will feel the pain of state budgetary deficits. They will be making choices about which programs, causes, and organizations to support from a pool of supplicants that will not only be larger, but for which each supplicant's needs will be greater than in the past.

Second, making those choices will require philanthropies to develop (and adhere to) increasingly rigid decision criteria. The wave of requests will be so great that the temptation to drift from core philanthropic interests or goals will be ever present. But once drift begins, demand will be so great that it will be managerially difficult to recapture focus. Hence, adherence to focus, and strict criteria about what does (and does not) fall within that focus will be necessary.

Third, hard feelings will ensue. Not all nonprofits constrained by budget cuts will find solace in local philanthropies. Indeed, some who enjoyed regular philanthropic support will find it more difficult to garner that support, if only because of the significant increase in demand.

A fourth consequence could result, and it is this consequence that is the most dangerous. Disappointment on the part of nonprofits, and a sense of being overwhelmed on the part of philanthropists, could erode trust. Whenever money is scarce, relationships between the haves and the have-nots can be tense. In states with major budget deficits and weak philanthropic records, nonprofits will be the have-nots. Philanthropies will be the haves. The fruit of frustration could be distrust. And that fruit could be bitter for years to come.

▨ SOURCES

Deficit data from the Center on Budget and Policy Priorities, Washington, DC, 2003.

State charity data from National Center for Charitable Statistics, 2002.

Drilling Down:
Deeper Revenue Sources
for Nonprofits

$\mathbf{T}$he United States has witnessed a 40 percent increase in the number of registered nonprofits over the last decade. Annual nonprofit revenues now approach a trillion dollars, an income stream larger than the gross national product of most nations. Where does all that money come from? And how will flows change (or be forced to change) in the future?

First, the numbers. Private giving and philanthropy account for only approximately 10 percent of nonprofit revenues. Government spending, contracts, and service reimbursement accounts for another 36 percent. But, overall, the largest source of nonprofit income is derived from fees charged for goods and services, including licensing fees.

Before we leap to the conclusion that there is not much difference between the financial lifeblood of the soup kitchen across town and that of the local Stop 'n' Shop, however, we need to make some distinctions. Because the catchall term "nonprofit" includes both hospitals and educational institutions, the gross numbers are misleading. "Fees" in these institutions include, for example, insurance reimbursements for hospital services, and tuition payments for higher education. The $35,000 "fee" at Harvard may skew the profile of revenue structure for purposes of nonprofit comparison. (It also skews many a family's wallet, but that is another topic…).

Within the nonprofit sector, healthcare receives only 5 percent of its revenue from private giving, and education only 15 percent. In contrast, arts and culture organizations are dependent on private giving for 41 percent of their revenue, civic organizations for 21 percent, and social/legal organizations for 20 percent.

Over time, the nonprofit revenue strategies are changing. As government funding plateaus at an approximate 3 percent per year increase (albeit after a real decline of over 8 percent per year in the 1987–1992 period), the real growth in revenues for nonprofits is coming from fees, not from private philanthropic sources.

Between 1990 and 1995, constant dollar income from fees increased by 62 percent. Although the trend may be influenced by inflation in tuitions and hospital reimbursement rates, it is by no means completely limited to pricing phenomena in these sectors.

Licensing, for example, is a growing source of revenue for nonprofits, especially arts and cultural organizations whose dependence on philanthropy is greater than in other organizations. Nonprofits license their names and logos to commercial products and services, establishing a brand link between the nonprofit and the commercial

EXHIBIT 3.7   NONPROFIT REVENUE COMPOSITION, 1998

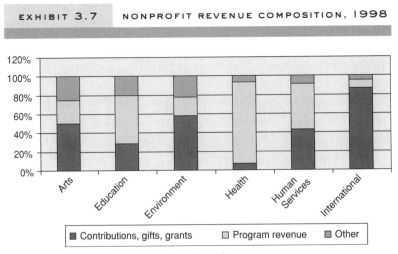

Source: U.S. Internal Revenue Service (Arnsberger)

entity. For example, the National Trust for Historic Preservation licenses its name to Valspar for a line of house paints based on plans from Colonial Williamsburg. The Sierra Club licenses its name for a wide range of clothing.

Art licenses accounted for an overwhelming share of the nearly $7 billion in annual licensing fees flowing to nonprofits. Revenue from art licenses increased 18.6 percent between 1992 and 2000. The increase in other nonprofit categories has been 16.7 percent.

But beyond licenses, there is really nothing particularly new about nonprofit revenues based on goods and services, sales, and fees. The Goodwill and the Salvation Army have always made money from sales. The market for used goods is fundamental to their financial viability. Auxiliaries at hospitals have long sold get-well cards in hospital gift shops. Museums and galleries charge entry fees. So, what is new or important here?

Three elements may make future revenue strategies different from the past. First, the sheer number of nonprofits will force even reluctant organizations to get into the revenue game. Expanding pools of philanthropy—which, happily, are expanding at a record pace—may be inadequate to cope with rising costs, burgeoning demands for services, and increased numbers of organizations providing those services. Slicing the charitable pie into ever-smaller pieces is not a viable funding strategy.

Second, the cadre of nonprofit managers is different in its background and experience compared to two or three decades ago. Top managers now frequently come to their jobs with experience in commercial enterprises. Many have MBAs, or at least graduate-level training in organizational management. Many universities now offer continuing education and even graduate and postgraduate degree programs in nonprofit management. Business schools now include nonprofit management as part of the core curriculum. The new generation of leaders will more easily translate the strategies of the marketplace into the language of the nonprofits and culture of commitment to cause.

Third, new experiments are moving beyond language. Some organizations are attempting not to wrap nonprofits in the cloak of commercial revenue strategies, but to create entirely new business models. Called *social enterprise* by some, *social entrepreneurship* by others, and *community wealth* by still others, these new models are experimenting with building classic businesses on the foundations of nonprofit causes. Juma Ventures in San Francisco reaches troubled youth and provides them with job training by owning and running small businesses of its own. In the nation's capital, the charity D.C. Central Kitchen serves the poor, in part, with revenues earned through its catering business, which turns a $300,000 profit each year. Even the Goodwill is experimenting; its used car lot in northeast Washington, DC sells more used cars than any other dealer in the region.

A variant on this strategy is called *cause-related marketing* which links corporate advertising budgets to nonprofit causes. Such marketing relates use or purchase of a sponsor's product to contributions of the sponsor to the cause. Although the business gain is clear, so is the societal gain. The win–win solution raises all boats.

Of course, new strategies are not without conflicts. If, for example, a nonprofit sells cars in competition with a for-profit, why should it not pay taxes? Does the government provide to the nonprofit a market advantage that impedes competition? Can wealth creation, the classic result of the marketplace, and wealth redistribution, the traditional "business" of charity be compatible in the long term? Are such strategies scaleable? Can the catering business achieve economies of scale and generate resources significant relative to the national problem of hunger? Or will such experiments continue to be successful only if they are sized to local control?

These and other questions remain to be answered. But, as with any experiment, the lesson is often not just in the results. It is in the discipline of experimentation itself.

◼ SOURCES

Arnsberger, P. "Charities and Other Tax-Exempt Organizations 1998," Special Studies Special Projects Section, Internal Revenue Service. In *IRS Statistics of Income Bulletin*, Fall 2001, Publication 1136.

Cannon, C.M. "Charity for Profit," *National Journal*, June 17, 2000 pp. 1898–1904.

Venture Philanthropy 2001: The Changing Landscape of Nonprofit Government Funding, Venture Philanthropy Partners, Washington, DC, 2001.

Weisbrod, B. (ed.) *To Profit or Not to Profit: The Dilemma of Commercializing the Non-Profit Center,* Cambridge, England: Cambridge University Press, 2001.

Nonprofit Compensation: Charitable Managers and Their Tax-Exempt Colleagues

Forbes magazine garnered its share of headlines in November 2002 when its charity survey revealed that, despite a slowing economy and rising unemployment, "nonprofits" were raising the salaries of their employees by 8.5 percent, with the raises concentrated in the suites of top managers. But *Forbes'* use of the term "nonprofit" was narrow, with its survey limited to 501(c)(3) charities. This is far from the nonprofit universe.

How does compensation differ across the full range of tax-exempt categories? And how do charities stack up relative to their non(c)(3) tax-exempt counterparts, such as trade associations and pension funds?

An IRS study produced comprehensive data on a 1998 sample of 216,514 tax-exempt organizations in categories 501(c)(3) through (c)(9). The returns were the most recent for which full data were available. The data are from Form 990 returns, hence the sample does not include organizations such as religious institutions that are not required to file. And because the data are from the full 990s, not the 990-EZ filed by small organizations, the profile portrays the structure of larger organizations. In that sample, the compensation differences are striking.

Among charities ((501(c)(3)), 46 percent of expenditures were taken up by compensation of staff and directors. For the 161,525 organizations in the sample (about a quarter of the active charities in the country), the dollar total was $325 billion. How big is that? Well, for perspective, according to the World Bank the 2001 gross domestic product of the Russian Federation was $310 billion. The compensation tab alone for even a quarter of U.S. charities is larger than Russia's annual GDP! And one year of just the payroll taxes of the sample would fund Costa Rica's whole economy! With a billion dollars to spare, no less!

How does the 46 percent of expenses spent on charitable salaries compare to other tax-exempt organizations? Not well. The percentage of expenditures allocated to compensation by (c)(3) organizations is higher than in any other category, and four times that of civic leagues or fraternal organizations. Even labor organizations spend a smaller portion on compensation.

EXHIBIT 3.8   5O1(c)(3) EXPENDITURE DISTRIBUTION, 1999

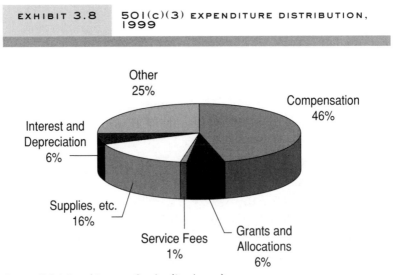

Source: U.S. Internal Revenue Service (Arnsberger)

The compensation of chief executives also differs radically across types of nonprofits. Among the most highly paid are CEOs of foundations, educational institutions, and health providers. Their mean annual compensation is double that of their counterparts in advocacy and consumer groups, chambers of commerce, and community development organizations.

Size does matter, to be sure. If one looks exclusively at 990-EZ organizations, then the expenditure structure changes markedly. Charities allocate only 20.6 percent of their expenditures to compensation, while labor falls from 40 percent to 27 percent. Across nonprofits, CEO pay also tracks size. CEOs of organizations with annual budgets between $25 and $50 million have median incomes over four times those of nonprofits with incomes under $250,000. Only voluntary employee beneficiary organizations see an inverse relationship between the compensation allocation within expenditures and organizational size. The differing pattern suggests that small may not always be beautiful, but it is certainly cheaper.

▓ SOURCES

Arnsberger, P. "Charities and Other Tax-Exempt Organizations," Special Studies Special Projects Section, Internal Revenue Service. In *IRS Statistics of Income Bulletin*, Fall 2002, Publication 1136.

Barrett, W. "Charity Begins with the Boss," *Forbes, www.forbes.com*, November 21, 2002.

Compensation in Nonprofit Organizations, 12th ed., Abbott, Langer and Associates, September 1999.

World Development Indicators, The World Bank, August 2002.

To: Nonprofit Human Resources Managers
From: Washington
Subject: Watch Your Back

Although it is generally true that the titles of reports emanating from Washington, DC, are as intriguing as old dishwater, there are exceptions. With an introduction by then Treasury Secretary Paul O'Neil, the National Academy of Public Administration's report on human resources in the federal government is titled "A Work Experience Second to None." The Part I subtitle is "Winning the War for Talent." A war, no less!

Among the challenges facing the federal government is the problem of aging. The hiring freezes over the last two decades, combined with the general marketing challenges inherent in selling professional opportunities in bureaucratic cubicles on the Potomac, have created a looming human resources vacuum. By 2006, depending on the agency, between a third and half of the nearly 1.8 million employees of federal executive agencies will become eligible to retire.

The exodus from the federal government will be difficult to staunch, although changing retirement options may slow the process. But even if delayed a few years, the cut in personnel will be equally difficult to restore. Labor force dynamics provide the sta-

EXHIBIT 3.9   PERCENT GOVERNMENT WORKFORCE
RETIRING BY 2007

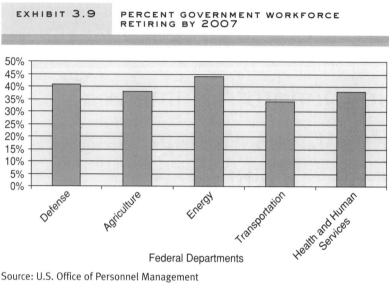

Federal Departments

Source: U.S. Office of Personnel Management

tistical barrier. Projections indicate that, if the economy grows by 2 percent, given the numbers of younger workers aged 24 to 45, the labor market overall will see a 30 percent shortfall in available workers in that age group by 2006. The entire market will compete for those workers. And, with its Partnership for Public Service initiative, the federal government has declared its intention to be in that market, and to be in it forcefully.

> "Alonso of Aragon was wont to say in commendation of age, that age appears to be best in four things—old wood to burn, old wine to drink, old friends to trust, and old authors to read."
> —Sir Francis Bacon
> Apothegms, 1624

Furthermore, the retiring federal workers will not all be brain surgeons and fighter pilots. The General Accounting Office (GAO) estimates that 30 percent of the government's program managers will retire by 2006, compared to 13 percent of its aerospace engineers. That means the government is in the market for the generalist.

Why should nonprofit human resources managers chew their pencils over the personnel woes of the federal government? Why does the federal government's declared intention to look for and attract the best talent give pause?

Because the pool of people the federal government seeks to fish in is the same pool from which nonprofits harvest their workers. While it can be argued that an increased demand for investment bankers or systems engineers does not necessarily increase competition for the kinds of people attracted to nonprofit careers, it is certainly true that increased demand for young generalists would. The motivations are similar. The services and issues are similar. The pay scales are similar. The benefits are similar. Indeed, with the pace of retirement, the upward mobility in government may be greater. Thus, the entry of an aggressive federal government in the human resources market may not worry Bear Stearns, but it should worry the nonprofit.

Of course, if only a handful of jobs were at stake, there would be less need to worry. How many jobs are we talking about? If we take the anticipated 2007 retirement rates of 2001 federal employees in five of the largest federal agency employers, the government will need to replace nearly 375,000 workers. How many is that? It is more than the entire nonprofit workforce of the State of Texas, more than twice the nonprofit employment of the State of Connecticut, and 73 percent more than the nonprofit workforce in the federal government's geographic cousin, the State of Maryland.

In fact, the competitive impact is probably even more intense than these general ratios would indicate. The state numbers include people such as brain surgeons via nonprofit hospitals and universities. In many states, this is a huge portion of the nonprofit workforce. In Maryland, healthcare is 49 percent of total nonprofit employment. Which means that federal demand is over three times the nonprofit workforce of Maryland. Clearly, the government's need (or ability) to suction up large numbers of young generalists will make it a major player in the human resources marketplace.

Which leaves nonprofits with two clear human resources tasks: develop aggressive marketing plans, and mandate that "employee retention" be the screensaver on every manager's computer.

■ SOURCES

Federal Civilian Workforce Statistics, U.S. Office of Personnel Management, 2002.

"Federal Employee Retirements: Expected Increase Over the Next 5 Years Illustrates Need for Workforce Planning," Report to the Chairman, Subcommittee on Civil Service and Agency Organization, Committee on Government Reform, House of Representatives. United States General Accounting Office, April 2001.

Office of Personnel Management, Partnership for Public Service, Washington, DC, 2001.

State employment data from Johns Hopkins University Center for Civil Society Studies of the Institute for Policy Studies, Maryland, 2003, Texas, 2002, Connecticut, 2002.

"A Work Experience Second to None: Impelling the Best to Serve. Part I: Winning the War for Talent." Human Resources Management Panel, National Academy of Public Administration, 2001.

Estate Taxes and Giving: Crepe Armbands versus Thinking Caps

Philanthropy usually flies through a great deal of rhetorical turbulence when the political debate focuses on revisions to the U.S. estate tax system. Predictions of nonprofit revenue doom abound. Without the prod of taxation, it has been said, the nation's wealthy would give in to deeper Dickensian tendencies. They would consume their wealth while alive, and die with what was left tucked safely in the family wallet. Throughout the first half of 2001, philanthropy prepared to wear crepe in mourning for the death of the death tax.

> "It takes a noble man to plant a seed for a tree that will someday give shade to people he may never meet."
> —David Trueblood

Parenthetically, few legal practitioners believe such taxes will actually be abolished in 2010, congressional claims aside. Indeed, many believe they may actually rise again, at least over the long term. To understand why, ask your trust and estates lawyer about the different policies Congress put in place for estates and for gifts.

The technicalities aside, estate tax change is upon us. Does subsequent philanthropic Armageddon appear likely?

First, a review of the numbers. There is little evidence that philanthropic behavior in general is tax-driven. Over time and despite wide fluctuation in the top marginal income tax rate (between 28 percent and 70 percent), the percentage of GNP allocated to philanthropy has stayed at between 1.7 percent and 2.3 percent. If philanthropy tracks anything, it tends to track economic performance (and then only weakly), not federal tax policy. Over the last 40 years, individual giving has vacillated between a low of 1.76 percent of personal disposable income and a high of 2.47 percent. Americans appear to be exceedingly reliable philanthropists, unimpressed with changes in tax codes or just about anything else.

Still, the concern over the link between bequest behavior and philanthropy is not trivial. Some 8.4 million American households have annual income of over $150,000 and net assets (not including primary residence) of over $500,000. In 1999, 8.2 percent of charitable contributions ($15.6 billion) came in the form of bequests. While that is the smallest source of giving, it is clearly not loose change out of the top drawer.

Moreover, charitable bequests have risen sharply in the last decade. Between 1986 and 1998, the number of estate tax returns that included charitable deductions increased by 117 percent. The total value of those deductions increased by 190 percent. Still, the percentage of total returns with charitable deductions remained exactly the same, 17.4 percent, while those deductions as a percentage of total estate value rose only from 6.0 percent to 6.2 percent. And if estate tax returns are viewed as a percentage of adult deaths, though history shows some variation, in no year between 1934 and 1993 (the years for which data are available) have the number of taxable estate returns exceeded 8 percent of the adult deaths in the nation.

The vast majority of bequest activity is out of the estates of the very wealthy. More than three-quarters of the value of bequests to charity is accounted for by estates in excess of $2.5 million. Hence,

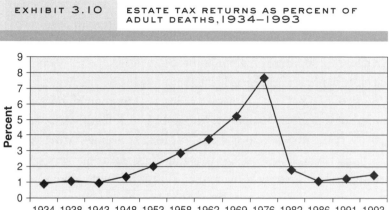

EXHIBIT 3.10   ESTATE TAX RETURNS AS PERCENT OF
ADULT DEATHS, 1934–1993

Source: U.S. Internal Revenue Service (Johnson & Eller)

what the very wealthy do (or plan to do) is key to anticipating the philanthropic effect of tax changes. One economic theory and two recent pieces of research indicate that the overall, long-term effect of tax change will not be significant.

> "[The inheritance tax of 1862 was] one of the best, fairest, and most easily borne [taxes] that political economists have yet discovered as applicable to modern society."
> —The Internal Revenue *Record*, 1869

Milton Friedman's "permanent income" or "overlapping generations" theory holds that families first determine how wealth will be transferred among generations. Only then are any charitable transfers allocated. Hence, among the wealthy, a reduction in estate taxes would actually redound to the credit of philanthropy, because this is where net additional resources are placed.

Paul G. Schervish, of the Social Welfare Research Institute at Boston University, has pointed out that the wealthiest Americans are moving increasing portions of their estates to charity. His own interviews have seen no tendency on the part of these philanthropists to change direction, irrespective of tax reform.

Similarly, a poll published in early 2003, and commissioned by HNW Digital, which owns Worth.com, indicated that nearly three-quarters of wealthy respondents did not feel that estate tax changes would alter their philanthropic plans. Another 19 percent felt tax changes would provide incentives to give more to charity, leaving only 8 percent predicting reductions in giving. The wealthy households planned to allocate about 11 percent of their estates to charity, compared to about 4 percent for the average American.

Of course, what is true "overall" and "long term" may not be true for any particular nonprofit here and now. Bequests tend to come in big chunks. In 1998, the average charitable deduction from an estate was $640,000, up from $459,999 a decade earlier. Clearly, the change of heart of even a single benefactor can leave quite a gaping hole in a nonprofit's revenue stream.

If the stakes are high, but the giving intent does not appear to be changing, times call not for mourning but for creativity. If the tax prod is not the source of philanthropic behavior for the wealthy, then the nonprofit strategy is best crafted to address deeper motivations. And those motivations are no surprise.

The Worth.com survey reiterates that wealthy Americans give when they feel strongly about a cause and when they have personal experience with the target organization. A compelling case experienced individually beckons far more effectively than federal policy. Additionally, the resources transferred within a family, rather than to a charitable bequest, do not disappear; they simply change hands. The art for the creative nonprofit will be to make its case as compelling for the kids as it was for Mom and Dad.

And that, in and of itself, may be the additional, largely unanticipated side-benefit to estate tax reform. Organizations that continue to refresh their commitment, that continuously reevaluate their relevance, that insist that both management and volunteers always serve with dynamism and an eye toward change, will thrive and grow.

If estate tax reform forces nonprofits to make an ongoing compelling case to the next generation in order to continue to access family philanthropy, it will generate a vibrancy of the nonprofit world that taxes never could.

■ SOURCES

Billitteri, Thomas. "A Taxing Dilemma," *The Chronicle of Philanthropy,* July 27, 2000, pp. 17–19.

Butler, Stuart M. "Why the Bush Tax Cuts Are No Threat to Philanthropy," *The Heritage Foundation Backgrounder,* March 8, 2001.

"The Economics of the Estate Tax," Joint Economic Committee Statement, U.S. Congress, 1999.

Giving USA 2003, AAFRC Trust for Philanthropy.

"If the 'Death Tax' Dies, Will Philanthropy Take a Hit?" *www.office.com*, November 2000.

Johnson, B.W., and M.B. Eller. "Federal Taxation of Inheritance and Wealth Transfers," Internal Revenue Service, March 2001.

Minton, Frank. "Reform, Don't Abolish Estate Tax," *Seattlepi.nwsource.com*, March 20, 2001.

"New Poll Shows How Wealthy View Estate Tax, Other Giving Issues," *The Chronicle of Philanthropy,* January 25, 2001.

Wasow, Bernard. "Repeal of Estate Tax Removes Incentive for Charitable Giving," The Century Foundation, 2001.

The Growth of the Nonprofit Sector: Is It Really Real?

Sometimes, an offhand question sparks curiosity. In chatting about the growth in nonprofits over the past decade, a skeptical colleague wondered aloud how true those numbers really were. That is, how many of these nonprofits were really operational and how many were just, if you will, cardboard cutouts without three-dimensional organizational depth.

There is no way to answer that question directly—at least absent cooperation from the FBI and the IRS. But the question did spark curiosity about what is underneath the growth data. If one cannot answer definitively the "is it real" question, it is at least possible to disaggregate data by size.

The hypothesis would be that the smaller the income stream of an organization, the smaller its operations. An overwhelming presence of tiny organizations would lead one to suspect that growth in numbers does not necessarily imply growth in economic clout.

Using the Guidestar database, one can distinguish between "public charities"—501(c)(3) organizations with service/product provision operations—and foundations. The lowest-income category in the database is "less than $25,000" in annual revenue. While $25,000 is admittedly not zero, it is pretty small as an annual operating base.

Of the 897,383 public charities listed in Guidestar, a whopping 71 percent have incomes less than $25,000 per year. The reason this element of the nonprofit constellation is not picked up in other studies, of course, is that these small organizations are not analyzed because they are not required to report to the IRS in detail.

States with a lower percentage of the smallest nonprofits are not particularly surprising: They tend to be larger states on the East Coast—Massachusetts (62 percent), New York, and Pennsylvania (66 percent)—and Washington, DC (65 percent). Somewhat surprisingly, Vermont also falls into this category, with only 66 percent of its nonprofits being in the smallest category.

States with 77 percent or more of their nonprofits in the smallest category share not regional location but agriculture. Top seed goes to South Dakota, where 80 percent of nonprofits have less than $25,000 in annual income, closely followed by South Carolina (79 percent) and Iowa, Nebraska, and Oklahoma (78 percent). Of the 14 states in which three-quarters or more of nonprofits are in the "smallest" category, all are dominantly rural.

But that explanation lacks power. Maine and Alaska, for example, fall below the national average, with 68 percent of their nonprofits in the smallest category. Neither could be described as either industrial or urban.

Does substance matter? Here the picture is clearer. Organizations focusing on human and public services have fewer than half their organizations in the smallest category, perhaps because the shift of public service provision to nonprofits has created huge government financing revenue streams in these subsectors.

In contrast religious, conservation, and animal protection categories are dominated by small organizations, with between 75 percent and 78 percent of their nonprofits taking in less than $25,000 per year. No other substantive categories come close to this concentration.

One suspects then that, despite the gross national percentages that hint at a dominance of smallness, much of nonprofit growth *is* real. Substantive categories with the largest numbers of organizations have the lowest percentages of extremely small organizations. Substantive categories with the largest concentration of extremely small organizations constitute only 8 percent of Guidestar's database.

When Philanthropy Demands Evidence and Results: Developing a Compelling Rationale for Funding

Successfully obtaining philanthropic funding for nonprofits requires multidimensional effort. One element of that effort involves solicitation of grants for specific programs or endeavors. This element—known in the parlance of the profession as "grant-writing" is, in fact, not a task, it is a process. As such, it is a funding element that is widely misunderstood hence often unsuccessful.

Traditionally, grant-writing has been a straightforward matter: Identify a program and write about how much good it does, being sure to make its needs for funds explicit. It is not overly facetious to suggest that the grant-writing product of the past approximated the following:

We are a fine organization doing good things.
We have a program that is also fine and does good things.
We like this program and so do the people who use it.
Please send money.

In some cases, where the sponsoring organization is well known to a donor, who has a special relationship to the people or programs of the organization, such a rationale is sufficient. Relationships matter a great deal in philanthropy, and program funding can trade on such relationships.

> "Writing is easy. All you do is stare at a blank sheet of paper until drops of blood form on your forehead."
> —Gene Fowler
> (Attributed)

Increasingly, however, except for the closest boosters, philanthropies take a much more critical view of funding solicitations. The proposing organization must justify its existence, the program's existence, the program's effectiveness and efficiency, impact, and long-term sustainability. In addition, the argument for a particular program must place that effort within a context, in effect demonstrating not only that there is a problem, but that the problem is important in a larger economic or societal context.

Grant-writing, then, is really not a matter of writing at all. Rather, it is a process of analytics, dominantly but not exclusively quantitative. That process has at least seven steps:

1. *Define the problem.* What is the problem being addressed? Why does the problem exist? How big is that problem in the location of the home organization? How big is it nationwide, or regionally? Therefore is it more or less important to the economy and society that the program touches?

2. *Define the implications of the problem.* Is the problem increasing in importance? Is it filtering out to new populations, new groups, new institutions? Therefore, is immediate action important? Measure wherever possible, even with surrogate evidence. Which problem will worsen if the program is not in place? By now much? Compared to what (nation, region, other cities, etc.)?

3. *Define the program approach.* Describe the program in detail. How does this program propose to affect that problem? Is this a new approach or an extension or replication of an existing

approach? If this is a totally new approach, measure the failure of previous approaches, define the innovation, and how the innovation addresses inadequacies of other approaches. What is the evidence that the proposing organization has the capacity to mobilize and implement that approach?

4. *Measure the impact.* What has been the measurable impact of the approach on the problem, either via data from the existing program or via data from a similar program in another place? If the problem is increasing, is the approach scaleable? That is, is there evidence that more of the same approach will effectively address a problem that is growing or changing? What will change if the program is in place and successful?

5. *Define and defend the need.* Why does the program need support? What has the program done to meet its own needs? What has been done to ensure efficiency of resource allocation? What is the level of support needed? Why this level? How does this compare with the past? What is the prospect for the future?

6. *Address sustainability.* Has the organization thought through options for achieving financial sustainability for this program? Are other revenue options being evaluated? What are the financial projections for such options? Even at best estimates, what is the uncovered financial need? Build a funding scenario. What happens if only 50 percent of the program budget is raised?

7. *Present the budget.* What is the total resource flow of the overall organization? What is the total resource flow of the program? What is the total need? Of that, how much is the organization willing to meet from its own central resources? What is the request? What percentage of the total need is represented by this request? Where will the organization go (or where has it successfully gone) to meet the remainder of the need? Draw up a specific line-item budget.

Only when the entire analysis is completed is grant-writing a matter of writing. Of course, then, the grant fairly quickly writes itself.

> "The only thing I was fit for was to be a writer, and this notion rested solely on my suspicion that I would never be fit for real work, and that writing didn't require any."
> —Russell Baker

Not every program will have compelling data in each of the seven areas. Alternatively, some may have a "case" that can be made on additional dimensions. But the general parameters needing analysis are likely to approximate these seven.

This process allows the organization to triage its needs. In fact, when analyzed, it may be that some needs are less defensible (in a program sense) than others. The strongest cases can then be pursed with grant proposals, with the weaker cases cross-subsidized out of budgetary overhead, central resources, or relationship resources. The process allows an organization to put forward its strongest cases for foundation proposals, increase its funding success rate, build foundation momentum for subsequent proposals, and use non-program funding to subsidize areas that "present" less well in the grant-writing community.

What History Teaches
about the Root Systems
That Nourish Philanthropy

The literature on the history of philanthropy is surprisingly deep. With all the societal and media attention to whiz-bang technology (you can no longer really ever escape your office), deep-space probes (recently, Mars has seemed more and more attractive as a residential option), and the likelihood that we will all soon be able to live to be 120 (well, perhaps not us, but certainly our grandchildren), it is startling that there are people actually giving fairly scholarly attention to the origins of modern philanthropy.

Moreover, the work is quite instructive. As many in philanthropy wonder whether (or how) the outpouring of goodwill engendered by the unspeakable evil of September 11, 2001, will be translated into deeper, lasting involvement in philanthropic leadership, a look back might be useful.

"History, we can confidently assert, is useful in the sense that art and music, poetry and flowers, religion and philosophy are useful. Without it—as with these—life would be poorer and meaner; without it we should be denied some of those intellectual and moral experiences which give meaning and richness to life. Surely it is no accident that the study of history has been the solace of many of the noblest minds of every generation."

—Henry Steele Commager

Two particular studies provide insights, one examining the emergence of the "Manchester Man" in English philanthropy in the Victorian Age, and the other examining the emergence of philanthropy in Bordeaux, France, during the late 1800s and early 1900s. The emergence of long-term commitment to community philanthropy in those early days was clearly tied to social acceptance. Interestingly, in Manchester, those who would become long-term leaders were not natives of Manchester. They were businessmen, many of whom were German, who had migrated to Manchester. They were relatively few in number, and comprised the middle-class elite. They were affluent but not necessarily titled.

Once engaged in philanthropic work, their influence spread widely. Of the 3,908 individuals known to be philanthropic or charitable leaders in Manchester, nearly 10 percent were members of at least three charitable organizations; 25 were members of more than 10 organizations each. In nearly all cases, those who became involved established permanent links to Manchester and became long-term community leaders.

In Bordeaux, the establishment of charitable institutions to serve the indigent dates to 1871, well in advance of the Third Republic decrees of 1893 providing free medical care to the indigent. By 1879, the city had added nighttime emergency medical services to its charitable network. Between 1870 and 1914, the population of Bordeaux grew by 35 percent; the number of charities grew by more than 70 percent.

What is interesting about the two cases is the degree to which they teach complementary lessons. In Manchester, the institutionalization of philanthropy was a result of changing social structure. Long-term charitable commitments provided social standing to a relatively new business elite, a way to achieve social standing commensurate with corporate success. In Bordeaux, the critical trigger appears to have been the local government's recognition of its inability to respond to the needs of the poor with its limited resources. Local government took a much more aggressive stance in encouraging local private leaders to establish service alternatives and to engage in charitable fundraising to combine private resources with public funds to finance those alternatives. With the prod of public policy, private leaders created charitable responses to everything from healthcare to after-school programs for working families.

What does it take to transform goodwill into deeply rooted institutional behavior?

On the one hand, one should never underestimate the motivational power of recognition. "Doing good" is often most easily long term and entrenched when it also does well. Extraordinarily deep leadership emerged in Manchester from very small initial seeds, in part because there was private social benefit to be had on the societal commons.

On the other hand, long-term private initiative often cannot be divorced from public encouragement. Policy matters. Local government support for, even financial partnership with, charitable initiatives provides the promise of stability that can transform episodic responses to need into long-term institutional advancement.

Of course, on at least one dimension, trends over a century ago differ markedly from modern experience. In Manchester, there was not a single woman among the ranks of charitable leaders; 50 of the 98 charities had no women in any position of active or honorary involvement. In the United States today, 41 percent of Americans earning $500,000 or more per year are women, and women give as much of their income to charity as men. Moreover, they are both financial and management leaders. A 1998 Council on Foundations survey found that women held half the foundation CEO positions and 68 percent of the program officer posts.

Certainly, today's philanthropic leadership is more representative of gender distribution in society. And that is an essential asset in and of itself. But the harder question is whether the leadership shifts have been accompanied by differences in the outcomes or targets of philanthropy itself. Does gender leadership matter? If women had played a more notable leadership role 100 years ago, would any need that was not met have been addressed? If they did not today, would philanthropic targets be different? Dissertation anyone?

■ SOURCES

Beaudoin, Steven M. "'Without Belonging to Public Service': Charities, the State, and Civil Society in Third Republic Bordeaux, 1870–1914," vol. 31, *Journal of Social History,* March 22, 1998, pp. 671–699.

Schumell, Donna Gardner. "Financial Advisors Heed the Call: Women Are Giving More Than Time," *Trusts and Estates,* April, 1, 2001, pp. 35–37.

Shapely, Peter. "Charity, Status, and Leadership: Charitable Image and the Manchester Man," vol. 32, *Journal of Social History,* September 22, 1998, pp. 157–178.

Philanthropy and Healthcare

INTRODUCTION TO THE ISSUES

By 2002, healthcare expenditures had risen to over 13 percent of the GDP of the United States. The industries and institutions that produce and provide healthcare, from the research bench to the hospice bedside, comprise the most powerful engine of innovation ever seen on the face of the earth. They have brought to human-kind undreamed of innovations, and hope for life and health be-yond any experienced in history. Their promise is that of a future increasingly free of early death and hopeless suffering.

> "I will apply dietetic measures for the benefit of the sick according to my ability and judgment; I will keep them from harm and injustice . . .
> Whatever houses I may visit, I will come for the benefit of the sick, remaining free of all intentional injustice. . . ."
> —Hippocrates 460–377 B.C. Physician's Oath

They are also complex, varied, disparate, bureaucratic, expensive, and, increasingly, in serious financial difficulty.

The federal government remains the overwhelming factor in determining how the nation's healthcare system will evolve, and how it will be paid for. While only 243 of the nation's 5,801 regis-tered hospitals are owned and operated by the federal government, Medicare and Medicaid pay for nearly 60 percent of hospital

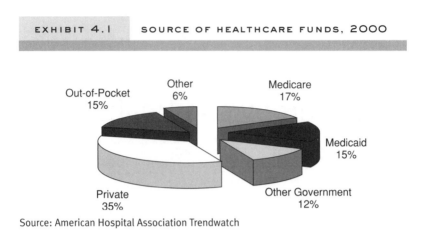

EXHIBIT 4.1   SOURCE OF HEALTHCARE FUNDS, 2000

Out-of-Pocket
15%

Other
6%

Medicare
17%

Medicaid
15%

Private
35%

Other Government
12%

Source: American Hospital Association Trendwatch

admissions. The hand that controls the purse strings can be expected to have significant control over decisions about how and where money is spent.

In the grand drama of American healthcare, private philanthropy does not take a starring role. Of the $1.4 trillion in healthcare expenditures, over a third is financed by private insurance, 45 percent is financed by government, and 15 percent is paid for out-of-pocket. Philanthropy is part of the remaining 6 percent of the funding stream.

Yet there are many tendrils to the relationship between private philanthropy and healthcare in the nation. Philanthropy is a key source of capital for improvements in hospitals. It is also an important source of meeting the healthcare needs of the nation's poorest citizens. In its noncash mode, voluntarism represents an important cost-containing element of service provision for all types of community healthcare institutions.

"It requires faith and courage to recognize the real human soul under the terrible mask of squalor and disease in these crowded masses of poverty, and then resist the temptation to regard them as 'clinical material.' The attitude of the student and doctor to the sick poor is a real test of the true physican."
—Elizabeth Blackwell, 1890
in *The Influence of Women in the Profession of Medicine*

The problem for philanthropy, of course, is how to craft and maximize its role as cost escalation exceeds its own growth, and as, therefore, it becomes an even smaller partner in the healthcare enterprise. These problems are compounded by the growing insolvency of many community healthcare institutions. Developing philanthropic strategies to raise money for institutions whose financial days are numbered is not simply a fundraising challenge. It is a challenge to healthcare management and to the financial transparency and openness of the community facilities under siege. Philanthropy as last financial resort can become philanthropy without full disclosure.

The essays in this section examine the size and role of philanthropy in the various dimensions of healthcare, from community to academic halls to the global commons.

▧ SOURCES

Hospital Statistics 2003, American Hospital Association.

Trends Affecting Hospitals and Health Systems, November 2002, American Hospital Association.

Healthcare in the Twenty-First Century: Why the Charity Gap Will Grow

$\mathbf{S}$ince 1990, American healthcare has been the recipient of about 17 percent of U.S. foundation grantmaking, representing about 9 percent of all philanthropy, each year. In 2002, that translated into $18.87 billion in resource transfers into healthcare institutions. In inflation-adjusted dollars, that is a doubling of annual giving for healthcare in the four decades between 1962 and 2002. Healthcare garners 7.8 percent of the philanthropic dollar. All of this would be impressive but for three facts.

First, the nation's total healthcare bill is over $1.4 trillion per year, or one-seventh of the nation's economy. Philanthropy, then, represents only 1.31 percent of healthcare resources in the nation.

Second, cost escalation in healthcare is projected to heat up. After being held to 3 to 4 percent annual increases in the mid-1990s, healthcare expenditures are projected to rise by 6 to 7 percent per year in the coming decade. That, at times, will likely be faster growth than the overall economy. Although there is some indication that cost-containment efforts may slow that rate to 5 percent in the 2003–2005 period, expenditure escalation will inevitably speed up. The crossover between the rate of healthcare cost increases and GDP increases that took place in 1997 has not been reversed.

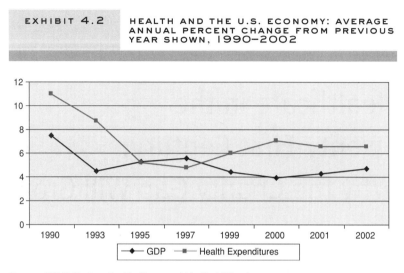

EXHIBIT 4.2   HEALTH AND THE U.S. ECONOMY: AVERAGE
ANNUAL PERCENT CHANGE FROM PREVIOUS
YEAR SHOWN, 1990–2002

Source: DHHS Centers for Medicare and Medicaid Services

In part, that inevitability is driven by technology advances. Genetically engineered therapeutics, for example, are expensive to produce and will be equally expensive to bring to the bedside. Pharmaceutical cost escalation already represents one of the fastest increases within the nation's healthcare bill, and demand for (as well as the promise of) new therapies will only bolster that trend.

But, in part, cost escalation is inevitable because of a phenomenon over which few of us have any choice at all—aging. The sad but true fact is that we are getting older. By 2020, 20 percent of the population will be on Medicare. The healthcare costs of each person over the age of 65 are three times those at younger ages. And those over age 85 cost three times those aged 65 to 74.

Unless healthcare philanthropy can grow at better than 7 percent per year in real terms, the gap between charity and costs will widen. But, in fact, healthcare philanthropy has slowed. Between 2000 and 2001, philanthropic allocations to healthcare declined by 2.1 percent in nominal terms and by 4.8 percent in inflation-adjusted dollars.

Third, not all of the $18.87 billion in healthcare philanthropy finds its way into actual care. The fastest-growing recipients of foundation health giving are policy organizations, focusing on assess-

EXHIBIT 4.3   GROWTH IN U.S. ELDERLY POPULATION BY
               AGE GROUP

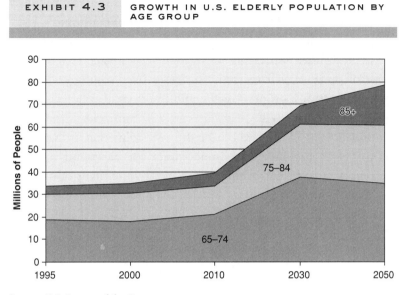

Source: U.S. Bureau of the Census

ments of alternative approaches to the provision and payment for
healthcare within evolving national policy. The healthcare philanthropic dollar is in danger of being found not at the bedside but in
the conference auditorium and the congressional hallway.

Two conclusions can be reached. First, philanthropic healthcare
resources are increasingly dear relative to healthcare costs. Growing
these resources, and attempting to focus them back on prevention
and service provision, will be an important mission for philanthropic
leaders in the next decade.

Second, as is usually the case, what is true in general is not
necessarily true in particular. While perhaps a tiny portion of total
healthcare resources, philanthropy can nonetheless represent a
critical element of viability for any individual institution. This is
especially true in these days of market-driven competition for the
ever-smaller managed-care dollar. Particularly for community and
nonprofit hospitals, the dollar value of voluntarism and charitable
donations can mean the difference between financial viability and
the "For Sale" sign.

Moreover, philanthropy carries great symbolism for community healthcare. The involvement and commitment of community leaders, political and corporate, to something as central to community life as healthcare represents more than just dollars. It represents unity of purpose. Whatever the divisions over zoning codes, cell tower regulations, property taxes, and the myriad other disagreements, large and small, that can tear a community apart, clear commitment to healthcare can be the core value that pulls a community back together. The opportunity for clear and steadfast commitment to health of the community by the titans of industry and those who may be titans only of their backyard grill provides a stability of shared interest.

In this sense, building philanthropic capacity at the local level will continue to be a central healthcare need, irrespective of national cost trends. Indeed, it is not simply a need, it is an obligation.

SOURCES

Bureau of the Census, 2003.

Giving USA 2003, American Council of Fund Raising Executives.

National Health Expenditure Projections, U.S. Health Care Financing Administration, 2001.

Hospital Philanthropy: David versus Goliath

With continually increasing healthcare costs (6.6 percent overall and 18.4 percent for pharmaceuticals in the past few years) and despite a concomitant ferocious focus on cost containment, hospital financial margins are shrinking from "low already" to "ready for the red ink." With the resultant narrowing of their resource pool, hospitals must increasingly look elsewhere for the capital needed to fund new programs, research, and infrastructure.

Historically, one source of such funds has come from investment income. The booming stock market of the 1990s lifted the bottom line of hospitals along with those of all other organizations and enterprises. Indeed, the boom came at an opportune time, given the reimbursement reductions for healthcare included in the Balanced Budget Act of 1997. The 1997 act set out a multiyear process for reductions in federal payments for Medicare services, and reductions in subsidies for teaching hospital costs. Medicare and Medicaid account for over 60 percent of all hospital admissions, so Federal policy is fairly critical to hospital financial well-being. By 2001, nearly two-thirds of all U.S. hospitals have negative overall Medicare margins, up from 46 percent in 1997.

Recent declines in investment returns, combined with falling reimbursement rates, have squeezed the total financial margin of hospitals, which dropped from 6.7 percent in 1997 to 4.6 percent in 2000. Indeed hospitals pursue their core business—delivering

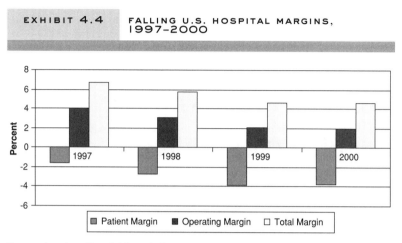

EXHIBIT 4.4   FALLING U.S. HOSPITAL MARGINS, 1997–2000

Source: American Hospital Association

patient services—at a deeper and deeper financial loss. Further-more, accessing capital in the marketplace is also becoming difficult. In 2001, six times as many hospitals had bond downgrades as had bond upgrades. In 1997, upgrades far outpaced downgrades. Thus, hospitals will increasingly turn to philanthropy to fill the gap.

A further question, however, is, "For whom does the bell toll?" The U.S. hospital "system" is actually a highly diverse patchwork of nonprofit, for-profit, community, and teaching facilities. Approx-

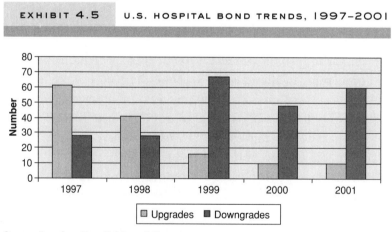

EXHIBIT 4.5   U.S. HOSPITAL BOND TRENDS, 1997–2001

Source: American Hospital Association

imately 90 percent of all hospital expenses are at community hospitals, but it is the large urban teaching hospitals that tend to draw the most public attention. The impact of changing financial parameters can, therefore, be different across hospital type and location. Who is losing badly? Hence, where will the philanthropic imperative be most critical?

Two measures can help to sort the institutional need. Total margin is the excess of revenues over expenses divided by total revenues net of allowances and uncollectables. It reflects profits from both operations and nonoperations. Earnings before interest, depreciation, and amortization (EBIDA) is often used in valuation to provide a better estimate of cash flow.

In 1999, total margins for hospitals nationally averaged 5.4 percent. In the Northeast, that slipped to 4.1 percent; for hospitals with fewer than 100 beds, it was 4.4 percent; and for teaching hospitals, it was 5.1 percent. But the real loser was New York, which ranked 50 among 50 states. The average total margin for New York's hospitals was 2.2 percent. Alarmingly, many hospitals have seen their margins slip into the red. The problems are particularly severe for the flagships of New York's healthcare system—its teaching hospitals—most of which are national research and training centers. Their higher cost structure, based on the costs of research, teaching, and uncompensated urban care, exceeds the reimbursement structure of both private insurers and, increasingly, federal programs.

Nationally, the EBIDA-to-revenues rate for hospitals is 12.5 percent. The regions underperforming the national average are facilities in the Northeast and the far West. The most seriously affected, however, are small rural hospitals whose rate is between 5 and 9 percent. Unfortunately, these are the very facilities for which the philanthropic reservoir is relatively shallow. The largest foundation pools, and the deepest individual philanthropic pockets, tend to be located in urban areas and in populous regions. Because most of this money is tied to funding its own geographic locus, the philanthropic flows will not naturally cross regional lines. Small rural facilities are in for a tough philanthropic slog.

The future will see a philanthropic footrace between the nation's healthcare Davids and its Goliaths. The larger, urban, teaching facilities will have the advantage of being proximate to deeper, more diverse sources of giving. The small rural facilities will need to develop creative, flexible, and compelling fundraising strategies if they hope to use philanthropic flows to staunch financial red ink.

■ SOURCES

Cleverly, W.O. *Almanac of Hospital Financial and Operating Indicators*, Ohio State University, 1999.

Hospital Statistics, American Hospital Association, 2003.

"The State of Hospitals' Financial Health," American Hospital Association, 2002.

Fighting Disease
with Philanthropy:
Who Gets the Funds?

We are an aging nation, it seems, newly aware of our own mortality. The pervasiveness of the public consciousness over its health is evidenced by the presence of medical commentators and commentaries in nearly every form of the media. Every network, every cable channel, and most major print media outlets have their consulting physicians to interpret trends, warn of dangers, and celebrate medical good news. Indeed, in 2000 the Lasker Foundation gave its Mary Woodard Lasker Public Service Award to the Tuesday *Science Times* section of the *New York Times* for its contributions to public knowledge. That is the same award that was given the very next year to the physician who engineered the global eradication of smallpox!

Simultaneously, science is providing new and fundamental insights into the process of disease at its most fundamental level. The two—science and public concern—feed one another: The more we care, the more attention we pay and the more science invests. The more science finds, the more attention we pay and the more we care.

"No, a thousand times no; there does not exist a category of science to which one can the name applied science. There are science and the application of science, bound together as the fruit of the tree which bears it."
—Louis Pasteur *Revue Scientifique, 1871*

The result of the two trends is a nation of individuals bound and determined to fight their own mortality on every front. A cardiologist colleague is fond of remarking that, for the average American faced with disease, death is no longer an acceptable outcome. That is as true of Americans at age 85 as it is at age 45.

"Justice will not come to Athens until those who are not injured are as indigent as those who are."
—Thucydides, 455 B.C.

The same determination that transformed a cluster of colonies into a continental nation, the same "can do" approach that gave us everything from the cotton gin to the space station, now has put its collective shoulder to the wheel of medical advance. Although the ethical dilemmas are myriad, and attention to their complexity is mandatory, progress will almost certainly ensue.

Where is philanthropy in this equation? The power to address the nation's disease patterns, of course, is held by the federal government and private industry. Together, they account for about 82 percent of the $12 billion in research funding in academic health centers. Philanthropy and voluntary funding represent about 9 percent. But, as Purnell Choppin, past president of the Howard Hughes Medical Institute has written, such funding is key because it tends to be less bureaucratic than government sources, more flexible in application, and longer term in commitment.

There is no comprehensive mechanism for examining the disease targets of U.S. philanthropy. Individuals represent the vast majority of philanthropy, and the directions of their giving (and volunteering) are a matter of speculation—at best. It is possible to gain some insight (but only some) by tracing the grants patterns of private foundations. Again, there is no comprehensive, fully reliable data source for such a query. But an approximation may be possible.

Using the Foundation Center's grants retrieval system, I examined just over 5,000 foundation grants for disease-specific programs, either in research or in prevention/education. I sought to illuminate three questions: What are the relative disease targets of U.S. philanthropy? How reliable is the funding? How large is the role compared to public sources?

WHAT ARE THE TARGETS?

Eight diseases or conditions were selected for examination: paralysis, stroke, asthma, diabetes, Alzheimer's disease, deafness/hearing-impaired conditions, cancer (all types), and HIV/AIDS. A total of 5,012 grants were identified, with a funding total of just over half a billion dollars ($503.9 million).

In the sample, giving was amazingly concentrated. Taken together, cancer and HIV/AIDS were the target of 72 percent of the grants, and garnered 76 percent of the total funding. However,

EXHIBIT 4.6   PERCENT SURVEYED TOTAL FUNDING BY SELECTED DISEASES

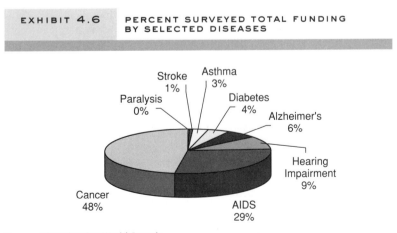

Source: Changing Our World Sample

while the two conditions were relatively even in grant receipt (38 percent of the total for HIV/AIDS and 34 percent for cancer), the dollar total for cancer ($238.85 million) was two-thirds again as large as for AIDS. The other six conditions paled in comparison, with deafness/hearing conditions coming in third with 555 grants totaling $47 million.

HOW RELIABLE IS THE FUNDING?

Often, research, prevention, and public education must take place over long periods of time. Philanthropy that is token is welcome, of course, but it cannot be considered a central force in disease prevention or cure. It is on this measure that HIV/AIDS funders tower over their colleagues.

Of foundations making grants for HIV/AIDS, 70 percent are multiple funders (i.e., made more than one grant in this disease area). Only 58 percent of cancer donors were multiple funders. For many diseases, foundation funding is often token: Only 4 of the 46 foundations making donations for asthma made more than one grant for this disease; only 5 of 28 in the stroke category, only 5 of 21 in the paralysis category, and only 47 of 136 in diabetes.

EXHIBIT 4.7   PERCENT SURVEYED FOUNDATIONS MAKING GRANTS TO SELECTED DISEASES

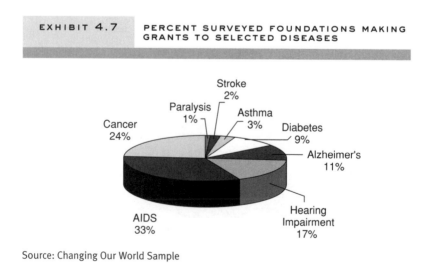

Source: Changing Our World Sample

HOW SIGNIFICANT IS THE FUNDING?

The average grant in the sample examined ranged from $57,000 (paralysis) to $169,000 (asthma.) A number of six- and seven-figure grants for research infrastructure pushed the cancer average to $139,000. Interestingly, while AIDS funders are loyal to the category, the $75,000 average grant placed AIDS funding second from the bottom on this measure.

For some diseases, notably cancer and HIV/AIDS, total philanthropic funding in this sample was fairly significant in the overall national picture. Although the comparisons are not exact, because the grants examined were not purely for research, the picture is still impressive. The 2001 total budget request for the National Cancer Institute, for example, was $5 billion, of which $2.34 billion was for research grants. The grant sample funding was about 10 percent as large. The National Institute for Allergy and Infectious Diseases (NIAID) had a total AIDS allocation of $1.2 billion; the grant sample was 12 percent as large.

For others, however, philanthropic funding clearly plays ball in the minor leagues. The National Institute of Neurologic Disorders and Stroke allocated $879 million for project grants; funding from the grant sample was only 0.6 percent as large. The National Institute of Diabetes and Digestive and Kidney Diseases allocated $1.186 billion for non–AIDS project grants; funding from the grant sample was only 1.8 percent as large.

As the nation's attention becomes focused on all that is possible via medical advances, and as it struggles with how to apply that potential in ways consistent with its ethical beliefs, the role of philanthropy will likely grow. For some disease categories, building a more significant presence from that trend will clearly require some heavy lifting.

▓ SOURCES

Grant sample taken from the online grants database of the Foundation Center, 2003.
"How to Fund Science," American Association for the Advancement of Science, 2001.
National Institutes of Health, budget submissions, 2003.

Picking Targets: Healthcare Philanthropy's Unenviable Task

There is good news and bad news for America in healthcare spending. After at least three decades of seemingly inexorable rises in the percentage of the nation's GDP consumed by (some would say, and arguably so, "invested in") healthcare spending, the period 1993 to 2000 saw a flattening of the trend. Although spending itself increased absolutely, so did GDP, at equal or better rates. So, although healthcare spending rose in the decade of the 1990s, its share of the national economic endeavor did not.

The bad news is that the resulting $1.3 trillion in expenditures is hardly mall money. It is, by anyone's measure, a considerable sum. The problem for philanthropy, which represents just less than 2 percent of healthcare spending, is how to craft a significant role in the shadow of such a gorilla. For any particular funder—even for healthcare philanthropy's behemoth, the Robert Wood Johnson Foundation, with $400 million in healthcare expenditures—the problem only gets worse. After all, $400 million is only 0.03 percent of the nation's healthcare appetite. It is only 0.1 percent of the total federal expenditures on Medicare and Medicaid. A short stick indeed for getting the attention of a very large beast.

"Health is worth more than learning."
                            —Thomas Jefferson

How can any philanthropy pick targets that can be measured by effectiveness metrics, when the total resource flow so overwhelms the investment?

The problem in healthcare is even more complex than the mere recitation of resource disparities would indicate. Over a third of the nation's health expenditures flow to physicians or other professionals for service provision. This is generally not a subject of philanthropy. The distribution of resources in the remainder of the healthcare system is diverse: Hundreds of thousands of beds and doctors serve 280 million Americans day in and day out; millions of individual decisions are made every day about where to go for care and what care to give or get; millions of other decisions are made to put off those decisions, and, in turn, increase the complexity of the ultimate healthcare choices to be made.

Philanthropy is not well engineered to be a rationale manager of resources in this environment. Philanthropy is not a sharpshooter

EXHIBIT 4.8   DISTRIBUTION OF U.S. HEALTHCARE
               EXPENDITURES, 2001

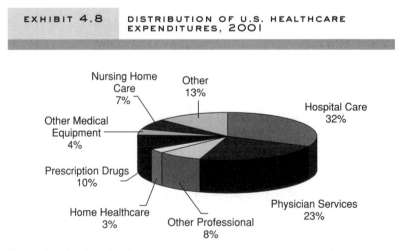

Source: American Hospital Association

with a single target called "healthcare" in its crosshairs. Rather, philanthropy is a handful of institutions, some large, most small, and a much, much larger mass of individual Americans. Each institution, and each individual, makes individual and separate decisions about what to care about, and, therefore, what to fund. And whatever those individual decisions, the flow of resources will almost certainly be small relative to the problem and relative to other kinds of resources also flowing to the problem. Hence, the ability to trace philanthropic results will be compromised.

Can healthcare philanthropy be rational in picking its targets? For argument's sake, let's say that philanthropy arbitrarily did pick a target. In reality, because institutions are easier to think about in common action than are individuals, let's say that all foundations decided to pick a target.

What if every foundation that spent healthcare dollars agreed to shut down its giving portfolios tomorrow and reprogram all healthcare resources to relieve the prescription pharmaceutical needs of the nation's elderly? This would be a finite target, capable of being defined, for which there could be little dispute either on the matter of the subject audience (most people's age can be documented) or on the matter of healthcare category (most independent observers would agree on what a prescription pharmaceutical is). There is, of course, the possibility of disagreement over the definition of "need" (are we to trust the judgment of prescribing physicians? Is there to be an incomes test?) and on the definition of "the nation's" (are we to include greencard or visa residents?). Still, let's assume we could agree to these parameters as well. In round numbers, let's say that the "elderly" would total about 16 percent of the U.S. population, or about 44.8 million people; and that by "need" we mean all of their physician-prescribed medicines.

The federal government estimates that the average American under age 65 uses seven prescriptions per year, for a total expenditure of $267. Those over 65 average 29 prescriptions per year, for a total annual per capita cost of $1,185. If foundations chose our intrepid but ill elderly as their target, would they represent critical mass? Foundations spend about $4.46 billion on healthcare programs annually. If all of that money were allocated to elderly drug needs, the result would be $99.55 per capita, or 8 percent of Aunt Millie's needs.

So, even narrowing the universe of healthcare to a very focused target does not raise philanthropy's resource asset to a level of critical mass. Helpful, yes. Definitive, hardly.

> "The demands of (the) public are not reasonable, but they are simple. It dreads disease and desires to be protected against it. But it is poor and wants to be protected cheaply."
> —George Bernard Shaw, 1913

There is a tension here that extends beyond healthcare. On the one hand, philanthropy—individual allocation of individual resources on the societal commons for purposes of the larger common good—is a treasured national asset. Because philanthropy (and the philanthropist) is given tax-free status, however, the tax burden of the rest of society increases. Society agrees to that burden, provided that philanthropy pursues the common good effectively. Yet, when the philanthropic resources available pale in comparison to the total investment being made by individuals (and their agents—insurers, employers, and governments), how should targets be chosen? And, if the demands of effectiveness lead to the selection of marginal targets (because the smaller the target the larger the de facto role of philanthropy), does that also violate the public covenant with the taxpayer?

There are unquestionable problems in the way the nation allocates its healthcare expenditures. The solutions themselves are fraught with questions. How philanthropy fits into both questions and solutions is fair game for debate.

SOURCES

Baker, Samuel L. "U.S. National Health Spending, 2002," University of South Carolina School of Public Health, Department of Health Administration, July 2002.

Lawrence Steven. "Health Funding Update 2001," The Foundation Center, 2001.

"Study Highlights Implications of Prescription Cost-Sharing Strategies for the Elderly," Express Scripts Outcomes Conference, 2000.

"Trends Affecting Hospitals and Health Systems," American Hospital Association, November 2002.

Philanthropy and the Academic Medical System: Cavalry to the Rescue? Or, Hope Springs Eternal?

The U.S. academic medical system is made up of 125 medical schools and their 160 clinical treatment facilities. Growth in academic medicine has been notable. Between the mid-1960s and the mid-1990s, the number of U.S. medical schools increased by half, enrollment doubled, and faculty increased tenfold. The academic medical system conducts 28 percent of the nation's biomedical research (most of the remainder being in private industry). It graduates all of the nation's 18,000 medical students each year, and trains 50 percent of interns and residents. Its clinical facilities represent only 3 percent of acute care hospitals, but their specialties are critical: they house 68 percent of the nation's burn units and 52 percent of its trauma centers. They also provide as much as 30 percent of indigent care in major U.S. cities. Simply put, academic medical centers are crucial to the health of the nation.

Many are in serious financial peril. There is considerable debate about who or what is to blame. The problem is variously attributed to historical mismanagement and failure to understand cost structures, to necessarily high cost structures that cannot be finan-

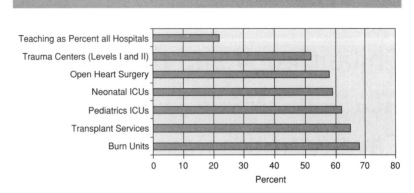

EXHIBIT 4.9   PERCENT SPECIALTY SERVICES LOCATED
               AT TEACHING HOSPITALS, 2000

Source: American Hospital Association

ced by market-driven public or private reimbursement rates, and to that convenient and comfortable villain, federal policy.

The responses to the yawning gap between costs and revenues have run the spectrum, from cost containment to faculty reduction to mergers and acquisitions to the outright sale of teaching hospitals to for-profit hospital corporations. Some things work; some things don't. When Tulane and George Washington Universities sold their hospitals to for-profit chains, at least part of the problem was solved. Problems of medical school funding, of course, could not be so easily swept away, since the private for-profit market for training doctors is imperceptible. Laying off 15 to 20 percent of their workforces bought Penn and Stanford some time. Mergers and acquisitions have a spotty record; many have been abandoned, with the only truly successful merger being between Brigham Women's Hospital and Massachusetts General.

As David Blumenthal, Professor of Health Care Policy at Harvard, has pointed out, whatever the source of the financial problem, academic institutions will likely need to figure out their own solutions. No public white knight is on the recession-clouded budget deficit horizon.

Reading through academic medical center strategic plans, one is struck by the talk of relying on private philanthropy to solve the problem. Is philanthropy likely to be the cavalry that saves the academic day? Or is such hope beyond any probability that might be suggested by historical experience?

First, some numbers. The academic medical enterprise totals about $40 billion in annual revenue, about half of which is wrapped up in teaching and research, the other half in service provision. Of that total, nearly 50 percent of medical school revenue is accounted for by the medical practice plans of the hospitals; and over 80 percent of hospital revenues are accounted for by public and private reimbursement for patients. Philanthropy accounts for between 2 percent and 5 percent of medical school nonresearch revenues, 5 percent of hospital revenues, and an unknown portion of research revenues. To gain an order of magnitude of what it would take for philanthropy to fill the academic revenue gap, let's say that private philanthropy accounts for half of these research revenues. Considering recent increases in research funding from the National Institutes of Health, this is probably a generous estimate.

Given the revenue structure of the $40 billion, then, this means that philanthropy accounts for about $5 billion of teaching and research revenues and about $1 billion in hospital revenues. Overall, healthcare philanthropy has recently been increasing at about 4 percent per year in real terms. How long will it take $6 billion in philanthropy to increase to, let us say, $10 billion, which would then approximate one-quarter of the academic revenue pie (assuming, of course, the total revenue need does not itself increase)? About 14 years.

Today's philanthropic role will have to increase at a significantly faster pace if it is to be anywhere close to approaching today's answer to the academic medical funding crisis. In medicine—not to mention in the fortunes of ill patients—14 years is a long time. Philanthropy may be the cavalry, but it is clearly not the mechanized cavalry.

Which is not to say that increases in philanthropy are not important. They clearly are. Private giving can provide essential financial flexibility, particularly if the giving is not tied to narrow purposes. But, it is unlikely to substitute for tight organizational management, new institutional alignments and efficiencies, and reimbursement reform.

▪ SOURCES

Aaron, H.J. "The Plight of Academic Medical Centers," Brookings Institution Policy Brief, no. 59, May 2000.

Annual reports and strategic plans of the Medical College of Wisconsin *(1999)*, Johns Hopkins Medicine *(1999)*, The University of Kansas *(2001)*, University of Minnesota Medical School *(2000)*, and University of Connecticut *(2000)*.

Blumenthal, D. "Unhealthy Hospitals," *Harvard Magazine,* 103:4, March–April 2001, p. 29.

Casper, G. "The University's Academic Medical Center: A View from the President's Office," Address to the Association of American Medical Colleges, April 19, 1997.

Frymoyer, J.W. "Academic Medical Centers in Trouble," *Bulletin of the American Academy of Orthopaedic Surgeons,* 44:3, July 1996, pp. 1–2.

Giving USA 2002, AAFRC Trust for Philanthropy.

Johns, M.M.E. "Viewpoint: Taking Stock: Partnerships, Philanthropy Key to Medical Centers' Futures," *AAMC Reporter,* 9:10, July 2000, p. 1.

Krakower, J.Y., T.Y. Coble, D.J. Williams, and R.F. Jones, "Review of U.S. Medical School Finances, 1998–1999," *Journal of the American Medical Association,* 284:9, September 6, 2000, pp. 1127–1129.

Mental Illness: Major Health Burden; But Is It a Philanthropic Priority?

Ten years ago, a massive undertaking by the World Health Organization, the World Bank, and Harvard University resulted in the development of a new set of measures to assess the state of the world's health. The measures, called Disability-Adjusted Life Years (DALYs) assessed what the authors termed the "global burden of disease." They measured not who was sick and who dies, but rather, lost years of productive life, whether that loss was from premature death or disability. The methodology was complex, and, as could be expected, not without its critics. But DALYs are now used in parallel with mortality data to characterize disease patterns throughout the world.

Measuring disease not by death but by disability resulted in several unexpected findings. What surprised many observers was the degree to which mental health took "pride of place" in the world's disease burden. Mental illness, including suicide, accounts for 15 percent of the burden of disease in industrialized countries, more than the burden of disease from all cancers and nearly as much as the burden from all cardiovascular disease. Indeed, unipolar major depression is second only to ischemic disease as a source of lost life years.

EXHIBIT 4.10   DISEASE BURDEN IN INDUSTRIALIZED
NATIONS: PERCENT DALYs

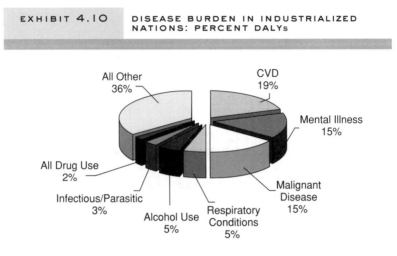

Source: The Global Burden of Disease

In 2001, the health sector in the United States received $18 billion in private philanthropy. That represented an inflation-adjusted 46 percent increase in the decade of the 1990s. Sectorally, it ranks third, after religion and education, as a recipient of American philanthropy. Where does mental health fall as a philanthropic priority?

The simple answer to that question is that there is no answer. Philanthropic data do not allow an accounting of resource flows by detailed subject matter. Alternatively, a sample of 5,021 grants for mental health coded into the Foundation Center's database were examined to attempt to tease out the parameters of grant-making for mental illness. These 5,021 grants were overwhelmingly (over 95 percent) for domestic organizations. Giving for mental health appears to be fairly broad, reflecting the portfolios of 623 foundations.

However, though the flow comes from a large number of foundations, there is tremendous concentration. Nearly 20 percent of the grants made are traceable to one of only three foundations: the California Endowment, Robert Wood Johnson Foundation, or The McCormick Tribune Foundation. Moreover, the grants are overwhelmingly small: 20 percent of the grants are for $10,000 or less and total less than $1 million. Only 2 percent of the grants were awards of $1 million or more. Grants of that size aggregated into $202 million in total awards. There are many very small grants totaling not much money and a few large grants totaling a great deal of money.

Furthermore, there is tremendous geographic concentration among grant recipients. Several hundred grants in California and striking concentration in the Boston-Washington corridor and the upper Midwest stand in stark contrast to the virtual absence of grants in the South, with the exception of Texas.

Still, there is some interestingly good news. There is a mental health grant "middle class," the vast majority of the grants awarded from $50,000 to $500,000. Furthermore, a surprisingly large portion of the grants crossed geographic boundaries. One of the problems with mobilizing philanthropy to address national problems is that the great majority of foundations do not make grants at the national level. Philanthropy is predominantly a local phenomenon; foundations respond to the needs of their communities or their home cities or states. If, to quote the late Speaker of the House of Representatives Tip O'Neil, "all politics is local," it is also true that most philanthropy is local.

That said, in the case of mental health, a third of the grants were made to grantees in states other than the headquarters state of the grantmaking foundation. Mental health grants from smaller funders, even those that made only a handful of grants for this purpose, tended to flow more freely across the nation's community borders.

So, mental health nonprofits should take heart. If the sample funding pool is viewed not from what foundations say they do, but from the perspective of what they actually do, the picture is brighter than one might think. Even though only 12 foundations categorize themselves as being national in scope and interested in mental health, the pool of sample grants had reasonable award levels and showed a propensity to cross the usual geographic limitations of grantmaking.

▨ SOURCES

Brousseau, R.T., D. Langill, and C.M. Pechura, "Are Foundations Overlooking Mental Health?" *Health Affairs*, September 2003, pp. 222–229.

Grant sample taken from the online database of the Foundation Center, 2003.

Giving USA 2002, AAFRC Trust for Philanthropy.

Murray, C.J.L. and A.D. Lopez, eds. *The Global Burden of Disease and Injury Series,* vol. 1. Cambridge: Harvard School of Public Health, on behalf of the World Health, Organization and the World Bank, 1996.

Philanthropy and Education

INTRODUCTION TO THE ISSUES

A half century ago, at the close of World War II, America embarked on a phenomenal educational adventure. Young children had always been enrolled in public schools, but the advent of the GI Bill, the aging of the population, and the emergence of technology as the base of the national economy together generated a surge in demand for higher levels of education. America of 1949 was a nation where readin', writin', and, 'rithmatic set the standard of educational achievement. By 2000, America had become a nation of biotechnology, nanotechnology, and genetic engineering; and the subject matter of the average high school project in the national Intel Science Competition was incomprehensible to the average adult.

In 1949, education accounted for only 3.3 percent of the GDP. By 2000, that had more than doubled to 7.1 percent. The 2000 educational tab for the nation was nearly three-quarters of a trillion dollars. Before World War II began, only 6.6 percent of the nation's young adults aged 20 to 24 were in school. By 2000, 32.5 percent were enrolled in degree-granting institutions. In 1949, less than 1 percent of people in their early thirties were enrolled in educational institutions; by 2000, nearly 7 percent were still in school.

American education today is big business. It is also clearly something about which Americans have cared deeply since the founding

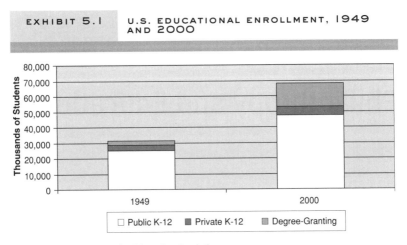

EXHIBIT 5.1   U.S. EDUCATIONAL ENROLLMENT, 1949 AND 2000

Source: National Center for Education Statistics

of the Republic. The depth of that concern is reflected, in part, in the relationship between philanthropic giving and education.

> "Learning is not attained by chance, it must be sought for with ardor and attended to with diligence."
> —Abigail Adams
> Letter to John Quincy Adams, May 1, 1780

Philanthropic giving to education is estimated to have totaled just over $31 billion in 2001. As several essays in this section note, this is almost certainly an underestimate. The educational recipients of U.S. philanthropy run the full gamut of institutions, from research universities all the way to local public school districts. While private educational institutions have always been in the education game (the first capital campaign was organized by Harvard in 1643), public institutions are new to the game. Public universities are organizing nonprofit foundations to receive donations. Even local communities are organizing local nonprofit educational funds to attract local community philanthropy to improve public schools.

None of these figures includes the value of the voluntarism that is so key to most educational institutions.

The essays in this section provide an overview of trends that knit philanthropy into the larger stream of revenues supporting the great American educational experiment.

■ SOURCES

Digest of Educational Statistics 2001, U.S. Department of Education National Center for Education Statistics.

Giving USA, 2003, AAFRC Trust for Philanthropy.

With College Costs Rising Quickly, Can Philanthropy Close the Gap?

After the good news that comes with college acceptance letters across America comes the bad news. Costs are rising. In the past decade, the private college price tag (tuition and fees only) has risen 67 percent, and now averages over $26,000 per year. Price tags in excess of $40,000 per year at the nation's top schools no longer even raise eyebrows.

Although still much less expensive, America's public colleges and universities now charge nearly twice the entry fee of a decade ago, on average over $9,500 compared to about $5,000 in 1990. Moreover, projections by the College Board are that private college tuition costs will grow at 5 percent per year, and one year of tuition and fees will take the princely sum of over $51,000 per year 15 years from now. The tab will be even more alarming at the nation's most elite schools. The privilege of studying the great philosophers in Harvard Yard could cost you a quarter of a million dollars. Only a few schools have vowed to freeze tuitions; most have not.

Of course, families often do not actually pay these full prices. The published bill is somewhat akin to an automotive sticker price—the price the manufacturer wishes it could get you to pay. Surveys indicate that parents on average contribute 55 percent of college costs, down from 69 percent in 1986. However, the average loan needed by the 25 percent of parents who use debt to finance a child's college costs is up by 50 percent over the last five years. Indeed, in the period 1987–1996, the cost of a college education, net of all student aid, nearly doubled at public four-year institutions and increased by two-thirds at private four-year institutions.

So, there are two problems. First, inflation-adjusted incomes have not kept pace with college costs. One estimate calculates the average inflation-adjusted income in the last decade has risen 10 percent compared with a 48 percent rise in tuition. The second problem is that other sources must be found to fill that gap.

In 2001, "voluntary support" to higher education totaled about $23.9 billion. Nearly a third of that support came from alumni, and over half from the alumni and other individuals. Total voluntary support for higher education has doubled in real terms in the last 30 years and now represents between 15 percent and 20 percent of the expenses of institutions of higher learning. Yet there is instability. The 2001 giving was down from $24.2 billion in 2000, the first time in 15 years that voluntary giving to higher education had declined.

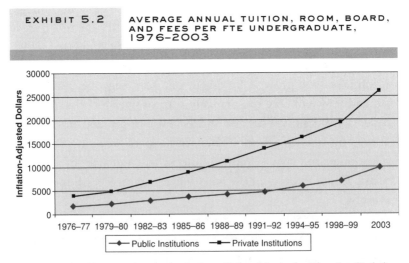

EXHIBIT 5.2   AVERAGE ANNUAL TUITION, ROOM, BOARD, AND FEES PER FTE UNDERGRADUATE, 1976-2003

Source: Data combine 2- and 4-year institutions. National Center for Education Statistics and the College Board

But even in the good years, growth can be somewhat misleading. Only 10 percent of voluntary giving is unrestricted, down from 13 percent in 1997. So, giving is increasing, and, while not precisely keeping pace with inflation, voluntary support continues as a respectable pace. However, the overwhelming majority of that giving is restricted to particular programs or purposes, and about half is tied up in "bricks and mortar" and in endowments. Hence, the cost line on the higher education graph is rising faster that voluntary support, and that support is decreasingly likely to be flexible relative to costs.

Philanthropy is clearly not the solution to the growing gap between tuition and family income. The financial weight of the gap will continue to fall on parental shoulders.

As tuition costs continue to outstrip the resources of all but the most affluent Americans, there may be a cry for accountability. And that cry may extend not simply to the cost structure of higher education itself, but to the use to which philanthropic funds are put. Greater pressure for allocating available resources to take the sting out of costs not just for the disadvantaged but for the middle class can be expected. And, much as many colleges and universities would like to deny it, education is a market. The institution that commits at least part of its philanthropy to making attendance possible for that middle class will find itself well advantaged in the marketplace for student talent.

SOURCES

"2003–04 College Costs" College Board, *collegeboard.com*.

Council for Aid to Education, A.E. Kaplan, Voluntary Support of Education, 2002, New York: Council for Aid to Education.

Kline, Gil. "Finance: Who Will Pay?" *Hispanic Outlook in Higher Education*, January 29, 1999, p. 13.

National Postsecondary Aid Study, 1996, U.S. Department of Education.

Scholarship Grants: You Can't Always Get What You Need

American college campuses are diverse places. Minority students account for 21 percent of baccalaureate degrees and 15 percent of masters degrees. Women earn 57 percent of BAs and 58 percent of MAs. More than 55 percent of all American undergraduates received some form of financial aid in the 1999–2000 academic year, up from 49.7 percent in 1995. And the average award is increasing as well, totaling $6,265 in 1999–2000, a 25 percent increase over 1995. Still, that average was less than the nearly $9,000 average need of families requesting financial aid.

Moreover, if the accounting change instituted by the Department of Education in June 2003 holds, grants as a portion of family income may decline. The shift alters the amount of family income that can be considered discretionary by reducing the amount that families can claim as payments to state and local taxes. By increasing discretionary income, the formula will decrease grant aid.

With so much riding on student aid, do educational grants (net of loans and work study) level the playing field in higher education? Much private philanthropy goes toward student aid, and it would be instructive to know if the flow of funds tracks need.

In general, aid inversely tracks income. Overall, 70 percent of students from families with total income of $20,000 or less received aid, compared to 24.5 percent of students from families with $100,000 or more annual income. After aid, the average net price for a year of college was 12 percent more for high-income families than for low-income families in public institutions, and about 60 percent more in private institutions.

"There are lots of young men and women we would love to have as students, the Nobel Prize winners, the Lasker Award winners of the future. It would be a sin if society is deprived of the fruits of their work down the road because those of us, today, who could have helped, didn't."
—Michael Bloomberg,
regarding his $45 million donation to
Johns Hopkins University

Focusing only on grants, it would appear, however, that public grants are more leveling than institutional grants. At the federal level, two-thirds of those with family income of less than $20,000 received grants, while only 0.4 percent of those with incomes over $100,000 received grant aid. This is not particularly surprising, as these are predominantly Pell grants, limited by law to low-income families. The equivalent percentages for state grants were 33.1 percent and 5.3 percent. However, grants provided from within college/university resources display an entirely different pattern.

EXHIBIT 5.3   AVERAGE GRANT PER DEPENDENT STUDENT BY FAMILY INCOME LEVEL, 1999–2000

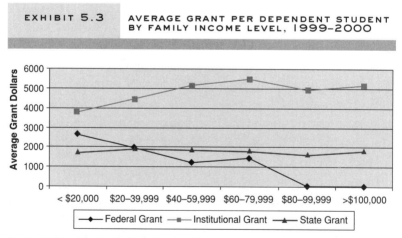

Source: National Center for Education Statistics

Of the lowest-income students, 20.4 percent received grants, but so did 20.3 percent of the highest-income-range students.

Moreover, although federal grant levels are inversely related to income, both state grant levels and those from within institutional resources are not. The student from the highest-income category will get more grant aid than the student from the lowest category. For internal resources, the dollar-value difference is nearly 25 percent in favor of the highest-income category.

Looking at the diversity profile of grant aid leads to other observations. The average grant to a woman is 4.8 percent greater than to a man. The average grant to an Hispanic undergraduate is 9.8 percent less than the overall average, but the grant to an Asian student is 42 percent greater.

That said, much grant aid may be given on the basis of academic standing or academic specialty rather than on the basis of need. Rewarding merit is, of course, right and good. Making sure the best and brightest of the nation's academic talent succeeds is a priority both for academic institutions and for the nation.

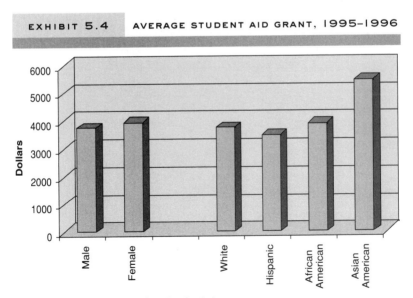

EXHIBIT 5.4   AVERAGE STUDENT AID GRANT, 1995–1996

Source: National Center for Education Statistics

Still, 60 percent of all aid is in the form of grants. These grants are, in effect, philanthropy. Should philanthropy, positioned on the societal commons, be concerned about the pattern of characteristics of its recipients? And how can education square this need with the need, described in the previous essay, to relieve the financial burden for higher education borne by the increasingly encumbered American middle class?

■ SOURCES

1999–2000 National Postsecondary Student Aid Study, U.S. Department of Education, National Center for Education Statistics.

1996 National Postsecondary Student Aid Study, U.S. Department of Education, National Center for Education Statistics.

Digest of Education Statistics, 2000, U.S. Department of Education.

"Disparities Continue for Women and Minorities in Degree Completions," *Higher Education and National Affairs,* American Council on Education, Vol. 51, 1 January 14, 2002.

"New Report Looks at Unmet Need of Undergraduate Students," *Higher Education and National Affairs*, American Council on Education, Vol. 50, 13 July 16, 2001.

Winter, G. "Change in Aid Rule Means Larger Bills for College Students," *New York Times,* June 13, 2003, Section A, p. 1, Col. 1.

University Foundations: Memo to the Dean: After the Faculty Meeting, Check the Dow

Over just the last five years, philanthropic funding to institutions of higher learning in the United States has increased by 35 percent. Of that total, approximately 46 percent flowed to public colleges and universities. But, two-thirds of undergraduates enrolled in universities or four-year colleges are in public institutions, and 95 percent of the enrollment in two-year programs is public.

The disproportionate flow of philanthropy to private institutions is, in part, a function of structure. Private schools are nonprofit institutions, hence easy targets for giving. Public institutions, for which state budget subsidies have stagnated or declined in constant dollars in the past decade, have responded with innovation.

> "To place your name by gift or bequest in the keeping of an active educational institution is to ... make a permanent contribution to humanity."
> —Calvin Coolidge

Many colleges and universities have formed affiliated but independent foundations to support their resource needs. The largest have formed multiple foundations, geared to raise funds for specific programs or schools. Many research-based universities have formed private foundations, which manage patent rights and redirect licensing fees back into university research programs. Moreover, these foundations are far from marginal to higher education's financial viability. At the University of Virginia, for example, the revenue from the Law School Foundation accounts for 40 percent of the law school budget, and the Darden School of Business Foundation operates the executive education program and meets 50 percent of Darden's revenues.

How big is the university foundation world? There are no comprehensive data, though it is possible to aggregate data from the Form 990 filed annually for each foundation. If you knew the names of all the foundations, and if time hung heavily on your hands, then the matter would be researchable.

As an alternative, a sampling of university foundations was developed using Guidestar. There appear to be about 500 such foundations nationwide. Foundations from six states were examined: New York, Connecticut, Florida, Alabama, Illinois, and Utah. Statewide assets of these foundations appear to range from $300 to $500 million in smaller states to $800 billion in larger states. Then there is the South, where public education is the overwhelming norm and where alumni appear to be exceedingly loyal. For example, Alabama's foundations supporting public higher education institutions have assets in excess of $1.1 billion. This is nearly a third again as large as the entire state annual subsidy of higher education, and larger than the annual higher education outlay of the Alabama's Educational Trust Fund.

Matching average asset size to state size in the United States, one estimates that foundations supporting public higher education institutions hold about $50 billion in assets. This is equivalent to the entire gross national product of New Zealand, or approximately the global market value of the American Express Company.

But $50 billion does not just represent a base for revenue flows to public higher education. It is also a powerful economic engine. Of course, foundation investment strategies differ. What is optimal

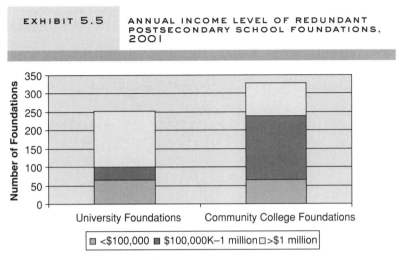

EXHIBIT 5.5   ANNUAL INCOME LEVEL OF REDUNDANT
POSTSECONDARY SCHOOL FOUNDATIONS,
2001

University Foundations   Community College Foundations

□ <$100,000 ■ $100,000K–1 million□ >$1 million

Source: Changing Our World Sample from Guidestar

for the University of Florida Foundation, with its $800 million in assets, may not be viable for Athens State College and its $1 million. Still, the sample of foundations indicates that between 60 percent and 90 percent of assets are held in securities. Thus, university foundations are institutional investors in the U.S. economy to the tune of between $30 billion and $45 billion.

That is one of the beauties of philanthropy. Resources invested not only serve the public good, they also create financial reservoirs that, reinvested in the marketplace, generate the economic strength necessary to keep the philanthropic imperative alive and well.

■ SOURCES

Breaking the Social Contract: The Fiscal Crisis in Higher Education, Council for Aid to Education and the RAND Corporation, 1998.

Education data from *Digest of Education Statistics,* 1999, U.S. Department of Education.

Foundation data from Guidestar, 2002.

Voluntary Support of Education 2000, Council for Aid to Education, 2001.

Philanthropy in K-12 Education: A Minor Player Missing a Major Opportunity

Ｉt is a rare occurrence, indeed, when politicians of widely varying stripes agree on anything. So the current consensus on the importance of educational improvement in the United States is worth writing home about. True, only time will tell whether agreement in principle leads to agreement in fact. But, years (if not decades) of erosion in K-12 public education performance in the nation, contemporaneous with the increased importance of education in employment, seem to have focused the political mind.

If agreement in fact emerges, there will be a mad rush by organizations of all types to jump on the policy bandwagon. It behooves philanthropy to take advantage of this interim period of policy exploration amidst (fleeting?) bipartisan good will to examine its own role, to explore its possible future role, hence, to be counted among the leaders.

There is good reason for the examination. The K-12 public education enterprise in the United States consumes about $300 Billion in public resources annually in about 87,000 schools operating within 14,500 school districts. Of the 53 million schoolchildren in the nation, about 47 million are in public schools. So public education expenditures are about $6,500 per K-12 student per year. Of

EXHIBIT 5.6   DISTRIBUTION OF THE K-12 PUBLIC
EDUCATIONAL DOLLAR, 2000

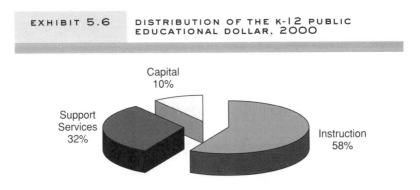

Capital
10%

Support
Services
32%

Instruction
58%

Source: National Center for Education Statistics

that amount, about $3,400 is spent on direct instruction, $1,900 on support services, and $600 on capital infrastructure. The expenditure range, of course, is wide, varying by geographic location and income group.

Educational philanthropy from private, corporate, and community foundations in the United States totals about $2.5 billion per year. Of that, about $625 million is for K–12 education. This represents about 6.4 percent of all foundation giving (down from 7.5 percent in 1994). Not all of this is for public education, of course. But the actual distribution of grant monies across school types is difficult to disentangle from the totals. Let's assume that philanthropy flows in parity with public/private student ratios—that is, that 89 percent of K-12 philanthropy is for public education. This is clearly an overestimate.

Still, the resultant figure is about $560 million per year. This represents about $12 per public education K-12 student per year, or about 0.2 percent of total per-pupil public expenditures in these grades. Against a $300 billion annual investment by the nation's public financial coffers, private philanthropy appears to hold a very minority stake. However, the totals may mask the situational importance of private philanthropy. Many private foundations operate only in the specific communities in which they are located. The importance of philanthropy, therefore, is probably much more acute at the level of the individual school or school system than it is in the larger arena of educational reform. Private philanthropy, it appears, is following that maxim to "think globally; act locally."

The educational rubber meets the instructional road in the neighborhood classroom, not in the congressional cloakroom. Hence, private philanthropy can assert a very significant leadership role in the current effort to improve educational performance. Philanthropy can provide the *sur la terre* resources to test and disseminate actual innovations that are targeted at improving quality and ensuring accountability. In that sense, Washington may be the one to talk the talk, but it is private philanthropy that can help individual schools walk the walk.

And formal, organized private philanthropy can do so by reaching out to, and partnering with, a largely forgotten informal private philanthropic resource in K-12 education: parent volunteers. In its 2000 Survey on the Condition of Education, the National Center for Education Statistics found that 38 percent of parents of K-12 students volunteer at their public schools. The rates are higher for higher income, more highly educated parents, 50 percent, for example, when household income is above $50,000 and parents

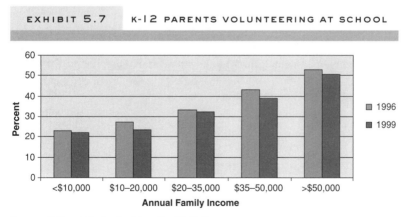

EXHIBIT 5.7   K-12 PARENTS VOLUNTEERING AT SCHOOL

Source: National Center for Education Statistics

hold a bachelor's degree or above. That said, the rates at lower-income levels are not paltry. Even when household income is $10,000 or below, 22 percent of parents volunteer at their K-12 school; and even for those parents with only a high school or GED diploma, 27 percent volunteer.

How many people is this? To derive an order of magnitude, let's say that the nation's 47 million K-12 school children come from 20 million families. Let's also say that these families represent 30 million parents, single parents, stepparents, or other relatives who are raising the 47 million children. A 38 percent volunteer rate yields about 11 million annual volunteers. Because the estimate is rough, and because it always pays to be conservative, let's say that the actual yield is between 9 and 10 million people who annually walk the talk of educational commitment. To push the point a bit further, we'll assume that each of these volunteers gives about 1.5 hours per month during the school year, or 13.5 hours per year, for a total of 135 million hours annually, or the equivalent of about 3.4 million 40-hour workweeks. Valued at the Independent Sector's 2002 dollar for volunteer time ($16.54 per hour), those K-12 volunteer hours total $2.2 billion of effort per year. That is a huge pool of human capability with extraordinary value. It also represents an extraordinary amount of personal time that is largely disconnected to the world of K-12 philanthropy (let alone educational policy in general).

> "You must give some time to your fellow men. Even if it's a little thing, do something for others—something for which you get no pay but the privilege of doing it."
> —Albert Schweitzer

Private philanthropy's unique contribution to the K-12 education, therefore, could be not only its role on the ground, but as a commitment to reach out to and improve the effectiveness of this vital parental resource.

▓ SOURCES

The Condition of Education 2000, U.S. Department of Education, National Center for Education Statistics.

Foundation Giving Trends, 2000. The Foundation Center.

National Association of Independent Schools, 2002.

Sommerfeld, M. "What Did the Money Buy?" *The Chronicle of Philanthropy*, May 4, 2000, p. 1.

"Value of Volunteer Time," Giving and Volunteering in the United States, Independent Sector, 2001.

Learning to Be Charitable: Is It a Girl Thing?

Coming out of a decade of self-absorption, there is renewed interest in raising a generation of young people who perceive and act upon larger societal need. There is a renewed sense of community in the nation, and carrying that renewal into the future will be the privilege and burden of the next generation.

That general trend, and personal observation, led me to expect to find little difference between the learning experiences of young men and young women in becoming acquainted with charity and service. My son as a West Point cadet voluntarily had his paycheck docked each month to donate to children's charities. My youngest son's all-boys school is awash with service do-gooders—the market limitation for service is not willingness, but finding enough moms to do the driving! Ditto for my daughter's all-girls school. Young men and young women are equal partners in learning to bear tomorrow's philanthropic responsibilities, right? Wrong.

Measured by school participation or future plans, girls have a greater affinity for charity. A 2000 survey found that 27 percent of high school girls participate in service or volunteer groups through school, compared to 18 percent of boys. A 2001 survey found that, while equal percentages of girls and guys expected to get a job after high school, the percentage of girls anticipating joining a volunteer organization was double that of boys. While 86 percent of teenagers feel it is important for corporations to contribute to charity, 60 percent of girls but only 40 percent of boys are involved in any philanthropic activity.

If learning to be charitable, then, is a "girl thing," why is that so? In part, perhaps, it is just that teenage girls are more likely to be joiners than guys. Overall, 82 percent of girls, but only 71 percent of boys, participate in school-related activities in high school, including sports. There is an argument to be made, however, that the gender difference is not erased with time and distance from the in-group and not-in-group pressures of high school clubs. The Independent Sector reports that 52 percent of adult women are involved with charitable causes, compared to 45 percent of men. True, the gap narrows from 11 percentage points in high school to 7 percentage points in adulthood, but it still persists. The Department of Labor Bureau of Labor Statistics found, in 2002, that the gender difference also persists in voluntarism. In the interim population census, 31.1 percent of women sampled volunteered, compared with 23.8 percent of men.

Is that persistence somehow related to experience? Why do high school boys not join the service club as readily as girls? Perhaps the problem is communication. Service in high school is seen as separate from so-called guy-stuff. You join a service club or volunteer for a particular cause; but, often, that is apart from other activities guys do. More boys than girls are involved in high school sports (sadly); more guys than girls are members of science and math clubs (also sadly). Band, orchestra, and drama tend to attract equal portions of boys and girls.

Perhaps there is a tendency to have a silo mentality about service and charity. Perhaps service and philanthropy are treated as whole unto themselves, unrelated to other aspects of a young person's life.

Rather than relying solely on service as a freestanding activity, perhaps high school boys would respond more readily to the message and opportunity if it were linked to what they already do: football-team organized food drives; band concerts as fundraisers, and the like. In turn, that would mean that the adults who lead these activities would need to be the role models. The basketball coach or band director as co-head of high school service might send a message that service, charity, and philanthropy are not parallel activities in the living of life; they are a part of life itself.

■ SOURCES

Department of Labor, Bureau of Labor Statistics, September 2002.

"Kids Prefer Brains Over Money," *Youth Markets Alert*, XIII(2), February 8, 2001, p. 8.

"Seven in 10 Households Contribute to Charity; Over Half of Adults Volunteer," *EPM Communications Research Alert*, 17(23), December 3, 1999, p. 1.

"Teens Are More Likely to Support Companies Involved with Charity," Youth Markets Alert, 8(12) December 2001, p. 1.

"Today's Teens Are Focused on Friends and the Future," *Youth Markets Alert*, XII(11), November 2000, p. 1.

"Women Focus Their Charitable Giving," *About Women and Marketing*, 12(2), February 1999, p. 1.

Philanthropy and National Academic Research Funding

Innovation in science and technology now provide the fuel for much of economic and societal progress. And the catalyst for innovation is research. The United States spends a quarter of a trillion dollars each year on research and development, 2.8 percent of national gross domestic product. Where does that money come from? And how important is philanthropy?

Taken in its most general terms, U.S. research and development is predominantly a private affair. Private industry funds $160 to $170 billion of the $260 billion total expenditure (about 70 percent). The federal government funds another $80 billion. Philanthropy would appear to be a very minor actor.

That conclusion, however, fails to make the distinction between basic and applied research and development. In 2000, basic research garnered $47.7 billion in funding, applied research $55.65 billion, and product/technology development, $161.65 billion. Private industry is the key source of funding for applied research and product development (nearly 90 percent). But over 77 percent of basic research (research targeted at unlocking fundamental scientific problems) is funded by the federal government.

Total foundation funding for research is about $2.2 billion per year. It is difficult to determine the research flow from individual philanthropy. Individuals account for 70 percent of all U.S.

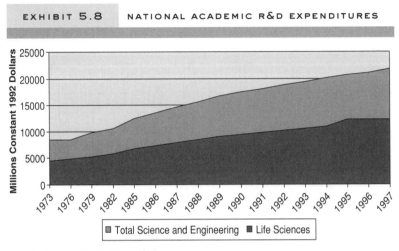

EXHIBIT 5.8   NATIONAL ACADEMIC R&D EXPENDITURES

□ Total Science and Engineering   ■ Life Sciences

Source: National Science Foundation

philanthropy, so they are probably also important in research. For argument's sake, let's say that individuals account for another $1 billion in research giving. The vast majority of philanthropic funding is for medical research, an area that is also dominant in the nation's basic research activity, representing some $30 billion of total public basic research funding. Let's say, then, of the total $3.2 billion likely annual research philanthropy, $3 billion is for medical research.

Compared to $250 billion, $3.2 billion does not stand out. But compared to $30 billion, $3 billion does make private philanthropy a major research force. The promise of research for creating societal opportunity has not been lost on major foundations. Moreover, with their streamlined decision making and ability to focus on well-defined problems or approaches, foundations can target on specific diseases or seek particular scientific impact. The Dana Foundation, for example, is targeted wholly on neuroscience. The Doris Duke Charitable Foundation has become a primary source of funding for young scientists and for scientific research that is at a preliminary stage, hence not eligible for funding from the National Institutes of Health (NIH). Edna McConnell Clark Foundation focuses on trachoma. The Ellison Medical Foundation targets aging research. The list could go on.

EXHIBIT 5.9   SUPPORT FOR ACADEMIC R&D BY SECTOR

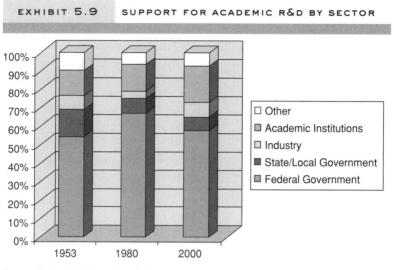

Source: National Science Foundation

Problem specificity has its price, though, especially when it comes to scientific research. Science increasingly recognizes that problems are interlinked. In response, scientific endeavors are increasingly interdisciplinary. Physicists and cell biologists are finding common ground. Genetics crosses disease groups. Too much focus may miss cross-disciplinary opportunities. Philanthropy that is targeted in theory may be myopic in reality.

The problem for research philanthropy in the future may not be motivating more giving for research; rather, the challenge may be in finding ways to ensure that the benefits of specific goals and targets are combined with the benefits of philanthropic cross-fertilization. The key need may be for greater interphilanthropy communication and greater coordination with the greater federal efforts via the NIH.

"Science is built up with facts, as a house is built with stone. But a collection of facts is no more science than a heap of stones is a house."

—Jules Henri Poincaré
La Science et l'Hypothèse, 1903

Perhaps what is needed is the research equivalent of Grant Makers in Health, a formal organization that would provide a regularized network of foundations supporting research and a way for individuals to ally their own giving with the information, insights, and lessons-learned of major foundations.

Still and all, private industry is the dominant player in overall national R&D, and the federal government is the dominant player in basic research support. So, as you are lacing up your sneakers for that walkathon, be sure to buy a couple of shares of stock in research-based industries. Oh, and also be sure to pay your taxes.

■ SOURCE

Science and Education Indicators, National Science Foundation, 2002.

U.S. Philanthropy
in an International Context

INTRODUCTION TO THE ISSUES

To observe that the world is getting smaller and more integrated is, by 2004, not news, in fact, approaches the obvious. Still, measures of globalization provide a metric for how far we have forged an interconnected world.

The inflation-adjusted value of U.S. merchandise trade more than doubled in the decade of the 1990s alone, and now totals over $2 trillion. In that decade, the value of U.S. merchandise trade grew at an annual rate of 8 percent, compared to an average rate of only 3 percent for the U.S. economy overall. Over 40 percent of the world's economy depends on trade.

People as well as goods are on the move. Outbound international travel from the United States increased by over 30 percent in the decade of the 1990s. In 2000, there were 171 million outbound international trips from U.S. embarkation points. Destinations with the largest increases were Eastern Europe, the Middle East, and South America. And, although the number of travelers was smaller, bidirectional travel to Africa increased more than travel to Western Europe.

The world of skills and ideas is also more tightly knit. The United States represents only 42 percent of global Internet users; Asia and Western Europe taken together account for half. America

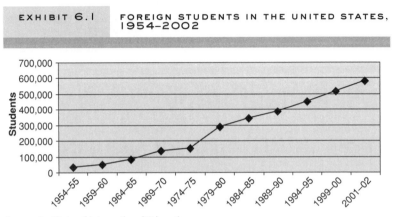

EXHIBIT 6.1   FOREIGN STUDENTS IN THE UNITED STATES,
1954-2002

Source: Institute of International Education

has long been a global educational force. The number of foreign students studying annually in the United States has increased more than twelve-fold since the mid-1950s. Growth in the decade of the 1990s continued apace, with the number of foreign students at U.S. institutions increasing by more than half in that decade alone.

American philanthropy, too, is increasingly international. In part that is because we remain a nation of immigrants. It is also because, as the nation's perspective has turned global, so has its charity. In 2001, U.S. giving to international charities and causes rose by

EXHIBIT 6.2   U. S. GIVING FOR INTERNATIONAL AFFAIRS,
1988-2001

Source: Giving USA 2003

$4 billion, or 13 percent. International giving experienced the second-largest percentage increase of any subsector, nearly as much as the increase in giving to U.S. domestic human services charities. Of course, the events of September 11, 2001, cast a pall over much that is outward-looking in the nation. New questions were asked about the relationship between the nation's security and its international role. The essays in this section, and those in Section Eight, address some of these new realities. But whatever the near-term difficulties, the nation's longer-term prospects remain unchanged. The globalization tide cannot be turned back. Too much of economics and culture has become bound together. Philanthropy, too, will continue to be global, not just in the flow of U.S. charity across our own national borders, but also in the deeper and more robust development of philanthropy in other nations. As people find themselves free to express and pursue their dreams, and to dream for their children, they also are becoming themselves increasingly committed to the future of their communities.

The combination of democracy rising throughout the world and closer ties being forged among nations may mean that a global golden age of the expression of community commitment through philanthropic giving is on the horizon.

◼ SOURCES

2002 World Development Indicators, World Bank, 2002.
Giving USA 2003, AAFRC Trust for Philantrophy.
Institute of International Education, 2003 Enrollment Profile.
U.S. International Travel and Transportation Trends, Bureau of Transportation Statistics, 2003.

America's International Giving: Search Elsewhere for Scrooge

$\mathbf{M}$uch has been made (and will likely continue to be made) about U.S. stinginess based on data from the Development Assistance Committee (DAC) of the Organization for Economic Cooperation and Development (OECD) in Paris. In sum, the data purport to measure the flows of Official Development Assistance (ODA) from industrialized nations to the developing world, both in dollars and as a percent of GDP. Accusatory fingers are pointed when the calculations show the United States as a "donor" of just 0.25 percent of its GDP, fourth from the bottom among DAC members. We are surpassed, in our miserliness it is said, only by Ireland, Australia, and Japan. The ensuing rhetoric about wealth and responsibility then becomes enflamed.

The problem, of course, is that the data are wrong. ODA purports to measure, in the DAC's own words, "the total net flow of financial resources from DAC countries to developing Countries and multilateral organizations." It does no such thing. ODA as published reflects only government appropriations for development assistance, whether bilateral or multilateral, and "net grants from nongovernmental organizations." Only the government appropriations figures are relatively complete, and even these do

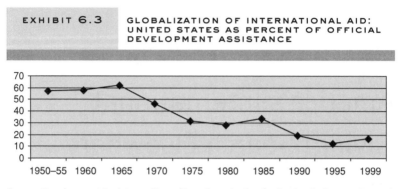

EXHIBIT 6.3   GLOBALIZATION OF INTERNATIONAL AID:
UNITED STATES AS PERCENT OF OFFICIAL
DEVELOPMENT ASSISTANCE

Source: Development Assistance Committee, Organization for Economic Corporation and Development

not include some measures of resource transfer (e.g., for scientific research partnerships). The nongovernment figures are incomplete, and much is not measured at all.

> "Facts do not cease to exist because they are ignored."
> —Aldous Huxley, *Proper Studies*, 1927

So, are we really Scrooge? To answer that question, some perspective is helpful. In constant dollars, total U.S. official government development assistance has risen from $1.1 billion in 1955 to $9.9 billion in 2000, making the United States the largest supplier of public foreign assistance, not the smallest. And that figure does not represent all U.S. government transfers to developing countries; such areas as NIH research funding are not included, for example; nor is aid to countries such as Russia and the Ukraine. The flows counted by the DAC represent less than half of U.S. government outflows. Simply, the DAC number is incorrect. Morever, the U.S. portion of total government assistance from all DAC nations has declined from 57 percent in 1955 to 15 percent in 2000. That means there are more players with more money in development than decades ago.

Finally, ODA itself is of decreasing importance. In the last two decades, ODA has dropped from 55 percent to a current 30 percent of total financial flows. Hence, it measures less and less about resources moving into poor nations. In contrast, private investment in 1999 represented 47 percent of such flows, up from 13 percent in the early 1980s. Thus, even if the data for official government flows are right, their purported meaning is not. But, more importantly, no measures—whether from the OECD or even from U.S. agencies—adequately track the behavior of the United States relative to international poverty and development needs. America is a complex organism, with myriad points at which private resource choices are made. Truly measuring the "donor" behavior of the nation would require moving beyond government and pursuing a complex accounting that traced resources from a number of U.S. financial sources.

First, an accounting would need to trace flows of current cash and capital assets, including those from:

- *Foundations*, both private independent foundations and the foundations of private and professional associations.
- *Corporations*, both from central corporate giving programs and corporate foundations, as well as from the giving of U.S. corporations via the independent philanthropy of their overseas branches and subsidiaries.
- *Educational institutions*, via grants and scholarships to international students.
- *Individuals*, both via direct giving to secular nonprofits (including ePhilanthropy) and individual giving to religious organizations and orders in the United States that makes its way overseas. Nearly half of all U.S. cash philanthropy flows to religious organizations, but its ultimate destination is not well documented.
- *Direct giving*, by immigrants to the communities from which they came or diaspora gifts made directly to institutions in home countries.

Second, an adequate accounting would have to trace not just current flows, but also *future* flows cash or assets (or income from assets) originating in:

- Bequests to international nonprofits or to religious groups with operations in poor nations
- Other planned-giving mechanisms
- Individual investments in funds targeted at emerging markets

Third, a full accounting would need to trace not just cash but also donated commodities. In some sectors (e.g., disaster relief), donated goods (food, tents, clothes, blankets) can be as significant as cash in reflecting the philanthropic urge. An accounting would need to monetize the values of the flows of good from:

- U.S. corporations of all types and sizes
- Noncorporate institutions (e.g., hospital surgical supply recovery programs that donate opened but unused surgical supplies to developing country health systems)
- Individuals and associations of individuals (schools, Boy and Girl Scout troops, and the like)

Fourth, philanthropy is expressed not just in cash and commodities but also in the value of time. Voluntarism is a fundamental part of philanthropy. Indeed, for many people, time is more valuable than money. Hence, a full accounting of the transfer of resources must include monetized values for the flows of services from:

- *Corporations.* Employees and managers providing skills, advice, and other services in their headquarters or branches in poor nations.
- *Unaffiliated individuals.* Those volunteering abroad and in the United States for programs targeted at the needs of poor nations.
- *Affiliated individuals.* Nonpaid or partially paid employees of religious or other nonprofit organizations abroad or in the

United States serving for programs targeted at the needs of poor nations.

Such a complete accounting for U.S. "donor" resource flows in these "spreadsheet" terms has never been attempted. Clearly the task would be difficult. But, it is also not be possible. Would it make a difference? That is, would such an accounting substantially change the "total net resource flow" picture as painted by the DAC? Short of actually carrying out the analysis, of course, one cannot say for sure that it would. A study in 2002 by the U.S. Agency for International Development looked at just a few of these indicators and calculated that private aid is one and a half times as large as the U.S. government transfer of resources.

An experiment with just three line items from this hypothetical spreadsheet might provide some indication of whether (and, if so, by how much) the resource pattern would change. One obvious item for examination is foundation behavior because it is easier to count than more amorphous flows of individual dollars. In 2002, foundations spent just over $4.62 billion on international affairs. In constant dollars, this was four times their 1988 grantmaking in this category. The growth, in part, reflects a general increase in global

EXHIBIT 6.4   U.S. RESOURCE TRANSFERS TO DEVELOPING COUNTRIES, 2000

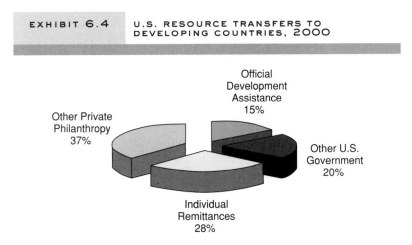

Source: Foreign Affairs in the National Interest, U.S. Agency for International Development

awareness; it also reflects the entry of two major philanthropists, Bill Gates and Ted Turner, into global development issues.

Of course, one cannot allocate all $4.62 billion to international economic development purposes or grants. Some "international" grants are for European affairs, of U.S.-Japan studies, or the like. Unfortunately, there is no reliable way to sort among all foundation grantmaking to isolate for specific grant purposes. So, let's say only half of the resource flow is poverty-or developing-nation-oriented. That adds $2.32 billion to the DAC's $9.9 billion total for the United States, or a full 23 percent.

Taking a more difficult measure, what about the resource flows from U.S. immigrants to their home nations? The U.S. Department of Commerce has been collecting data on remittances only since 1986. In that period, total remittances have grown to an estimated $18 billion. Between 1991 and 1996 international money transmissions from the United States grew at 20 percent per year. The remittance total is nearly twice DAC-measured official development assistance.

Do such remittances really aid in development? At a macro level, it is hard to see how they could not. Remittances from U.S. immigrants account for 10 percent of the GDP of six Latin American countries, and 13 percent of the GDP of El Salvador. At the micro level, surveys from Mexico indicate that about 75 percent of those who received such remitted resources used them in part to supplement family healthcare resources. Hence, the remittances are not being used to buy DVDs, and can, in part, be counted as meeting economic/societal needs of communities. It is no surprise, then, that several Latin American nations have made concerted efforts in the U.S. to increase financial flows from their United States immigrants to support local economic development.

> "Rather than love, than money, than fame, give me truth."
> —Henry David Thoreau

To press the point, let's do one more quick piece of math in an area that no international development study has tried to examine: Socially screened investment funds in the United States are growing in both size and clout. In 2001, such funds totaled $2.38 trillion, or 12 percent of the $19.9 trillion in assets under professional management in the United States. Socially screened funds were only 9 percent of all assets in 1999. In the first quarter of 2003, socially screened funds gathered $185.3 million at the same time that all diversified equity funds in the United States experienced a net loss outflow of $13.2 billion.

Such screened funds are of many types and invest in many opportunities, domestic and international. There are no hard data for links to developing nations' products, but certainly an investment bias toward, for example, rain-forest-sensitive industries positively impacts the environment in developing nations. Since environment is one of the concerns of governmental assistance in poor nations, one could argue that such funds complement ODA. Again, let's be very cautious and say only 2 percent of the $2.38 trillion has such a developing-nation effect. That total is $47 billion, more than four times DAC/ODA estimates for the United States.

To review, having taken only three line items from our hypothetical spreadsheet, we have tallied $67 billion in uncounted U.S. resources flows to the international development process, more than six times official development assistance counted by the DAC. A full accounting of the hypothetical spreadsheet would almost surely reveal more, perhaps eight times more than the DAC counts.

Scrooge, America is not.

▓ SOURCES

Blumenthal, R.G. "Good Vibes," Barrons, July 7, 2003, pp. L2–L6.

"Conversations with Disbelievers," The Conference Board, 2001.

DeSipio, Louis. "Sending Money Home . . . for Now: Remittances and Immigrant Adaptation in the United States." Working paper of the Inter-American Dialogue and the Tomas Rivera Policy Institute, January 2000.

Foreign Aid in the National Interest: Promoting Freedom, Security, and Opportunity. U.S. Agency for International Development, 2002.

Giving USA, 2003, AAFRC Trust for Philanotrophy.

"Non-Bank Financial Institutions: A Study of Five Sectors," Coopers and Lybrand, February 28, 1997.

Orozco, Manuel. "Remittances and Markets: New Players and Practices." Working paper of the Inter-American Dialogue and the Tomas Rivera Policy Institute, May 2000.

U.S. Census Bureau, data from U.S. Census 2000.

The International Scope
of the Nonprofit Sector

These are difficult times, filled with uncertainty and caution. National tragedy and war tend to focus the mind and raise questions and cautions about what had been basic assumptions. That new spirit of caution touches the nonprofit world in a most fundamental and sobering fashion.

Since the mid-1990s, the CIA has been conducting a global trends analysis every five years that forecasts trends 15 years in the future. The document provides a series of scenarios for future national security concerns and assesses the forces that will influence the directions of international trends. The second analysis, Global Trends 2015, takes notice of the rising importance of nonprofit organizations in both human services and democratic evolution around the world. The CIA notes, "Nonprofit networks with affiliates in more than one country will grow through 2015, having expanded more than 20-fold between 1964 and 1998."

Further, the analysis points to changes that will characterize this growth and its influence. First, nonprofits will have more resources than in the past, hence will become more confident political players, within and among nations. Second, with higher incomes, Asia and Latin America will see particular nonprofit growth; but the knife can cut two ways. Recognizing the increased legitimacy of nonprofits, autocratic governments with resources to spare will begin creating and/or supporting such groups to carry out their international policies via other means. Finally, and in contrast, their rising profile and credibility will lead nonprofits to be expected to meet new standards for public accountability.

Independent data would seem to indicate that the CIA is spot-on in terms of nonprofit growth. Of course, actual growth rates depend on definitions and on time periods measured. There is no central mechanism available for estimating the total growth of nonprofits. Each country has different standards and definitions. But it is certainly huge, especially since the rise of democracy and the international assistance to the creation of "civil society" institutions in newly open nations.

In terms of nonprofits with an international orientation, one source of data is the Union of International Associations, which tracks the formation of organizations working across national boundaries. If one focuses only on the category nongovernmental organizations (NGOs), which excludes such things as intergovernmental organizations, the numbers are striking. In 1909, there were just 176 international NGOs worldwide; in 1996, the most recent year for which comprehensive data are available, the number was 38,243. In the single decade 1986–1996, the number of NGOs increased by 78 percent.

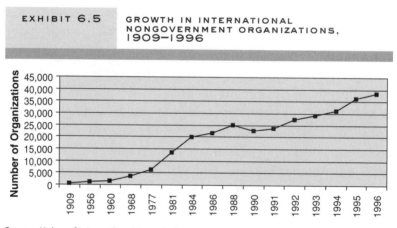

EXHIBIT 6.5   GROWTH IN INTERNATIONAL NONGOVERNMENT ORGANIZATIONS, 1909–1996

Source: Union of International Associations, 2000

Perhaps more interesting and telling is the growth rate of NGOs since the expansion of foreign assistance programs. The U.S. Foreign Assistance Act of 1974, which still underpins U.S. programs—albeit with amendments that total several inches of paper—committed U.S. resources to social as well as economic development abroad. Since that time, the number of international NGOs has increased by a whopping 515 percent.

The point is, Global Trends 2015 is certainly right: The nonprofit community internationally is becoming a force to be reckoned with. This is a good thing with, perhaps, not-so-good potential.

Nonprofits represent the expression of citizen commitment to the societal commons. They are mechanisms for individuals to contribute to a perceived mutual interest of the society that allows them to exist while exempting them from paying the taxes that fund the body politic's common interests. In exchange, the expectation is that nonprofits will provide goods and services to advance the common interest, or at least some swath of the common interest.

At its best, the nonprofit community does exactly that. In the United States, nonprofits mobilize 20 billion volunteer hours annually to address a plethora of needs. Their hours of commitment are valued at a quarter of a trillion dollars. Because much of this effort is locally generated to address local needs, effectiveness is perhaps better served than via central government effort. The taxes forgone are well worth the policy.

But numbers and growth rates of organizations do not illuminate content of action. It is this issue that drives the CIA analysis. If the nonprofit moniker becomes a cloak for self-interest, the principal rationale for nonprofit status is threatened. To the extent that rapid rise in nonprofit formation is not a reflection of a group voluntary response to larger societal needs, but, rather, to narrow group interests (or worse), the classic argument for nonprofits as actors on the commons is weakened. It is a slippery slope. As the concept of tax-free status in exchange for societal service erodes, the legitimacy and credibility of nonprofit status can then be thrown about the shoulders of all manner of narrow self-service. It can be (and has been) also thrown about the shoulders of organizations committed to violence. The street riots and property destruction during the trade negotiations in Seattle and Genoa involved nonprofits. Ironically, it was (in part) nonprofits who engaged in violence that endangered the commons itself.

These are serious issues. The rapidly expanding leadership of the nation's nonprofit community would do well to think deeply about them.

■ SOURCES

Global Trends 2015, Central Intelligence Agency, 2001.

Yearbook of International Organizations, 1909–1996, Union of International Associations, Brussels 1997.

The Globalization
of Education: How Important
is Philanthropy?

A quarter millennium ago, the founding fathers well understood that the foundation of freedom is deeply dependent on what people know and how they come to that knowledge. In this increasingly interdependent world of free peoples, where both the best and the worst of human experience cross borders with the speed of an electron, knowledge is power. And knowledge of others— of cultures, perceptions, propensities, strengths, and weaknesses—is critical to global growth and future prosperity. Education is not only a matter of life-long learning, it is a matter of global experience.

"A popular Government, without popular information, or the means of acquiring it, is but a Prologue to a Farce or a Tragedy; or, perhaps both. Knowledge will forever govern ignorance: And a people who mean to be their own Governors, must arm themselves with the power which knowledge gives."
—James Madison

America is, and has long been, an educational beacon for the world. Despite current worries over national security, that beacon is not likely to fade in the eyes of the rest of the world. Nor will the importance of global intellectual exchange likely fade as a means to achieve understanding and prosperity.

How strong is the role of private philanthropy in ensuring the continuation of that essential intellectual exchange? There are two optics through which that question can be viewed, that of students and that of faculty.

Annual total foreign student enrollment in U.S. institutions of higher learning has increased fifteen-fold since 1954. The number now stands at some 548,000 students, representing a tripling of international students as a percentage of all students on campus since 1954. The United States Department of Commerce estimates that higher education overall is the fifth largest services export sector for the United States, and that international students annually contribute some $11 billion to the economy in tuition and expenses.

How important is philanthropy in enabling that educational flow? Overall, 67 percent of foreign students in the United States get the majority of their funds directly from family. Only 2 percent to 5 percent turn to private philanthropy for the majority of their resources. Of course, this is a bit simplistic because since 1 percent to 2 percent get their funding from home or sponsoring institutions, some portion of which reflects philanthropy (net of market appreciation of endowments, a product of markets as well as charity). Still, the importance of family and government (together representing the major funding sources for three-quarters of the students) overwhelms the philanthropic role.

The pattern is even more striking for the undergraduates, where 80 percent of students rely on family and public funds for resources.

What is ironic is that the states with the largest numbers of foreign students are also the states with the strongest philanthropy. Five states (California, New York, Texas, Massachusetts, and Florida) account for half of all foreign students. These states are also the leading sources of philanthropy in the nation.

If, then, expanding philanthropy and the growing globalization of education are disconnected for students, what happens when, to

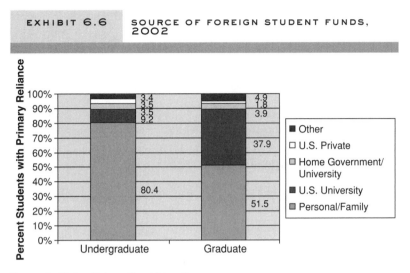

EXHIBIT 6.6   SOURCE OF FOREIGN STUDENT FUNDS, 2002

Source: Institute of International Education

coin a phrase, the book is in the other hand? Intellectual flows and understanding are not just important from the lectern to the blue book; they are also important among peers.

The picture does not change appreciably. In the United States, only 5 percent of higher education faculty exchanges are financed by foundations. Nearly two-thirds are financed by government, home institutions, or faculty themselves. A study of exchanges among the NAFTA nations of Canada, Mexico, and the United States finds a similar regional pattern. The exception is Canada where the government/academic/personal sources still represent two-thirds of funding, but foundations fund 17 percent of exchanges.

It is true: Given the time, a placid lake at sunset, and a crisp chardonnay, anyone could sit and dream up all manner of things for philanthropy to do. And it is arguably an excellent outcome that families are the primary investment sources for their children's education. Still, the power of education, the imperative of global understanding, and the growing importance of newly pivotal (but not newly wealthy) nations to America's future do seem to argue for a reassessment of the global elements of educational support among America's philanthropists.

SOURCES

Open Doors 2001, Institute for International Education, November 2001.
Survey and Evaluation of North American Higher Education Cooperation, Institute for International Education, 1997.

Indigenous Philanthropy: Poorer Nations Also Give

$\mathbf{M}$uch is made, and rightly so, of the fundamental philanthropic streak that runs through American culture. Much is also increasingly made of the growing philanthropic organizational infrastructure in other industrialized nations, as well as foundations within industrialized nations (e.g., the Grameen Foundation USA) focused on resource transfers to developing nations. What is less appreciated is the degree to which philanthropy is alive and well, in some cases amazingly so, even in the poor nations of the world.

There is no central data source for global giving that would allow rigorous analysis to be made. Case material is available, however, and it provides a hint at the degree of current giving within developing nations. It suggests that the forest is indeed much bigger than previous tree-counts would suggest.

In October 2000, for example, the Aga Khan Foundation and the Canadian International Development Agency (CIDA) organized the Conference on Indigenous Philanthropy, held in Islamabad, Pakistan. Included in that conference was a report on the first-ever National Survey of Individual Giving in Pakistan, conducted in 1998. The household survey resulted in an estimate of the monetized value of individual cash gifts and voluntarism in Pakistan of 70 billion rupees. It did not include corporate or other organizational giving.

At January 2002 exchange rates, that individual giving totals a whopping $1.165 billion. This, be assured, is not loose change out of Pakistan's top drawer. It means that an average Pakistani makes philanthropic contributions of $8.63 per year out of personal income/time. With a per-capita income of $460 per year, that, in turn, means the average Pakistani gave 1.9 percent of personal income in 1998, or *MORE THAN* the average 1999 American's cash giving of 1.8 percent

> "Never doubt that a small group of committed citizens can change the world; indeed, it is the only thing that ever has."
> — Margaret Mead

Of course, one would prefer to have a whole range of surveys from a whole range of countries before jumping to any conclusions, thus our feet shall remain firmly planted on the ground. Still, the depth of indigenous philanthropy appears to suggest more careful examination is in order.

There are obvious differences when comparing such data among nations. As an Islamic state, much of Pakistan's individual giving is probably in response to the charitable dictates of Islam, which requires private philanthropy by all belivers. But much of America's individual giving is also to religion—American adults give 77 percent of their philanthropic dollars to churches.

A study of Latin American philanthropy notes that, although formal philanthropy is on the rise in increasingly democratized societies, its roots are still shallow. Giving is often not linked to larger issues of poverty or social need. Rather, it is tied to individual linkages to particular nonprofits. Further, nonprofits rely on more creative approaches to revenue generation than their cash-giving-based U.S. counterparts. Latin American philanthropy lacks deep fundraising expertise and precedent, and it faces greater public skepticism about its ultimate intent.

Still, concerted effort in Latin America has borne fruit. In Brazil, the Group of Institutions, Foundations, and Enterprises (GIF) now counts 40 institutions as members, which together donate $300 million annually in cash and human resources to social welfare. In Colombia, the Maria Santo Domingo Foundation, established in 1960, now has offices throughout the country, and an endowment both gives grants and generates income through microcredit programs. The Salvadoran Foundation for Health and Social Development, in partnership with the Salvadoran American Health Foundation, distributes $10 million per year for healthcare throughout El Salvador. The Hogar de Cristo Foundation, founded in Chile in 1944, has nearly 500,000 members, a volunteer corps of 3,765 people, and 50 affiliates located in Chile's 11 regions, as well as 3 in metropolitan Santiago. It receives between $3 million and $5 million in individual cash donations each year.

Philanthropy is truly increasingly global, and indigenous philanthropy is on its way to claiming a seat at the philanthropic leadership table. U.S. philanthropy and bilateral and multilateral donors take note. You are not alone, and both leverage and sustainability argue that taking advantage of changing local capacity is in order.

▓ SOURCES

The Conference on Indigenous Philanthropy, Introduction to Proceedings, Aga Khan Development Network, October 2000.

"Strengthening Philanthropy in Latin America," David Rockefeller Center for Latin American Studies, Hauser Center for Nonprofit Organizations, Harvard University, February 1999.

"Sustainability through Earned-Income Strategies: A Diversified Approach to Self-Financing. A Case Study of Hogar de Cristo," New York: Synergos Institute, 2000.

North of the Border: Canada-United States Philanthropic Comparisons

There are no two nations so large, so culturally similar, and so well aligned as the United States and Canada. It is true that occasional political differences arise, occasional rivalries break out, and occasional hockey championships test geopolitical collegiality. Overall, however, the term "international" has a decidedly neighborly feel when applied to the Maple Leaf and the Stars and Stripes.

An examination of the philanthropic and nonprofit sectors of the two nations, however, reveals both striking similarities and striking differences. And a caveat is important from the outset: The precise nature of charity in the two nations, levels of voluntarism, and legal definitions may differ; comparisons can only reveal patterns and broad distinctions.

In at least three ways, Canadian and U.S. philanthropy are similar. Canadian private philanthropy appears to be as geographically checkered as its American counterpart. Canadian provinces differ widely in the number of charities operating and the giving behavior of the population. Saskatchewan has twice the number of charities per capita than, for example, Ontario. Quebec, with virtually the same population as Ontario, has 46 percent fewer charities and annually

EXHIBIT 6.7   FIVE-STATE DOMINANCE OF PUBLIC
CHARITY REVENUE

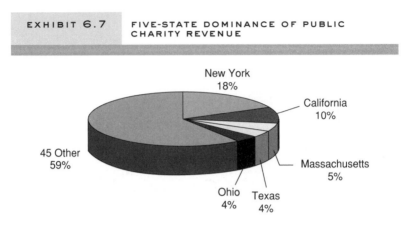

Source: IRS and the National Center for Charitable Statistics, circa 1997

donates 33 percent less per 1,000 people than Ontario. Similarly, in the United States, geography matters to philanthropy. Five states (New York, California, Massachusetts, Texas, and Ohio) alone account for 40 percent of giving to public charities in the nation.

Many of Canada's charities are also young. None of Newfoundland's foundations, for example, existed before 1983. In the United States, more than half of all foundations were created after 1980.

✗ Finally, wealth does not necessarily correlate with giving behavior. In the United States, those making $30,000 to $40,000 per year gave 2.17 percent of their income to charity, compared to 1.6 percent for those making $75,000 to $100,000 per year. In Canada, the median annual gift from those declaring charitable contributions in Quebec was $100 (Canadian), where annual income was $32,240. The equivalent pattern in Prince Edward Island was a median of $220 on $26,800 income. Even where incomes are approximately equal, (Quebec and Newfoundland), giving behavior differed markedly. In Quebec, the median gift was $100; in Newfoundland it was $250.

On three counts, however, Canadian and U.S. philanthropy appear to differ markedly. First, the targets of giving contrast significantly. In Canada, 56 percent of giving is for hospitals and teaching institutions. Only 6 percent finds its way to religious organizations. In the United States, in contrast, 44 percent of private giving is targeted at religion, while only 25 percent flows to health-care and educational organizations.

> "That long (Canadian) frontier from the Atlantic to the Pacific Oceans, guarded only by neighborly respect and honorable obligations, is an example to every country and a pattern for the future of the world."
> —Winston Churchill, 1939

Second, U.S. philanthropic institutions appear to be much more diverse than in Canada. There are only about 3,300 private foundations in Canada, compared to about 45,000 in the United States. Taking economic size into account, this is still a significant difference. The U.S. economy is about nine times as large as that of Canada, and purchasing power parity corrected for per-capita income is about half again as large. Yet the United States has 14 times the number of foundations.

Third, tax policy appears to correlate more with giving behavior in Canada than in the United States. Changes in Canadian tax law in 1996 and 1997 allowed tax filers to increase the amount of charitable deductions claimed. In that period, claimed contributions rose 6.4 percent, and the total value of contributions claimed rose 14.2 percent. In the United States, the relationship to tax policy is far less clear. People do not necessarily give to charity to avoid taxes. Between 1982 and 1989, when tax rates fell consistently, giving to charity by individuals rose by 27.8 percent.

Still, the comparisons are unsatisfying. Problems with definitions and data comparability lead one to suspect that the differences between Canada and the United States may not be so different, and the similarities may not be so similar.

▓ SOURCES

Adams, R.M., J. Confort, E.J. Finley et al. "Forecast for 2001: Hazy, Some Clearing by End of Year," *Trusts and Estates,* January 1, 2001, pp. 20–21.

Bozzo Sandra L., and Marcus Parmegiani. "Trends in Individual Charitable Donations: 1984–1997," *Canadian Centre for Philanthropy Research Bulletin,* 6:1, Winter 1999.

Dover, Sandra. "A Picture of the Donor in Canadian Society Today," Canadian Fundraiser, February 12, 1996.

Giving and Volunteering in the United States: Findings from a National Survey, Independent Sector, 2000.

Hall Michael H., and Laura G. Macpherson. "A Provincial Portrait of Canada's Charities," *Canadian Centre for Philanthropy Research Bulletin,* 4:2–3, Spring/Summer, 1997.

Macpherson, Laura G. "Who Gives More? Individual Donations by Region," *Canadian Centre for Philanthropy Research Bulletin,* 3:3, June 1996.

Statistics Canada, 2001. Raw data can be found at *www.statcan.ca.*

Is Europe Poised for a Golden Age of Community Philanthropy?

From the point of view of gross statistics, it would appear that philanthropy continues to be a characteristic of American social economics not shared by our neighbors across "the pond." Data comparability are poor, but whereas the United States devotes about 2.3 percent of its GDP to philanthropy, the comparable percentages in Europe are between 0.2 percent and 0.8 percent. Per-capita European annual giving ranges from $27 to $150 per year, depending on the country. The U.S. average is between $500 and $1,500 per tax return, depending on the state.

But that may be an incorrect point from which to view the changes afoot in European philanthropy. Historically, European social policy was dominated by government support for social services. From cradle to grave, communities relied on the public purse for healthcare, education, social welfare, and retirement. And, for decades, governments kept those promises. Three converging trends have made those promises increasingly untenable, however.

First, Europe is aging rapidly. By 2050, the median age in Europe will be 52.3, up from 37.7 today. In Germany, 12 percent of the population in 2050 will be over age 80, compared to 2 percent today. The ratio of German workers to retirees will shrink from two to one to just about one worker for one retiree. And that aging means

EXHIBIT 6.8   POPULATION DECLINE IN EUROPEAN NATIONS

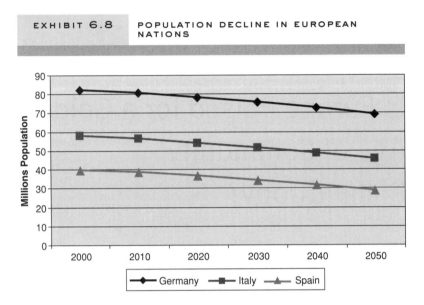

Source: Centre d'Etudes Prospectives et d'Information Internationales

falling total populations. By 2010, the population of three of seven countries studied by the European Union will begin declining. By 2050, all seven will begin experiencing declines in population.

Second, European economies have been growing slowly, and often have not been growing at all. The reasons for the economic trough are many, but part of the problem is a dwindling labor force that must support the aging population. Part also is the tax structure, which, in Germany for example, claims half the average paycheck.

Third, globalization exacts a high price from those who cannot compete. The tax structure needed to support the social welfare system imposes higher costs of production on European industry, making its products expensive relative to its global competitors. As tariff and nontariff barriers to trade fall, more and more goods and services can be freely traded. High cost structure will always lose to lower costs, unless demonstrable differences in quality exist. And, because investments is global and electronics allow the transfer of standards and the oversight of production anywhere in the world, quality, too, can be competitive.

The result? Strikes in France, for one, to protest changes in the government's retirement policies.

But a counterbalance is emerging in Europe. Community foundations and philanthropies are beginning to emerge, not to replace government roles, but to supplement programs that reflect community priorities in the face of resource constraints. The number of such organizations increased 42 percent between 2000 and 2001 alone. Spain is among the leaders in the emergence of community foundations, but Italy has followed suit, with support from the Caripio Foundation, as has Germany, with support from the Bertelsmann Foundation. The community foundations are developing donation mechanisms similar to donor-advised funds, with grantmaking targeted either at particular areas of community need or specific service organizations.

There is no lack of outlet for European philanthropy. The nonprofit sector accounts for some 31 million jobs in Europe. In Spain, the nonprofit sector is seven times as large as the largest private commercial firm, and represents 4 percent of the GDP. In the Netherlands, nonprofits represent 12.6 percent of total nonagricultural employment. In Ireland, they account for 11.5 percent, and in Belgium 10.5 percent. As government resources shrink, this nonprofit sector will pitch in to encourage the evolution of private philanthropy. If it does not do so, its very survival is in question.

Two converging forces will boost European philanthropy. Government program decline in the face of continuing need will prompt communities to turn to philanthropy as a supplement. And the large nonprofit sector, feeling the pinch of cutbacks in the government resources that represent 55 percent of its income, will heartily join in encouraging that trend.

There is some evidence that aggressive promotion of philanthropic opportunities bears fruit. Britain is probably the most well-documented case in point. Charitable philanthropy began to decline precipitously in 1995. Even the creation of a national lottery, 28 percent of whose proceeds benefit charity, did not boost individual giving. The lottery gave a 50 percent boost to charitable resources, with startling effects for organizations, such as museums, that had long been starved for resources. The turnaround in personal giving came later, with revisions in the tax law, which favored gifts of capital to charity. Between 1998 and 2001, the average monthly charitable donation in Britain rose 30 percent.

The combination of reduced public resources, strong nonprofit institutions, and creative government policy is infusing vibrancy into British philanthropy. There is every reason to think that Europe will follow suit.

■ SOURCES

"Charitable Giving in 2001," National Council for Voluntary Organizations, London.

"Community Philanthropy in Europe: A Growing Phenomenon," European Foundation Center Conference Report, Barcelona, May 10, 2001.

Drucker, H.M. "New State, New Economy, New Philanthropy in Britain and Ireland," Universidad de Madrid, July 17, 2001.

"Europe's Demographic Evolution through to the Year 2050," *La Lettre du CEPII,* Centre d'Etudes Prospectives et d'Informations Internationales, Paris, France January 2003.

IRS Statistics Bulletin, Spring 2000, as compiled by the National Center for Charitable Statistics of the Urban Institute, Washington, DC.

Salamon, L.M. S. Wojciech, Sokolowski, H.K. Anheier, R. List, and S. Toepler, *Global Civil Society.* Baltimore: Johns Hopkins Center for Civil Society Studies, 1999.

Evidence of Philanthropic Impact: A De Novo Case from Poland and the Lessons It Teaches

Impact evaluation is risky business. Cause and effect are seldom closely linked, and evidence must often be teased out of tangled webs of human, financial, and technological action and interaction.

Evaluation of philanthropy is no less risky. For most nonprofit institutions, the financial roots of American philanthropy are deep and long-standing, but they are intertwined with other streams of finance, and nourish programs addressing historically complex ills. Pinpointing the specific, or even the relative, impact of philanthropic investments often sinks to the level of speculation rather than rises to the level of science. Which makes Warsaw, Poland, of all places, interesting.

In 1993, in the early days of democratic change in the former Soviet system, a small group of American advisors joined with a handful of Polish and American business and medical leaders to create the first private, independent philanthropic foundation in Warsaw. The target of its efforts was to be improvement in the largest children's hospital in the city. The philanthropy, Friends of Litewska Children's Hospital, announced its formation in 1994, and began funding major investments in 1995.

The story of the formation of Friends is long and complex; its motivation was a combination of healthcare needs and U.S. foreign policy concerns over the stability of democratization. (See Sources at the end of this essay for background reading.) History aside, led by its visionary executive director, Dr. Adam Jelonek, supported by its determined board of Polish, American, and European private corporate executives, and aided by hospital management courageous enough to be innovative in the face of political uncertainty, Friends began its groundbreaking work. Friends focused on improvements in three wards of the hospital, concentrating on infrastructure, training—especially of nurses—and community voluntarism.

In 2001, Friends paused to evaluate five years of its work. Because organized private philanthropy had been a new (but growing) concept in Poland, isolating the impact of Friends' funding was more straightforward than in an American context. Among the evaluation's findings was a stunning statistic: The death rate in those three wards had declined by 52 percent.

Obviously, every percentage point cannot be directly attributed to the presence of philanthropy. When the scope of concern in the private corporate community became widely public, the government reacted with changes of its own. That said, government action can be at least indirectly attributed to the pressure of private philanthropic leadership. But let's be conservative and say that, directly and indirectly, the presence of Friends as a prod and as a philanthropic resource accounted for half of the fall in pediatric mortality. That is still an impressive 26 percent decline.

What does this say to American philanthropy? De novo situations in this country are hard to find, hence comparing investments is difficult. So let's look instead at comparable need.

Mississippi perennially ranks last or next to last on many measures of U.S. healthcare. This is not to criticize Mississippi, only to indicate that there are deep and difficult problems that need solutions there, as in many parts of this country. Mississippi, for example, has the worst infant mortality record in the nation. Its rate of 10.4 per 1,000 live births is slightly higher than that in Poland, and approximately what the U.S. national average was two decades ago. Infant mortality is clearly a problem there.

What about philanthropy? This is a more difficult question to address. There are just over 250 private independent foundations in Mississippi—which, of course, grossly underestimates philanthropy. According to the Generosity Index compiled by the Catalogue of Philanthropy, Mississippi is first in the nation in generosity—that is level of giving relative to level of income. Still, it is difficult to know what to do with that measure, as it tells us nothing about which problems the money targets, or even if it stays in Mississippi.

So back to the only resource we have that can trace flows: data on organized philanthropy. According to the Foundation Center, of the 251 foundations in Mississippi, 36 made no grants in 2001. Of the 215 with grantmaking, only 18 had an explicit interest in health-care or medicine. If these 18 had chosen to dedicate *ALL* of their grants to healthcare (which they did not, as they have other inter-ests), this amount (about $8 million) would still have represented only 13 percent of the total grants made by Mississippi foundations.

Yet if Friends of Litewska is any measure, there is opportunity for Mississippi philanthropy in Mississippi healthcare, especially as regards the health of young children. There is a troubling discon-nect between Mississippi's healthcare ranking and its philan-thropic patterns.

But the message is more general. Private philanthropy that is underinvested in a clear and present problem misses a major oppor-tunity for change. If Litewska is to be believed, then the infusion of private philanthropic effort into significant, yet underaddressed problems can have effect. Perhaps it is at that intersection that pri-vate philanthropy should seek its targets.

■ SOURCES

2002 Generosity Index, Catalogue of Philanthropy.

Jelonek, A. M.D. "Community Philanthropy as a Source of Funding: How to Involve the Community in Financing Hospital Improvement," presented at the Eurasia Health Transitions Conference, Washington, DC, June 2002.

Raymond, S. "Corporate Voluntarism: Private Support for Social Policy," Economic Reform Today, Center for International Private Enterprise, November 4, 1996.

Raymond, S., P. Rader, A. Jelonek, and M. Hoffman, "Managing Capital Development for Health Care in Poland: Friends of Litewska Children's Hospital," The Journal of Health Care Administration, 12:4, Fall 1994, pp. 519–532.

State Health Rankings: An Analysis of the Relative Healthiness of the Populations in All 50 States, United Health Group, 2000 Edition.

World Health Statistics, World Health Organization, 2002.

Learning from International Conflict: Philanthropic Strategy Is as Important as Sympathy

The understandable emphasis in current American philanthropy on results and self-reliance has motivated many innovations in programming and management among nonprofits. Those innovations are directed at ensuring the measurement of impact, and that the objective of effort is to solve problems in a reasonable time frame, not simply to reinforce persistent dependence for generations. These are very important changes of philosophy and approach. Their utility in some areas of international philanthropy, however, may be slight.

The first issue is that much American philanthropy abroad is not motivated by careful problem identification and program planning. Giving responds to crisis; natural disasters and man-made conflicts stimulate an outpouring of giving. The objective of the public is to assuage suffering. The giving is premised on sympathy, not on strategy.

But, when the crisis is bred of conflict, will sympathy be enough? There is an argument to be made that more than sympathy must underpin giving. American philanthropy needs to take a strategic view of its role in international crises. The argument rests on two realities.

First, the storms of conflict into which America finds itself thrust are increasingly complex. They are conflicts bred of centuries of cultural animosities or of religious intolerances. They are not just conflicts among nation states, they are conflicts within nation states. Indeed, in their worst formulation, they are conflicts wherein the concept of the nation state has broken down entirely. The agony of many sections of West and Central Africa is of this last type; the Middle East typifies the former.

Where the roots of conflict extend deeper than any single paroxysm of violence, the consequences of the approaching storm may not just be the short-term dislocations of war. They may be deep, broad, longabiding, and outside of the geographic and cultural experience of most American philanthropies. Those whom sympathy seeks to help may face the future with perspectives, values, and assumptions that are distinct from those of American institutions. Indeed, where societies have splintered over decades or centuries, "American philanthropy" may be seen as an oxymoron by the very segments of the population that sympathy seeks to assuage.

We as a nation find these realities uncomfortable. We understand our reactions to be generous. It seems implausible that others do not. But violent and splintered cultures do not always react as we would predict. Headlines about murdered foreign nurses, kidnapped aid workers, and suicide bombers in refugee camps indicate that the world of generosity is more complex than three or four decades ago. Hence, philanthropy born of reactive sympathy may not only be an inadequate approach, it may also be a wrong approach. And charitable mistakes and missteps, however unintentional, will be susceptible to misinterpretation in social settings that are suspicious of America to begin with.

A second reason that strategy must accompany sympathy is embedded in the implications of time. History offers some lessons on the convergence of military action and philanthropy, specifically that achieving stability takes more time than anyone ever thinks. The Balkans provide an apt example, as does Russia, where the Peace Corps is only now closing its programs, more than a decade after that nation's political and economic upheaval. Haiti is the quintessential example. After political chaos, troop interventions, and decades of aid, virtually nothing has changed in Haiti's present, and its future remains bleak. Iraq is on its way to being a long-term philanthropic issue, where the central concern will not be assuaging disaster, but encouraging the emergence of a civil society grounded in tolerance.

> "With malice toward none, with charity for all, with firmness in the right as God gives us to see the right, let us strive on to finish the work we are in, to bind up the nation's wounds, to care for him who shall have borne the battle and for his widow and his orphan, to do all which may achieve a just and lasting peace among ourselves and with all nations."
> —Abraham Lincoln
> Second Inaugural Address, 1864

Philanthropy, whether it is denominated in government disaster assistance or private resource allocations, tends to flow longer than initially expected because the change that it either assuages or supports is nearly always slower than those caught up in its vortex expect it will be. Which is why strategy must accompany sympathy, strategy that seeks to link sympathy to the emergence of local social, cultural, and economic stability.

Merely reacting with airlifts of blankets to a regional crisis on the basis of good-hearted concern for the suffering poor will be an insufficient approach to the problem. Worse, business-as-usual reactions could be potentially destructive to the emergence of social and economic stability in a region long riven by distrust, bloodshed, and perceived betrayal.

Now, the plea. The long-term is not an unrealistic time frame for guiding American philanthropic decisions. In 1999, Serbian forces departed Kosovo under U.S. and European military pressure. Three years and $2.4 billion later, United Nations management remains. And Kosovo, tiny, ethnically homogeneous Kosovo, is a walk in the park compared to the Middle East or the tribal conflicts tearing Africa apart.

Over the long term in Africa and the Middle East, American philanthropies have the potential to be part of American national security—perhaps a smaller part than American forces, but a part nonetheless. They have the potential to do more than assuage immediate wounds. They have the potential to become an expression of civil society, symbols and funders of community commitment and stability, partners in the search for paths to democracy.

"Most people live, whether physically, intellectually, or morally, in a very restricted circle of their own potential being. They make use of a very small portion of their possible consciousness, and of their soul's resources in general, much like a man who, out of his whole bodily organism, should get into a habit of using and moving only his little finger. Great emergencies and crises show us how much greater our vital resources are than we had supposed."
—William James, 1906

But they also have the potential to do harm. If their reaction is merely an expression of sympathy in a crisis, merely the funding of blankets and wheat, then they risk doing worse than not enough. They risk doing harm, both by falling into unforeseen ethnic or religious divisions in the short term, and failing to assist in developing self-reliant societal and economic templates to stabilize the future in the long term.

In their own interests, in the interests of those they seek to help, and in the interests of the country, American philanthropies must inventory their assets and capabilities in light of potential needs and complexities in places like Africa and the Middle East. That inventory must take place on two levels.

To prepare for the short term, they have to do due diligence now on potential nonprofit partners in the region, and short-list those with whom they want to work. They need to determine now which target groups or population subgroups in which geographic locations they have competence to serve and understand. They need to put together contingency plans for mobilizing their resources to address those groups. They need to prepare their boards and staffs for the complexities and dangers of working in those locations. They need to tell U.S. government agencies about those plans. They need to put together communications plans that are sensitive to likely public perceptions and reactions. They need fallback plans for when and if things go wrong.

To prepare for the long term, an equally careful and searching internal analysis is needed. Philanthropies have to determine where they have long-term substantive strength of programmatic experience and the staying power of significant human resources and board commitment. Programs need to be outlined for the longer term. Potential programs need to be budgeted for, and investments in staff knowledge and professional networks in the United States and in the Middle East developed so that implementation is smooth.

America's philanthropies need to do all of this, and they need to have done it yesterday. What they do not need to do is to wait until the next crisis is upon us.

Corporate Philanthropy

INTRODUCTION TO THE ISSUES

Corporate America is a major actor on the U.S. philanthropic stage. It is also both a resilient and a complex one. Even when profits fall, corporate philanthropy does not necessarily follow suit. In 2002, corporate profits fell 2 percent, but corporate philanthropy rose to $12.19 billion, an inflation-adjusted 8.8 percent increase over 2001.

Even these estimates of corporate giving, however, understate the case. The flows of revenues from private enterprise to nonprofits originate in many reservoirs. Formal corporate giving programs and corporate foundations are but two such pools.

Increasingly, major corporations are engaging in "cause-related marketing," an approach that attaches their names/products to charitable causes. The consumer, then, supports the charity by supporting the product. The resources for developing these programs in support of charity come not from giving budgets, but from advertising or public affairs budgets. Hence, they are not included in normal estimates of corporate philanthropy.

> "I believe it is my duty to make money...and to use the money I make for the good of my fellow man according to the dictates of my conscience."
>
> —John D. Rockefeller, 1905

Second, many corporations encourage, even facilitate, voluntarism by their employees and executives. Nonprofits in areas with a corporate presence are often the beneficiaries of such programs. The result can be as simple as extra hands at the soup kitchen or as sophisticated as free help developing a Web site, setting up an accounting and financial management system, or developing more sophisticated communications, branding, and marketing systems. The market value of such assistance can represent hundreds of thousands of dollars to a nonprofit, but it is never counted in conventional inventories of corporate aid.

Finally, of course, America is a nation of small businesses. Most community efforts are support by the local dry cleaner and the Coffee Cup Cafe on Main Street. Much of this charity is probably not counted either. Small businesses do not have the managerial horsepower to capture every last donation to a local cause. But, any little league team will attest to the importance of the small business to American philanthropy.

■ **SOURCE**

Strom, S. "Gifts to Charity in 2002 Stayed Unexpectedly High," *New York Times,* June 23, 2003, section A, p. 14, col. 5.

Corporate Giving: A Workhorse in Small States

$\mathbf{E}$conomic prognostications, and hopes for their philanthropic effects, are rife with risk. In early 2000, the Dow Jones flirted with passing the 12,000 mark. By mid-2003, it was barely chinning itself up to 9,000. In the space of 36 months, the decade-long hope that ever-expanding corporate profits would translate into ever-greater corporate philanthropic largess began to dim.

Still, viewed in the long term, share value in the marketplace has performed amazingly well in historical terms. And corporate America is fundamentally solid. The same will probably continue to be true of corporate philanthropy. Corporations sponsor and fund about 5 percent of all foundations. Their giving represents just over 12 percent of all giving in the United States.

> "The highest use of capital is not to make more money, but to make money do more for the betterment of life."
> —Henry Ford

What is interesting, however, is how these data understate the importance of corporate giving in small, low-income states in America. In these situations, corporate philanthropy is often the bulwark.

A sample of five lower-income (largely rural) states, which are compared with Massachusetts and New Jersey, which are among

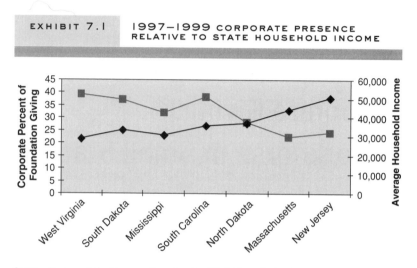

EXHIBIT 7.1   1997–1999 CORPORATE PRESENCE
RELATIVE TO STATE HOUSEHOLD INCOME

Source: Bureau of the Census; Changing Our World Foundation Sample

the most industrial and high-income states in the nation, indicates that the corporate presence is much more central to small rural states than to their wealthier, urban brethren. The lower income states display incomes as much as 28 percent lower than the U.S. three-year median household average. West Virginia's household average is 44 percent lower than that of New Jersey.

Clearly, in such situations, corporate philanthropy carries significance beyond the national averages. Representing between a third and two-fifths of foundations providing philanthropic funds, corporate foundations in poorer or more rural states can carry a disproportionate share of the funding burden. Moreover, even this data probably understates the corporate ratio. Independent foundation grants tend to be more comprehensively counted in national databases than do the gifts from local businesses on Main Street.

What is true on the aggregate at the state level is also true for individual institutions. The Foundation Center's database shows Mississippi State University, for example, receiving grants from seven corporate foundations for about $456,000, compared to grants from eight private independent foundations for $319,000.

Corporate foundations represented 47 percent of the foundation funders and 59 percent of the foundation funding.

Of course, to the nonprofit, a dollar equals a dollar. Aside from certain cases of principle or religious belief, nonprofits do not care where the grant originates. But for the overall state of philanthropy in nonaffluent settings, there is a larger implication: Economic policy matters.

In virtually no cases in the poorer states sampled was the corporate headquarters located in the state. Rather, the state was home to plants or branches of larger businesses. Policies that seem to attract and deepen corporate investment, therefore, will have a side-benefit: Nonprofits will become potential recipients of corporate philanthropy. And that philanthropy will be a critical income source relative to local philanthropy.

In the long run, of course, economic policy that seeks to boost private industrial investment also enhances private, independent philanthropy. The rising tide of investment, jobs, and income lifts all boats, and it permits the accumulation of assets, which then begets private foundation creation. In the near term, however, it is the presence of corporate investment that opens access to corporate philanthropy.

The lesson, however, extends far beyond American shores. Developing the capacity for local philanthropy is critical to sustainable economic and societal development. Philanthropy represents a community's investment in itself. Progress built on that foundation is inherently more likely to be sustained than progress that is owed to gifts from international donors. Moreover, the link between philanthropy and democracy is also clear. Communities that invest widely in themselves are also communities that value citizen participation and involvement. The two—philanthropy and democracy—go hand in hand.

What the state data cited here illustrate is how important corporate philanthropy can be in this equation in low-income situations. It is corporate philanthropy that can carry disproportionate weight at early levels of economic growth. And, therefore, economic policy, always critical to investment, can also be critical in the long term to philanthropic growth.

SOURCES

Foundation comparison data taken from the Foundation Center's online database, 2002.

Income data from the U.S. Bureau of the Census, U.S. Census 2000.

State foundation profile sample taken from data in Prospector's Choice, the Taft Corporation, 2001.

Gifts in Kind:
The Good of Goods

An important fuel for the rise in U.S. philanthropy has been product donations. Gifts-in-kind revenue to nonprofits has been rising at about 7 percent per year. In the 1980s, noncash contributions constituted about 20 percent of all corporate giving. By 2000, that figure was 33 percent. For some industries, product giving is dominant. In Silicon Valley, half of all corporate donations are in the form of product giveaways. In 2000, 73 percent of the giving of the U.S. pharmaceutical industry was in the form of products. In the computer and office equipment industry, 62 percent of giving was in product donations.

For example, the rising importance of gifts-in-kind led the Gates Foundation to give a cash grant of $2.75 million to Gifts in Kind International, an Alexandria, Virginia, nonprofit that provides charities access to product and services donations. The grant will help expand the goods donations programs worldwide.

A glance at U.S. tax law sheds some light on the popularity of goods donations. With the largest tax break, the donor can take up to twice the adjusted tax basis of the donated goods. Say, for example, a company has excess inventory in its warehouse with a market value of $100,000, and a tax basis value of $20,000. Depending on the type of corporation, the donation of that $100,000 worth of product could lead to a $40,000 deduction, twice its tax basis. In addition, the company reduces inventory, saves warehouse space

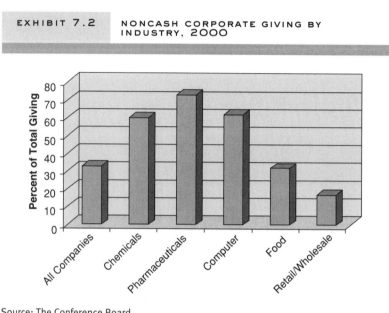

Source: The Conference Board

and costs, and/or frees up warehouse space for newer products. The nonprofit receives goods that allow its cash resources to be shifted to other, nonprocurement line items, and, in the process, to increase its service capacity and effectiveness.

The problem, of course, is obvious. From the nonprofit's point of view, the utility of the product donation is in direct proportion to a combination of the utility of the product and the ability of the nonprofit to effectively insert the product into its programmatic or service chain. Computer and software donations without teacher skills are suboptimal inputs to education. Medical supplies without adequate storage and distribution capacity on the part of the nonprofit risk simply spoiling in a warehouse other than that of a company. The more complicated or sophisticated the product, the greater the problem. Recipient capacity is the key to product effectiveness.

That concern is, increasingly, the focus not only of the nonprofit recipients but also of the corporate donors. Corporate donors with sophisticated products are becoming equally sophisticated in their approaches.

Apple Computer, for example, sponsors competitions among nonprofits to develop new ways to use its technology. U.S. West uses philanthropy to point to technologies that lie in the future. More often, software donations are given in conjunction with the technical assistance that nonprofits need to adapt and use it effectively. Before its corporate demise, the WebMD Foundation developed a project to found a global public health communication called the InterNetwork. The foundation's donation was not denominated in dollars; rather, it was a commitment to provide many multiples of the professional capacity necessary to design and manage the Internet platform and communications system that would be adaptable to the needs of the developing world. That professional commitment had an equal, or perhaps greater, value than cold cash.

In education, IBM meets early on with both potential education recipients and with potential philanthropic partners to understand core problems of educational institutions. Together, the participants determine how technology can best be integrated into each other's organizational problems, and they evaluate the capacity of technology to address current needs. On the basis of that understanding, IBM targets the donation of its technological capacity (goods and services) to meet needs effectively. The benefits flow two ways.

EXHIBIT 7.3   VALUE OF NONCASH CORPORATE
CONTRIBUTIONS, 1990–2000

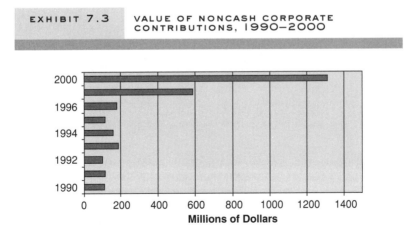

Source: The Conference Board

Educational recipients receive technology assistance that reflects their priorities and responds to both needs and capacities. IBM (and its partners) receives guidance into the problems of educational institutions that can guide future technological development (and market relationships) and can foster other types of business tie-ins.

With virtually all industries becoming more technology-based, and virtually all nonprofits having to expand their technological capacity, the evolution of sophisticated approaches to the donation of goods and services is likely to become more rapid.

▊ SOURCES

Clolery, Paul. "Non-Cash Gifts Boosting Bottom Lines," *NonProfit Times,* August 1998, p. 17.

"Corporate Contributions in 2000," The Conference Board, 2001.

"Corporate Contributions: The View from 50 Years," The Conference Board, 1998.

Smith, Craig. "Turning Product Donations into an Art Form," Corporate Philanthropy Report, 1999.

Corporate Giving and Tax Policy: Let's Do the Math

As with many things, the level of corporate giving depends on what you count and what you compare. The most frequently cited data are that corporate giving currently represents 1.0 percent of U.S. pretax income. This measure has shown modest rate increases in recent years, but is still far below the historical high of 2.6 percent in 1986. Whether the ramp-up to this high is causally related to the 1981 change in deduction level is debatable, as even 2.6 percent is a far cry from 10 percent (or even 5 percent). The ceiling could have been reached without the policy change.

Moreover, the 1.0 percent is the brightest light in which to portray the giving. Measured by consolidated pretax income (pretax income acquired from U.S. and global operations), contributions were only 0.7 percent of income. The highest industrial category using this measure was pharmaceuticals, at 1.5 percent. Regardless whether the ceiling is 10 percent or 15 percent, there is clearly room to grow. It is not clear, however, that federal tax policy drives corporate giving levels. Indeed, the data seem to indicate that it does not. Giving seems more driven by market economics than by federal policy.

> "The results of philanthropy are always beyond calculation."
> —Mariam Beard, *A History of Business*, 1938

Source: The Conference Board and Giving USA

But what about the 75 percent of U.S. corporations that do not indicate any contributions on their tax filings? Would change motivate them? That they do not report, of course, does not mean that they do not give, only that they do not capture the data on their reporting forms. If, however, their giving was anywhere near 10 percent, the rational behavior would be to report. So we can assume that any nonreported giving is below 10 percent, and hence unlikely to be motivated in an upward direction by a change to 15 percent.

Suspending reality for a moment, what would happen if the 15 percent policy were enacted and it did motivate giving at the 15 percent level? A sample of 15 companies was developed, representing mature and emerging industry categories from the following Standard Industrial Classification (SIC) subcodes: aerospace products, computer hardware, networking and communications devices, pharmaceuticals, automotive and transportation manufacturers, and telecommunications, Internet, and online providers. The companies were randomly selected; only those with positive operating income were included (admittedly, narrowing the choices for inclusion among emerging industry companies). The surveyed companies are as follows:

- Aeronautics Products: Alcoa, Curtiss Wright, Teledyne
- Computer Hardware/Networking: 3Com, Alcatel, Cisco
- Pharmaceuticals: Abbott Labs, Eli Lilly, Pfizer
- Auto Manufacturers: DaimlerChrysler, Ford, General Motors.
- Telecommunications Internet and Online: AOL (pre-Time Warner merger), AT&T, Qwest Communications.

Total gross profits (revenue less cost of products sold) in 2001 were $203 billion; net income was $73 billion. Again, definitions of "pretax income" determine the ultimate data, but 15 percent of $73 billion is approximately $11 billion. This is significantly more than all of reported corporate giving—hence, probably unrealistic.

An equally interesting question is whether giving (at current levels or, certainly, at a 15 percent level) ought to be disclosed to shareholders, who are, after all, the ultimate owners of a publicly traded corporation. Eight million Americans hold personal equity

EXHIBIT 7.5   PROFITS AND INCOME FOR INDUSTRIAL SAMPLE, 2002

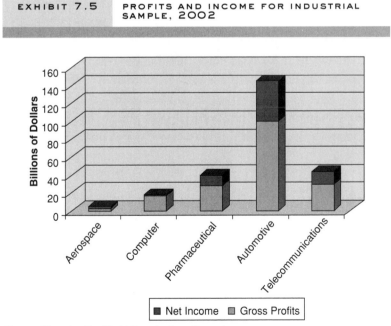

Source: Changing Our World Sample, from Hoover's

in U.S. companies. The 15 surveyed companies alone represent 22.9 billion shares of stock. Disclosure of major philanthropic initiatives and the details of their recipients are, therefore, both intellectually interesting problems and fraught with management complexity.

There are two dimensions to this problem. First is the question of the appropriateness of corporate philanthropy itself. Corporations exist to grow shareholder value. Because they have been charged with responsibility for investor money, use of that money should serve investor goals. Most investors invest to make money; hence, using money for any other purpose would not be appropriate. The counterargument, now widely accepted, is that philanthropy *does* increase shareholder value, by contributing to societal strength and stability—hence markets—and by ensuring that the marketplace views the company, its products, and its brand in the most favorable light possible. The more extended version of that argument holds that corporations have a "responsibility" for addressing social needs, apart from their investors' interests, because they represent such significant resource pools. This extension does create dispute.

The second dimension of the shareholder problem is less well debated. Must the company disclose to its shareholders, even *in advance,* both the level of its planned philanthropy and the nature of the recipients? Should shareholders, whose investments allow the company to exist, have some significant say—perhaps even a veto—over the philanthropic allocation of their resources?

Those who are argue for significant increases in corporate philanthropy should be careful what they wish for. Shareholders might then begin paying attention, and the outcome is not at all certain.

SOURCE

"Corporate Contributions in 2000," The Conference Board, 2001.
Giving USA 2003. AAERC Trust for Philanthropy.

Global Health and Corporate Philanthropy: Fickle Funder or Lasting Partner?

$\mathbf{C}$ontroversies often tempt participants to push the edges of statistical truth. What one wishes to be true can be very different from what *is* true. In the end, and as the lawyers are wont to emphasize, the facts are recalcitrant.

One such current controversy is the potential role of philanthropy in promoting global health. A recent report of a committee organized by the World Health Organization, and led by Jeffrey Sachs of Harvard University (now at Columbia), proposes, among other things, that a "cooperative and voluntary arrangement" among private companies and governments should be forged to contribute to pharmaceutical and vaccine availability in the developing world. It is a controversial proposal among global health advocates. Whatever its merits, it is a strategy that one advocacy group, quoted in the *New York Times,* December 21, 2001, characterized as follows: "Relying on goodwill or charity is a very frightening way to move forward. Companies can have their priorities change overnight."

Little in this world can be counted on to change overnight, and things that do usually have been unstable for some time. Could it be that "company priorities," in this case presumed to mean "company philanthropic priorities," are among the exceptions?

First, let us establish a sense of scale. U.S. corporate philanthropy was recorded as totaling $10.86 billion per year in 2000, a

12.1 percent increase over 1999. Noncash giving represented about 20 percent of this total, with the remainder being cash from corporate contributions budgets and foundation grants.

These data, of course, represent a gross underestimate. Only 25 percent of U.S. corporations bother to report contributions on their tax filings. Small businesses, involved in their communities via donations of goods and services or small cash gifts, often do not trouble to compound their tax-filing complexity by seeking exemption for such efforts. Because these businesses are tied to their communities, it is unlikely that their giving priorities "change overnight," unless their communities also change overnight—in which case, change would be a good thing, not a bad thing. Moreover, many corporate contributions are difficult to classify, and find their niche on balance sheets as expenses rather than charitable contributions. Finally, the estimate does not monetize corporate voluntarism, an increasing strategy for a business response to community needs, especially those that are technical.

> "The man who in view of gain thinks of righteousness; who in the view of danger is prepared to give up his life; who does not forget an old agreement however far back it extends—such a man may be reckoned a complete man."
> —Confucius
> *The Confucian Analects*

That said, then, what about the 25 percent that do register their contributions for purposes of exemption? The modern era of corporate charity on a large scale dates from 1953, when the New Jersey Supreme Court, in *A.P. Smith Manufacturing Co. v. Barlow, et al.* ruled that corporate contributions for purposes other than direct benefit to the business are legal. Where have these contributions gone? And do they reflect whim or commitment?

Over the last three decades, education and health have consistently represented between 65 percent and 75 percent of corporate philanthropy. In 1975, education was slightly behind, receiving 35 percent of corporate monies; health and human services organizations received 40 percent. The trend shifted in 1978, when education giving began to outpace that for healthcare; it shifted again in 1996, when health and human services regained the lead. But the two sectors have rarely been more than 10 percentage points apart.

For the past three decades, the arts have remained at a virtually unchanging 10 percent of contributions, and civic and community groups have garnered another 10 percent, with a notable rise in the 1982–1986 period, at the expense of healthcare.

Do these long-term trends mask year-to-year volatility? For health and human services, the single period of significant short-term change in corporate allocations was in the 1982–1986 period just mentioned, with a significant increase beginning in 1996. On a year-to-year basis, health and human services giving as a percent of corporate giving has never shifted by more than one or two percentage points.

Does this pattern apply to international giving? This is a difficult question to answer, as data do not break out neatly into categories that align with developing-nation aid portfolios. What is clear is that international giving is rising rapidly in many corporate sectors. Since 1987, the median annual international contribution of the United States has risen more than threefold, from $160,000 to well over half a billion dollars. Two-thirds of that giving is in health and human services, although data collection does not permit the examination of this ratio over the last three decades.

Do the last three decades predict the next three decades? The prognostication business is inherently risky. It is important to keep in mind a cautious warning of Deon Filmer, Jeffrey Hammer, and Lant Pritchett: "Answers to questions that do not begin 'it depends' mean that either the answer is wrong or the question was trivial." So, it depends.

Nevertheless, one has a certain level of confidence that past trends in corporate philanthropy stability will continue. Increasingly, corporate giving is being tied directly to corporate business expertise and interests. Hence, one would expect changes in corporate giving priorities where corporate business expertise changes. The focus (albeit not the exclusive focus) of the Sachs report is on partnerships, with the giving by international pharmaceutical and healthcare companies. A major change in priority, then, would be expected if these companies either (a) removed themselves from the healthcare business, or (b) abandoned international markets.

Is either eventuality likely? It depends. For example, for a pharmaceutical company to cease being a pharmaceutical company, it would either have to go out of business or become something else. Bankruptcy is certainly a known corporate destiny. But merger/acquisition (M&A) is a more typical outcome of financial difficulty, and M&A is common within the healthcare industry, in part because markets and patents are valuable to competitors. I am unaware of any company pursuing an alternative evolutionary fate, ceasing to produce healthcare goods and taking up, for example, the blue jeans business.

Are healthcare companies likely to abandon international markets? Nearly 60 percent of the market for U.S. pharmaceutical companies, for example, is outside the United States. Nearly 20 percent is in regions of the developing world. Few rational companies will wake up one morning and precipitously abandon 60 percent (or even 20 percent) of their business.

In conclusion, are those seeking to broaden coalitions for global health likely to see "corporate priorities change overnight?" It depends. Still, both past data trends and future scenarios would argue in the negative.

■ SOURCES

Altman, Daniel. "Diagnosis of World's Health Focuses on Economic Benefit," *New York Times,* December 21, 2001, Section w, p. 1, col. 1.

Filmer, Deon, Jeffrey Hammer, and Lant Pritchett. "Health Policy in Poor Countries: Weak Links in the Chain," Policy Research Working Paper, No. 1874, The World Bank, January 1998.

Giving USA, 2001. AAFRC Trust for Philanthrophy.

"Macroeconomics and Health: Investing in Health for Economic Development," World Health Organization, 2001.

Muirhead, Sophia A. "Corporate Contributions: The View from 50 Years," The Conference Board, Research Report 1249-99-RR, 2000.

Pharmaceutical Industry Profile 2001, Washington, DC: Pharmaceutical Research and Manufacturers Association.

Reflections on September 11, 2001

INTRODUCTION TO THE ISSUES

The essays in this section reflect some of the darkest days in this nation's recent history. The philanthropic outpouring in response to the terrorist attacks of September 11, 2001, was unprecedented. It was also not surprising. Anything less would have been alien to American culture. And, as the gifts poured into U.S. charities from around the world, it also appears that anything less is also alien to much of the world. One can hope that essays like these will never need to be written again. But life is unpredictable, and, as we have learned, full of hazard.

As throughout much of the nation's history, it was the average American who came forward. On the morning of September 11, 2001, 3,000 average people left for work or for long-planned trips, looked forward to the most exciting of days or the most uneventful of days. By noon that day, millions of Americans were reacting to the loss of those 3,000. And, by the time all the philanthropy was counted, it was individual Americans who stood again as the largest single source of philanthropic support.

EXHIBIT 8.1   SEPTEMBER 11 PHILANTHROPY BY SOURCE

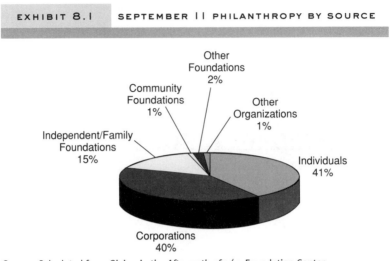

Source: Calculated from *Giving in the Aftermath of 9/11*, Foundation Center

There is little more to be said. There is much to mourn. And there is much of which to be proud.

SOURCE

"Giving in the Aftermath of 9/11," The Foundation Center, 2003.

Philanthropy Put to the Test

We all felt helpless. After the shock, after the horror, after the tears, we all felt helpless. We gave our blood, but even our blood was no longer critical. We gave our muscles, but soon even our hands and backs were sent home and the job was given over to professionals. Still we felt helpless.

After our prayers, which seemed the last (and still are perhaps the best) resort, we reached into the only remaining reservoir available to assuage the agony of our need to help. We reached into our wallets.

> "The only thing necessary for evil to triumph is for good men to do nothing."
>
> —Edmund Burke

The peoples of New York, New Jersey, and Connecticut, of Chicago, Atlanta, Los Angeles, London, Cairo, Moscow, Johannesburg, Tokyo, Sao Paolo—literally from thousands of towns, cities, villages, farms, households, and schoolrooms—reached into their wallets and gave. And gave. And gave. The weeks passed, and still they gave. Firefighters held out their boots in traffic for contributions, kids rode in bike-a-thons, veterans set up folding tables in front of shopping malls. And still they gave.

Since then, slowly, silently, ever so cautiously, the question is being raised: Now what? It whispers: Will our giving compromise our philanthropy? Will an outpouring of giving in the face of unspeakable evil supplant the philanthropic resource flows upon which so many nonprofits and charities rely for their services on the societal commons? Will a dollar in the firefighter's boot replace a dollar for cancer research?

It feels unseemly to be analytic in the face of horror, to give reasoned thought in the face of such unreasonable destruction. It seems trivial to worry about money amidst worries about war. Still, the question persists. Ignoring it will not make it go away.

Hence, I would make two observations, one about disaster and one about war. It strikes me that the outpouring of giving in response to the terror of September 11 will, in fact, not replace our national philanthropic traditions. Since that awful Tuesday, Americans (and our global neighbors) have given (and still give) from their wallets. They turned from their televisions and, through their tears, wrote checks. They drove to the grocery for milk and stopped at the firehouse with water and granola bars and five bucks. They went to school and sold ribbons and cookies to parents and teachers. The outpouring was spontaneous, unplanned. The source, by and large, was immediately available cash. No one took time to plan this giving. It had to be done, and it had to be done now.

> "The destiny of mankind is not decided by material computation. When great causes are on the move in the world ... we learn that we are spirits, not animals, and that something is going on in space and time, and beyond space and time, which, whether we like it or not, spells duty."
> —Winston Churchill, 1941

This is not how Americans usually give. They are selective in their largess. When they choose their philanthropic causes, they choose carefully and give generously. When the end of the year rolls around, the five bucks at the stationhouse, or even the thousand bucks from the bank account, will not replace the giving to organizations and causes that individual Americans have long supported out of tradition. Disaster will not supplant time-bound relationships between Americans and the charities they favor.

Which is not to say that there will not be a price. Corporations that allocate tens of millions of dollars to disaster relief may, indeed, find their philanthropic till a bit leaner when reviewing proposals for quotidian operational support by charities. The same will be true for large foundations, some of which have allocated excess funds to the disaster. The former is a problem. For the latter, the key word is "excess"; these are funds largely uncommitted or from discretionary accounts. The point is, normal giving portfolios have not been eroded by the disaster. Moreover, individual Americans represent 75 percent of charitable giving, and emergency giving out of immediate cash is not likely to impact greatly the annual philanthropic behavior of individuals.

The larger and longer-term question is whether a persistent war (either concretely against a particular foe or less concretely against the unseen foe of terrorism) will erode the philanthropic revenue streams upon which America's charities rely. A negative effect might flow from two circumstances: first, economic downturns common to wartime conditions, affecting both corporate giving and, if employment is affected, individual capacity; and, second, a redirection of individual giving away from domestic charities and to wartime needs.

With the markets in flux, judging the first of these circumstances is difficult. A significant downturn might affect total giving, but it is not clear that giving itself would turn away from the communities in which corporations operate and upon whom they depend for their workforce. Corporate philanthropy has always been bound up in local communities. A sense of solidarity in the face of war would likely reinforce, not erode, that tradition. As regards the second issue, if employment is seriously impacted, individual giving could fall (or be replaced with increased voluntarism), but its directions will not necessarily be affected. If communities suffer, the likely reaction would be for individual support of local communities. In

America, outside threats normally bind local institutions more tightly together; there is no reason to believe this would be less true because the enemy this time is faceless.

Is there any empirical evidence that would provide support to these views? Can we predict today and tomorrow from the experiences of yesterday? The data sets are poor, so conclusions must be offered cautiously. That said, looking at the Vietnam years, the last difficult, drawn-out, often-ambiguous war (at least in public opinion), there does appear to be some verification. Giving trends are like the stock market; point-to-point data are less revealing than trends over time. In the years between 1968 and 1973 (the beginning of a three-year recession), annual total giving increased by 6 percent in inflation-adjusted terms; individual giving increased by 9 percent. The one year of significant decline (3.7 percent between 1969 and 1970) was accounted for by a 16.6 percent dip in corporate giving, the largest percentage decline in the 30-year period 1968–1998. Organizationally in the 1968–1973 period, giving to public welfare and societal benefit organizations increased by 14 percent in real terms. Substantively, annual healthcare giving rose by 17 percent, although giving for human services programs, with a 4 percent increase, did not keep pace with the overall increase in giving.

If it is a long-term, often invisible, war upon which we as a nation are embarked, one can expect a sobering of philanthropy, marked not by declines but by modest growth. This is approximately what we have seen since September 11: growth of around 1 percent per year, with philanthropy as a percentage of GDP holding steady.

There is a deeper implication to be derived from all of this, as well. It is important to realize that maintaining philanthropic trends will rely heavily on the capability of nonprofits to make their case within the environment of national emergency and mobilization. Policy uproar and media attention, upon which many causes often rely for exposure, will not provide a convenient spotlight for their needs. The nightly news will focus on wartime issues and controversies, not on neighborhood drama. The local nonprofit may not be able to ride the coattails of the press.

This is not a bad thing, for it will require nonprofits to continue to evaluate their operations and position their services within more deeply felt societal needs, not the media-driven national "angst of the month." In the end, the need to articulate a forceful case deep within the philanthropic motivations of individuals will bear important fruit for us all, those who seek to give and make a difference and those we empower to act in our stead on the societal commons.

SOURCE

Data from Giving USA 1999 and 2003, AAFRC Trust for Philanthropy.

U.S. Diversity Creates Philanthropic Opportunity...and Risk

Despite the controversies over domestic legal policy after the September 11 attacks, we are and always will be a nation of immigrants. People will continue to move toward the beacon of freedom that stands in New York Harbor. Even reformed (one hopes, or at least permanently defeated) Afghan Taliban operative Mullah Amirjan Selabe told the *New York Times* on November 28, 2001, that his two priorities were to learn English and computers. Not that the Immigration and Naturalization Service will be approving a visa application from the Mullah anytime this century, but still the point is clear: Those who look to the future look toward opportunity.

In 1850, the U.S. Census Bureau estimated that immigrants represented 9.7 percent of the population. By 1920, that percent had risen to its all-time recent high of 13.2 percent. For the next half-century, the immigrant presence in the U.S. population dropped, to a low of 4.7 percent in 1970. But, by 2000, immigrants once again represented 11.1 percent of the population, nearly back to their levels of a century and a half earlier.

The nation takes pride in its diversity. It is, therefore, incumbent upon philanthropy to understand the cultural dimension of giving and volunteering that rests within the differing ethnicities and religions that make up an increasing portion of the American

EXHIBIT 8.2   IMMIGRANTS AS PERCENT OF U.S.
               POPULATION, 1850–2000

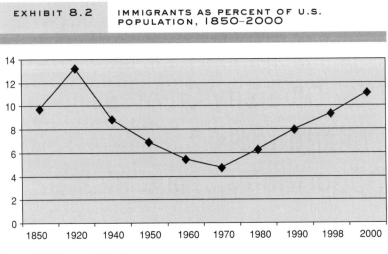

Source: U.S. Bureau of the Census

population. This could be the "growth sector" for American philanthropy over the next decade, and understanding what makes
giving and volunteering tick in it would be a wise investment of
time and effort.

And the cultural differences in perspective are not trivial. Let's
start with Islam, since that seems to be our national blindspot
right now. Mind you, I do not think it is our largest cultural blindspot, but it certainly is our most immediately salient. The caveat
in providing illustrations of the multicultural dimensions of giving and volunteering is obvious: The illustrations are based on my
admittedly limited knowledge. Thus, they are intended to under-
score the importance of understanding these traditions, not to
imply full knowledge.

Islam dictates two types of charitable giving. The Prophet
Mohammad advised that "charity is a necessity for every Muslim."
Zakat, which can be translated as "purification" is an annual alms
contribution, which must be paid on wealth as a condition of being
a practicing Muslim. To give alms is as central to Islam as declaring
one's faith. It is one of the Five Pillars of Islam, which are requisite
to all believers; Zakat is obligatory. Additionally, Sadaqa is the strictly
voluntary charity enjoined on all Muslims. Sadaqa is preferably given

anonymously. The U.S. philanthropic tradition of "naming opportunities" will not be attractive to Muslim charitable giving.

In Sikh culture, the word for volunteer service is "sewa." And while giving in the form of money is accepted, the highest form of giving is thought to be in personal service.

In the Parsi religion, Zarathushtra Spitama, one of the earliest prophets to teach monotheism, preached through the triple motto of "Good Thoughts, Good Words, Good Deeds." For the Parsi, some 5,000 of whom are resident in the United States, philanthropy and service are a mandate.

The list could go on. The point is that the diversity of cultures in the United States, and their growing presence in U.S. communities, provides an opportunity and a challenge for U.S. philanthropy. The opportunity is to meld American philanthropic traditions and institutions and cultural diversity, with a resultant resilience to address a wide spectrum of community problems across the entire patchwork of American society. The challenge is to adapt methods and institutions to the specifics of cultural perspectives and expectations.

Thinking through strategies for responding to these challenges is perhaps most well advanced in Canada. The development offices of many institutions there include cross-cultural subprograms to reach out to diverse communities for volunteers and fundraising. These programs tailor strategies to community preferences. The Volunteer Center of Calgary has even published a guide for such strategies, "Creating Bridges: A Practical Guide and Checklist for the Development of Cross-Cultural Volunteer Programs."

Now a word on the risks of reality. One need not pass judgment on recent national security concerns, nor on national concerns about the security of allies, to recognize that the diversity of the American population, and the cultural diversity of its philanthropic roots, raise complex risks. Even as they join the multicolored fabric of American society, immigrants retain their family, cultural, and religious roots to their home nations. This is not a new phenomenon; it has been true since the first Europeans set foot on these shores. Perhaps it was equally true for those who crossed the Bering land bridge millennia ago. With globalization, telecommunications, and international financial markets, the reality is clear. As the lawyers say, this is a true fact.

It is also true that this very interconnectedness of American philanthropy, across all manner of cultures and borders, entails risk. It is difficult to know exactly where funds flow and whom they ultimately benefit. By and large, no one pays it much heed. We are all, in many ways, free to give our philanthropic dollars to whomever we please—until and unless that flow threatens national security. And therein lies the problem: How will we know? And, if we can know, how will we gain that knowledge without compromising the very openness and diversity that makes this nation a global beacon to begin with?

The interplay of these two factors continues two years after September 11. Efforts to control and track philanthropic transfers overseas, borne of concern over national security, can constrain the good works of charities abroad that rely on U.S. support for their viability. There is an unmistakable price to caution, just as there is an unmistakable price to risk.

But life is full of risk. Some degree of risk must be accepted if we are to live other than in constant fear and isolation. But foolish ignorance of risk is deadly. With the free and open flows of philanthropic funds from all segments of an immigrant nation, where does risk cross over into foolish ignorance? This nation of immigrants, and its philanthropic and nonprofit leadership of all cultures and traditions, must face these questions head-on. It is time for philanthropies of all forms to call a caucus of leaders to acknowledge the risks in our global environment, and to provide realistic criteria and standards for policymaking that reflect both the openness of our traditions and the new realities of our world.

▧ SOURCES

Data from U.S. Bureau of the Census, 2002.

McClintock, Norah. "As Canada Becomes More Multicultural, So Does Its Voluntary Sector." *Front and Centre,* 1:2, 1996, pp. 14–15.

Strom, S. "Small Charities Abroad Feel Pinch of U.S. War on Terror," *New York Times,* August 5, 2003, section A, p. 8, col. 1.

Did September 11 Change Philanthropy Forever?

After two years, the scene from the viewing platform at Ground Zero in lower Manhattan is no longer one of devastation, but of rebuilding. Nevertheless, millions still come to see that hole, to remember what was or to imagine what must have been. No one has forgotten—but perhaps some have begun to ask what lessons have been learned.

In mid-2002, I was asked whether September 11 "changed philanthropy forever in this country." I hope not. September 11 revealed an ethic in America that is deeper than a single event, however horrific. There is a predisposition in this nation to step forcefully forward onto the societal commons when need is clear. The clearer the need, the more forceful the response. There are dozens of examples from the past two decades that this is so. Floods, earthquakes, even missing children in Utah have opened floodgates of both cash and voluntarism. Giving now tops $200 billion per year. This is not a one-time thing: this is a tradition.

"If to be venerated for benevolence, if to be admired for talents, if to be esteemed for patriotism, if to be beloved for philanthropy, can gratify the human mind, you must have the pleasing consolation to know that you have not lived in vain."
—George Washington, in a letter to Benjamin Franklin, 1789

That said, permit me to ask what I think is a more interesting question. By virtue of its size and devastation, did September 11 create a new perspective on the part of young people? Did the horror and helplessness of an entire people reach not just into their awareness, but into their sense of action so that it will create lasting behaviors? If so, then perhaps September 11 did not change philanthropy forever so much as preserve philanthropy for the next American generation.

Let me expand. I recall a picture from the days immediately following September 11. A young girl—perhaps seven or eight—had dressed up in her Irish step-dance costume, put a jar on a folding table in front of her house, and commenced to dance on the sidewalk for contributions to the relief fund. She dug deep down into her "asset portfolio" and put on the table everything she had—her dancing. Did September 11 and that experience of giving impress in her memory the importance of what she did? Did "doing something" become so overwhelmingly important to her in those days (as it did for all of us) that, when she is 37 or 38, she will have internalized her ability to "do something," hence make philanthropy a life-long matter of the heart? Which is, after all, what it should be. Did the carwashes, the flag sales, the cookie sales of all those nightmare days that followed create a wave of experiences for young people that will carry them forward more forcefully into a sense of their role in the larger need than would otherwise have been the case? For young people, did "me first" fall along with the Twin Towers? If so, then philanthropy was not changed, it was preserved.

A similar question can be raised about the generation of young professionals, whose ranks were diminished disproportionately on September 11. It has been said—although the data are mixed— that the young professionals of the "go-go 1990s" were (and still are) a self-absorbed, out-of-my-way-or-under-my-wheels group. I doubt it. But, to the extent that it is true, the question is whether the experience of loss and helplessness will provide a lasting memory of the importance of giving that will motivate young professionals to give as well as take. Again, if it does, this does not so much change philanthropy forever as provide a bridge for philan-thropy between that little Irish step dancer and her aunts', uncles', and grandparents' traditions of giving.

Unfortunately, none of the research that has been done asks these questions. Evidence abounds that September 11 giving did not supplant American giving; it was, by and large, new money. Whether it is one-shot new money is yet to be seen. If it is or is not does not change philanthropy forever either. However, if more of September 11 philanthropy came from young people, or younger generations, than traditional philanthropy has in the past, then per-haps we do have a phenomenon here—perhaps not a new phe-nomenon, but at least one that will ensure that two decades from now we will still have the luxury of asking "forever" questions about American philanthropy.

Index

A

AAFRC Trust for Philanthropy.
    See Giving USA
Aaron, J.J., 182
Abbott, Langer and Associates, 35, 133
Abelson, Reed, 19
Absorptive capacity, dilemma, 7–10
Abzug, R., 90
Academic medical system, philanthropy
    (relationship), 179–182
Academic R&D, support, 215
Accountability, 68. *See also*
    Nonprofit board of directors;
    Philanthropic accountability
    relationship. *See* Ethics
Accounting, 119
    compliance, 92
Adams, Abigail (quote), 188
Adams, John (quote), 78
Adams, R.J., 244
Adult deaths, estate tax returns
    (percentage), 141
Aeronautics products/companies, 271
Africa, tragedies, 79
African American households, income
    quintiles, 42
Aga Khan Development Network,
    239
Aga Khan Foundation, 237
Allen, Richard, 41–42
Altman, Daniel, 276
American Association for the
    Advancement of Science (AAAS),
    171
American Council of Fund Raising
    Executives, 162
American Council on Education, 198

American Express Company, global
    market value, 200
American Hospital Association, 157,
    166, 177
American philanthropy, status, 254
Anheier, H.K., 248
Annie E. Casey Foundation (UPS
    creation), 15–16
Annualized return on capital.
    See Thrift institutions
*A.P. Smith Manufacturing Co. v. Barlow,
    et al.*, 274
Apple Computer, sponsor, 267
Arenson, K.W., 85
Aristotle (quote), 21
Arnsberger, Paul, 66, 115, 128, 133
Art licenses, 127
Assets. *See* Foundation assets
    sale, 64
Assumptions, consequences, 95–99
Automobile manufacturers, 271

B

Bacon, Sir Francis (quote), 29, 136
Baker, Russell (quote), 150
Baker, Samuel, 177
Balanced Budget Act of 1997, 163
Bankruptcies, 276
    measurement, 48
Barrett, W., 133
Basinger, Juliana, 19
Bear Stearns, 137
Beard, Mariam (quote), 269
Beaudoin, Steven M., 154
Becker, M.M., 109
Behavior (stream), monetized value,
    65–66

Benchmarking. *See* Organizational
   benchmarking acceptance.
   See Nonprofits motivation.
   See Management
Beneficiaries, 43
Bequest. *See* Charitable bequests
   activity, 140–141
   size, 142
Bertelsmann Foundation, 247
Better Business Bureau of Metropolitan
   New York, 75
Billitteri, Thomas, 143
Blackwell, Elizabeth (quote), 156
Bloomberg, Michael (quote), 196
Blumenthal, David, 180, 182
Blumenthal, R.G., 227
Board of directors
   expectations. *See* Nonprofits
   independence, 93
   participation, distinction, 73
   responsibility, 71
Boris, Elizabeth, 62
Borkoski, Carey, 35
Boston University. *See* Social Welfare
   Research Institute
Bozzo, Sandra L., 244
Bradley, B., 90
Brousseau, R.T., 186
Brusa, M., 24
Budget
   deficit, 180
   presenting, 149
Budgetary overhead, 150
Buffett, Warren, 89
Bureau of Labor Statistics
   (U.S. Department of Labor),
   210, 211
Burke, Edmund (quote), 281
Business death, 47
Business media, watching, 78
Business operation, cost, 57
Business Roundtable, 75
Butler, Stuart, 143

C
Caffrey, Andrew, 20
Calhoun, Alexander, 31
California Endowment, 184
Camposeco, C., 120
Can do approach, 168
Canada/United States, philanthropic
   comparisons, 241–244

Canadian International Development
   Agency (CIDA), 237
Cannon, Carl M., 31, 129
Caripio Foundation, 247
Carnegie, Andrew, 27
Cash value trends, 96
Casper, G., 182
Catalogue of Philanthropy. *See* Generosity
   Index
Cause-related marketing, 128, 259
Center for Effective Philanthropy, The, 54
Center on Budget and Policy Priorities,
   124
Centers for Disease Control (CDC), 62
   Foundation, 60
Central Intelligence Agency (CIA),
   229–232
   analysis, 231
Central resources, 150
Charitability, learning (girl thing),
   209–211
Charitable bequests, 140
Charitable causes, 259
Charitable dollars, inflation-adjusted
   decline, 55
Charitable giving, 25
Charitable institutions, establishment, 152
Charitable managers, tax-exempt relations,
   131–133
Charitable philanthropy, 247
Charities
   business, 128
   gap, 159–162
   money, taking/making, 74
Charity, girls (affinity), 209–211
Choppin, Purnell, 168
Churchill, Winston (quote), 64, 84, 243,
   282
CIDA. *See* Canadian International
   Development Agency
Clark, P.A., 24
Cleverly, W.O., 166
Clolery, Paul, 268
Cobbs, L.S., 24
Coble, T.Y., 182
Cohen, Todd, 54
College Board, 191, 193
College costs
   increase, 191–193
   net price, average, 196
Colleges, minority students (percentage),
   195

Colvin, G., 24
Commager, Henry Steele (quote), 151
Communities
  benefits, 108
  facilities, 164
  foundations, 119
  wealth, 128
Community philanthropy. *See* Europe
  attracting, 188
  long-term commitment, 152
  relationship, 122
Company
  philanthropic priorities, 273
  priorities, 273
Compensation. *See* Nonprofit
  compensation
Competition, importance, 83–85
Competitive advantage, 107
Computer hardware/networking
  companies, 271
Conference Board, The, 268, 272, 277
Conference on Indigenous Philanthropy,
  237
Confort, J., 244
Confucius (quote), 274
Cook, W. Bruce, 31
Coolidge, Calvin (quote), 199
Coopers and Lybrand, 228
Coplin, W.D., 109
Core operations, 119
Corporate foundations, 8
Corporate giving
  pre-tax income, 270
  tax policy, 269–272
Corporate performance, disclosure, 73
Corporate philanthropy
  issues, introduction, 259–260
  netting out, 12
  recipients, 263
  relationship. *See* Global health
  trends, confidence, 275–276
  workhorse, 261–264
Corporate resources, 119
Corporate scandals, lessons/applications,
  91–94
Corporate strategy, 73
Corporations
  cash/assets, tracing, 223
  sponsors, 261
Cost accounting, 93
Cost-loading techniques, 120
Council for Aid to Education, 201

Council on Foundations, 94
Craven County Health Department
  Foundation, 59
Cross-cultural subprograms, 289
Cross-disciplinary opportunities, 215
Current reality, rank, 52

D
DAC. *See* Development Assistance
  Committee
DALYs. *See* Disability-Adjusted Life Years
Dana Foundation, 214
Darden School of Business Foundation,
  200
David and Lucile Packard Foundation, 51
D.C. Central Kitchen, 128
De Marco, Donna, 31
de Tocqueville, Alexis, 1
  (quote), 2
Death rates, 77
Decision-making criteria, 89
Delaney, Dennis, 31
DeSipio, Louis, 227
Desired future, rank, 52
Developing countries, U.S. resource
  transfers, 225
Developing nation effect, 227
Development assistance, U.S. involvement
  (percentage), 222
Development Assistance Committee
  (DAC), 221–222, 225
  estimates, 227
Dickens, Charles, 95, 99
Direct giving, cash/assets, tracing, 223
Disability-Adjusted Life Years (DALYs),
  183
Discretionary income, increase, 195
Diseases
  burden. *See* Industrialized nations
  foundations, grants (making), 170
  global burden, 183
  incidence, 77
  philanthropy funds, usage, 167–171
Diversity. *See* Governance
  profile. *See* Grants
Donations, double-counting, 91
Donor behavior, measurement, 223
Doris Duke Charitable Foundation, 214
Double-counting, 93
Dover, Sandra, 244
Drucker, H.M., 248
Due diligence, 256

Dugger, Celia, 44
Dwyer, C., 109

E
Earnings before interest depreciation and
    amortization (EBIDA), 165
E-commerce, impact, 7
Economic cycles
    problems, 65
    responses, 55–57
Economic downturn, 21, 64, 96
Economic growth, stakeholders, 89–90
Economic parameter, 21
Economic problems, resolution, 1
Edna McConnell Clark Foundation, 214
Education
    enrollment. *See* U.S. educational
        enrollment
    globalization, 233–236
    philanthropic giving, amount, 188
    philanthropy, 204
        relationship, 187–189.
        See also K-12 education
    power, 235–236
    room/board/tuition, average.
        See Undergraduate education
    voluntary support.
        See Higher education
Educational commitment, 206
Educational institutions, 3
    cash/assets, tracing, 223
Effectiveness metrics, usage, 174
Efficiency/effectiveness, expectations
    (increase), 105
Egodigwe, Laura Saunders, 20
Elasticities, 65
    variables, 63–66
Elderly population, percent change.
    See U.S. elderly population
Eller, M.B., 143
Ellison Medical Foundation, 214
Endowments, 193. *See also* Foundations
Enron Corporation, 71
    energy futures, trading, 78
    reality, 92
Entrepreneurial money/public scrutiny,
    combination, 97
Entrepreneurs. *See* Private entrepreneurs
Ericson, James D., 49
Estate tax returns, percentage.
    See Adult deaths
Estate taxes/giving, 139–143

Ethics, accountability (relationship), 67–69
Europe, community philanthropy,
    245–248
European Foundation Center Conference
    Report, 248
European nations, population decline,
    246
European philanthropy, outlet, 247
Expectations. *See* Board of directors;
    New York Philanthropic Advisory
    Service; Nonprofit board of
    directors; Organization for
    Economic Cooperation and
    Development; Philanthropists
    collision, 95
    conflict, 95
    directions, 96
    standard. *See* Philanthropy
Expenditures, 73
    contribution. *See* 501(c)(3)
External affairs, 119

F
Family income, grants (receiving),
    196–197
Fiduciary responsibility, 93. *See also*
    Owners
    breach, 74
Filmer, Deon, 275, 276
Financial accounting, integrity, 73
Financial oversight, 93
Finley, E.J., 244
501(c)(3), 112–115
    charities, 131. *See also* Tax-exempt
        501(c)(3) charities
    expenditure distribution, 132
    organizations, 112, 145
501(c)(9) category, 112
501(c) tax code category, 111
Five-state dominance.
    See Public charity revenue
Ford, Henry (quote), 261
Foreign born individuals (in U.S.), 44
Foreign students
    funds, source, 235
    (in U.S.), 218
Foreign-born residents, 43
Form 990, foundation filing, 200
For-profit facilities, 164
For-profit healthcare systems, 85
For-profit hospital corporations, 180
For-profit marketplace, personnel, 34

For-profit sector, regulatory/
  legal structure, 67
For-profit service providers, 85
For-profit status, 19
Foundation assets
  endowment erosion, 56
  growth. *See* Inflation-adjusted
    foundation asset growth
  size, percentages, 8
Foundation Center, The, 186, 207,
  264, 280
  database. *See* Mississippi State University
  grants retrieval system, 169
  philanthropy data, 62
  study. *See* Mississippi grants
  total U.S. philanthropic endowment
    base, 15
Foundation Directory, The, 10
Foundation Yearbook
  (The Foundation Center), 20
Foundations. *See* Communities; Corporate
  foundations; Independent foundations; University foundations
  annual income level. *See* Redundant
    post secondary school foundations
  board composition, 38
    female (religion), percentage, 38
  cash/assets, tracing, 223
  contributions, 64
  diversity, increase, 9
  endowments
    size, 15–20
    vulnerability, 15–20
  establishment/management, complexity,
    18–19
  funding, 170
  grants
    distribution, 118
    making, 159. *See also* Diseases
    portfolio, 53
  investment strategies, difference,
    200–201
  pools, 165
  preselection. *See* Grantees
  resources, 9
  risk-averse momentum, 53
  size, importance, 7–10
  support, attraction, 118
Fowler, Gener (quote), 148
Franciscan Sisters of the Poor Foundation,
  27
Franklin, Benjamin, 62

Friedman, Milton, 141
Friends of Litewska Children's Hospital,
  249, 251
Front-office management, 119
Frumkin, P., 2, 24
Fryes, B., 31
Frymoyer, J. W., 182
Funding percentage. *See* Total funding
Funding rationale, development, 147–150
Fundraising. *See* Private fundraising;
  Private philanthropy
Funds, individual investment, 224

G
GAO. *See* U.S. General Accounting Office
Gates Foundation, 265
Gender gap. *See* Philanthropic governance
Generosity Index
  (Catalogue of Philanthropy), 251
George Washington University, hospital
  sale, 180
GIF. *See* Group of Institutions
  Foundations and Enterprises
Gifts in Kind International, 265
Gifts in kind, 265–268
Giving. *See* Charitable giving; Individuals;
  International affairs; Private giving
  behavior, wealth (relationship), 242
  cash/assets, tracing. *See* Direct giving
  compromise. *See* Philanthropy
  pre-tax income. *See* Corporate giving
  tax policy. *See* Corporate giving
Giving USA (AAFRC Trust for
  Philanthropy)
  1999, 285
  2001, 277
  2002, 182
  2003, 99, 162, 189, 219, 272, 285
Global health, corporate philanthropy
  (relationship), 273–277
Global Trends 2015, 229, 231
Globalization. *See* Philanthropy
  impact, 246
Goodwill, 273
  increase, 151
  sales, 127
  transformation, 153
Governance, diversity/inclusion, 37–39
Government
  assistance, U.S. portion, 222–223
  challenges, 135
  connection. *See* Nonprofits

Government *(Cont.)*
  disaster assistance, 255
  grants, 63
  workforce (retiring), percentage, 136
Grameen Foundation USA, 237
Grant Makers in Health, 216
Grant per dependent student (average),
    family income level, 196
Grantees, foundation preselection
    (percentage), 12
Grantmakers, impact. *See* Societal
    dilemmas
Grantmakers for Effective Organizations,
    52, 54
Grants. *See* Unrestricted grants
  aid, diversity profile, 197
  monies, distribution, 204
  proposals, 150
  size, 184–185
    average, 171
Grants Committee, 27
Grant-writing process, 147–149
Greenfield, Karl Taro, 31
Gross domestic product (GDP)
  education, percentage, 187
  healthcare expenditures, percentage,
    155, 173
  philanthropy (percentage), 123, 245, 283
Group of Institutions Foundations and
    Enterprises (GIF), 238–239
Guidestar, 62, 88, 201
  database, usage, 145
  sampling. *See* University foundations

H
Haiti, political chaos, 255
Hall, Michael H., 244
Hammer, Jeffrey, 275, 276
Harvard University, 273
  health measures, 183
Hauser Center for Nonprofit
    Organization
    (Harvard University), 239
Health
  market, perfection, 23
  percent change. *See* U.S. economy
Healthcare
  cost-containment efforts, 159
  expenditures, 159
    distribution. *See* U.S. healthcare
      expenditures
    percentage. *See* Gross domestic product

funds, 156
future, 159–162
industry, 23
ranking, 250–251
relationship. *See* Philanthropy
resources. *See* Philanthropic
    healthcare resources
revenue, 126
state levels, 137
Healthcare philanthropy
  growth, 160–161
  rationality, 175
  task, 173–177
Hernandez, D., 45
Herodotus (quote), 52
Hewlett-Packard stock
  performance, 17
  value, decrease, 16
Higher education, voluntary support,
    192–193
Hippocrates, 155
Hispanic community, poverty rates, 42
HNW Digital, 142
Hoffman, M., 252
Hogar de Cristo Foundation, 239
Hospitals
  bond trends. *See* U.S. hospitals
  EBIDA-to-revenues rate, 165
  margins, decrease. *See* U.S. hospitals
  philanthropy, problems, 163–166
  sale. *See* George Washington University;
    Tulane University
  services, insurance reimbursements, 125
  specialty services, percentage.
    See Teaching hospitals
Household-directed nonprofits, 4
Households
  income, 140
    corporate presence. *See* State
    household income
    number, 43
    lower income limit, 42
Howard Hughes Medical Institute, 168
Human assets, 26
Human resources, 119
  management, hours-by-task basis, 117
  managers. *See* Nonprofit human
    resources managers
  staying power, 257
Human respect, moral response, 29
Huxley, Aldous (quote), 222
Hybridization, 90

I

IBM recipients, 267–268
Iglehart, J.K., 90
Immigrants
  minorities, 43
  percentage. *See* U.S. population
Immigration and Naturalization Service
  (INS), 287
Inclusion. *See* Governance
Income tabulations (U.S. Bureau of
  the Census), 45
Independent foundations, 8
  capital assets, 15
Indigenous philanthropy, 237–239
Individuals
  cash/assets, tracing, 223
  giving, 97
  initiative/behavior, impact. *See* Societal
    problems
  philanthropic behavior, 283
Industrial sample, profits/income, 271
Industrialized nations, disease burden, 184
Inflation-adjusted foundation asset
  growth, 16
Inflation-adjusted incomes, average, 192
Information technology (IT), usage, 88
Innovation Fund, 27
INS. *See* Immigration and Naturalization
  Service
Institute for International Education, 236
Institutional investors, growth, 89
Institutions, private industrial output, 4
Intel Science Competition, 187
Intellectual exchange, 234
Interlocking board rate, 39
Internal resources, dollar-value difference,
  197
Internal Revenue *Record*, 141
Internal Revenue Service, 61, 133, 143,
  145
  longitudinal data, 112
  requirement, excess, 18
  sample, 112, 114. *See also* Nonprofits
    statistics, 248
  study. *See* Tax-exempt organizations
International affairs, 225
  U.S. giving, 218
International aid, globalization, 222
International conflict, lessons, 253–257
International giving, 221–228
  pattern, 275
International grants, 226

International nongovernment
  organizations, growth, 230
International nonprofits, bequests, 224
InterNetwork, 267
Investment money, source, 88
Investor/investee, relationship, 26
Iraq, long-term philanthropic issues, 255

J

James, William (quote), 256
Jansen, P., 90
Jefferson, Thomas (quote), 174
Jelonek, A., 251, 252
John Hopkins University
  Center for Civil Society Studies, 138
  study, 25
Johns, M.M.E., 182
Johnson, B.W., 143
Jones, Absalom, 41–42
Jones, R.F., 182
Jordan, Barbara (quote), 88
Justice Department.
  See U.S. Department of Justice

K

K-12 education
  philanthropy, relationship, 203–207
  private philanthropy, contribution, 206
K-12 parents volunteer, 205
K-12 public education, 203
  dollar, distribution, 204
Kaplan, A.E., 193
Karatnycky, A., 24
Kellogg, W.K. *See* W.K. Kellogg
  Foundation
Kendizor, J., 120
Kennedy, John F., 52
Kim, M.T., 22, 24
Kline, Gil, 193
Knowledge
  decentralization, 7
  illusion, 111–115
  importance, 11–13
Koch, Ed, 37
Korn, Donald Jay, 20
Kosovo, problems, 255
Krakower, J.Y., 182

L

Langill, D., 186
Lasker Foundation, 167
Latin America, philanthropy (study), 238

Law School Foundation, 200
Lawrence, S., 120
Lawrence, Steven, 177
Leonard Davis Institute, 85, 108
Leonhardt, D., 49
Libman, Harvey, 35
Library of Congress.
    See U.S. Library of Congress
Licensing, revenue source, 126
Lies, acceptabililty, 77–81
Lincoln, Abraham (quote), 73, 255
Line-item budget, 149
List, R., 248
Local efforts, support, 61
Lopez, A.D., 186
Lord Tennyson, Alfred (quote), 78

M
MacArthur Foundation, genius
    grants, 53
Macpherson, Laura G., 244
Madison, James (quote), 233
Managed-care dollar, market-driven
    competition, 161
Management
    benchmarking motivation, 107
    problems, realities, 103
Manchester Man, 152
Maria Santo Domingo Foundation, 239
Markets
    management/survival, 55–57
    philanthropy, interference, 21–24
Mary Woodard Lasker Public Service
    Award, 167
McClintock, Norah, 290
McCormick Tribune Foundation, The,
    184
McCully, C.P., 5
Mead, C.I., 5
Mead, Margaret (quote), 238
measurement. See Official Development
    Assistance flow
Measurement-intense organizations, 30
Medicaid, federal expenditures, 173
Medicare
    federal expenditures, 173
    impact, 160
    margins, 163–164
    services, 163
Memorial Sloan Kettering, 85
Mencken, H.L., 97
Mental health nonprofits, 185

Mental illness
    health burden, 183–186
    philanthropic priority, 183–186
Meredith, Denise, 45
Merrill Lynch, assets, 17
Minority philanthropy, future, 41–45
Minton, Frank, 143
Mission statements, accountability, 77–81
Mission-driven nonprofits, 80, 89
Mississippi grants, Foundation Center
    study, 251
Mississippi State University (grants),
    Foundation Center database, 262
Moe, R.C., 90
Mohammed (prophet), advice, 288
Murray, C.J.L., 186
Mutual interest, partnerships, 98

N
NAE. See National Academy of
    Engineering
NAFTA nations, exchange (study), 235
NASDAQ implosion, 34
National academic R&D expenditures,
    214
National academic research funding,
    philanthropy (relationship), 213–216
National Academy of Engineering (NAE),
    60, 62
National Academy of Public
    Administration, 135, 138
National Association of Independent
    Schools, 207
National associations/conferences,
    macro-level, 99
National Bureau of Economic Research
    (NBER), 34–35
National Center for Charitable Statistics,
    103, 124
National Center for Education Statistics,
    198, 205, 207
National Council for Voluntary
    Organizations, 248
National Institute for Allergy and
    Infectious Diseases (NIAID), 171
National Institute of Diabetes and
    Digestive and Kidney Diseases, 171
National Institutes of Health (NIH), 53,
    171, 181, 214
    federal efforts, 215
    research funding, 222
National Science Foundation, 216

National Survey of Individual Giving
(Pakistan), 237–238
National Trust for Historic Preservation,
127
NBER. *See* National Bureau of Economic
Research
Need
defining/defending, 149
definition, disagreements, 175
Networking, 13
New American Alliance, formation, 43
New Jersey Supreme Court, 274
New philanthropy, 44
New York Academy of Sciences, 35
New York City, Nonprofit Sector, 48
New York City Nonprofits Project.
See Nonprofit Coordinating
Committee of New York
New York Metropolitan Opera, lawsuit,
97–98
New York Philanthropic Advisory Service
(NYPAS), 72
nonprofit expectations, 73
NGOs. *See* Nongovernment
organizations
NIAID. *See* National Institute for Allergy
and Infectious Diseases
Nicholson, S., 85, 109
NIH. *See* National Institutes of Health
Noncash corporate contributions, value,
267
Noncash corporate giving, 266
Non-corporate institutions, 224
Nondot-com philanthropic world, 27
Nongovernment organizations (NGOs),
230–231
growth. *See* International
nongovernment organizations
net grants, 221
Nonphilanthropic healthcare, 23
Nonprocurement line items, 266
Nonprofit board of directors, 83
accountability, 84
evolution, 74
expectations, 71–72
governance, 74
Nonprofit community, 231
Nonprofit compensation, 131–133
Nonprofit Coordinating Committee of
New York, 48
New York City Nonprofits Project, 56
Nonprofit credibility, core, 79–80

Nonprofit current receipts, 4
Nonprofit facilities, 164
Nonprofit funding, total resource base, 55
Nonprofit human resources managers,
135–138
Nonprofit income, sources, 63
Nonprofit institutions
public trust, 102
scrutiny, 68
transfer payments, 4–5
Nonprofit institutions serving household
(NPISH), 4
Nonprofit managers, change, 127
Nonprofit networks, 229
Nonprofit organizations
number, 102
percentage, 114
Nonprofit revenue, 125
composition, 126
predictions, 139
sources, 59, 64, 125–129
strategies, 126
Nonprofit sector
employment, percentage, 71
increase, 68
international scope, 229–232
problems, 108
Nonprofits. *See* Mission-driven nonprofits
balance sheets, IRS sample, 63
benchmarking, acceptance, 108
budget cycle, relationship.
See Philanthropy
current receipts, 5
definitions, diversity, 111–115
disappointment, 123–124
dominance. *See* Small nonprofits
economic importance, measurement,
3–5
expectations. *See* New York
Philanthropic Advisory Service
government, connection, 59–62
growth, 145–146, 230
industries, 33–34
infrastructure, 28
management dilemmas, 101–103
methods, change, 3–5
missions, 80
private industry output, percentage, 4
professional experience, vulnerability,
34
ROI, 74
savings behavior, 5

Nonprofits *(Cont.)*
services, sale, 65
shakeout, 47–49
small business trends, comparison,
47–49
state percentage, 146
status. *See* Organizational hybrids
stockholders, existence, 74
wages, 33–35
Nonurban philanthropy, 12
North American Industrial Classification
System, 4
NPISH. *See* Nonprofit institutions serving
household
NYPAS. *See* New York Philanthropic
Advisory Service

O
ODA. *See* Official Development Assistance
OECD. *See* Organization for Economic
Cooperation and Development
Official Development Assistance (ODA)
estimates, 227
flow, OECD measurement, 221, 223
O'Neil, Paul, 135
O'Neil, Tip, 185
On-lending (on-granting), 10
Organization for Economic Cooperation
and Development (OECD), 221.
See also Principles of Corporate
Governance
corporate governance framework,
72–73
enterprise expectations, 73
measurement. *See* Official Development
Assistance
Organization types. *See* U.S. tax-exempt
organization types
Organizational benchmarking,
management/performance
solutions, 105–109
Organizational goals, performance, 106
Organizational hybrids
fairness, 87–90
nonprofit status, 87–90
Organizational needs, 96
Organizations. *See* Sponsoring
organization
size/substance, 146
Orozco, Manuel, 228
Overlapping generations theory, 141
Owners, fiduciary responsibility, 74

P
Packard, David/Lucile. *See* David and
Lucile Packard Foundation
Parents, volunteer. *See* K-12 parents
volunteer
Parmegiani, Marcus, 244
Partnership for Public Service, 136, 138
Pasteur, Louis (quote), 168
Pauly, M.V., 85, 109
Peace Corps, involvement, 255
Pechura, C.M., 186
Performance
failure, 84
measurement, 105–106
objectives, 73
Permanent income theory, 141
Pharmaceutical Research and
Manufacturers Association, 277
Pharmaceuticals
cost escalation, 160
percentage, 163
Philanthropic accountability, 69
demand/risk, 51–54
Philanthropic cash, gift, 98
Philanthropic causes, 282–283
Philanthropic comparisons. *See*
Canada/United States
Philanthropic financial leadership, 23–24
Philanthropic funds, 262
Philanthropic governance, gender gap, 39
Philanthropic healthcare resources, 161
Philanthropic impact, evidence.
See Poland
Philanthropic inflation-adjusted dollars, 96
Philanthropic instinct, 59–62
Philanthropic investments, impact, 249
Philanthropic leadership, 153
entrants, 44
Philanthropic opportunity/risk (creation),
U.S. diversity (impact), 287–290
Philanthropic research centers, 94
Philanthropic strategy, importance,
253–257
Philanthropic support, 92
Philanthropic transparency, 69
Philanthropic wealth, competition, 80–81
Philanthropies
decision criteria, 123
tax-driven behavior, evidence, 140
Philanthropists
expectations, 101–102
tax-free status, 176

Philanthropy. *See* Community
philanthropy; Europe; Indigenous
philanthropy; New philanthropy
change, September 11 (2001) impact,
291–293
confidence, 2
democracy, relationship, 263–264
disease targets, examination, 168–169
economy, issues, 1–2
evaluation, 249
evidence/results, 147–150
expansion, 234–235
expectation standard, 98
flow, 199
funds, usage. *See* Diseases
future. *See* Minority philanthropy
gap, closing, 191–193
giving, compromise, 281–282
globalization, 239
healthcare, relationship, 155–157
importance, 205, 213, 233–236
increase, importance, 181
initiatives, 272
institutionalization, 152–153
interference. *See* Markets
international context, 217–219
international impact, 218
issues. *See* Corporate philanthropy
management, deficits, 121–124
minority leadership, 43–44
nonprofit budget cycle, relationship,
117–120
priority. *See* Mental illness
problems, 157, 173. *See also* Hospitals
ranking. *See* State deficits
rationale manager, role, 174–175
regulatory requirements, 52
relationship. *See* Academic medical
system; Communities; Education;
K-12 education; National academic
research funding
role, 181
growth, 171
root systems, history lessons, 151–154
sources. *See* September 11
status. *See* American philanthropy
success, 11
symbolism, 162
task. *See* Healthcare
tax-free status, 176
testing, 281–285
usage. *See* Venture philanthropy

Planned-giving mechanisms, 224
Pogrebin, R., 99
Poincaré, Jules Henri (quote), 215
Point-to-point data, 284
Poland, philanthropic impact (evidence),
249–252
Pot Bellied Pig Association Foundation,
16
Power, expectations, 68
Pretax income, definitions, 271
Prevention programs, donations, 61
Primary/preventive care, access, 23
Principles of Corporate Governance
(OECD), 72
Pritchett, Lant, 275, 276
Private entrepreneurs, 87
Private fundraising, 61
Private giving, 125
Private industry, funding, 213
Private overseers, 79
Private philanthropy, 156
access, 79
contribution. *See* K-12 education
fundraising, 61
growth, 59
importance, 214
minority stake, 204–205
success, 60
Private social benefit, 153
Private stockholders, influence, 83–84
Problems
defining/implications, 148
specificity, 215
Profit/not-for-profit distinction, 73
Program approach, defining, 148–149
Prospector's Choice (Taft Group), 11,
39, 264
Public charity, 145
revenue, five-state dominance, 242
total net income, 49
Public consciousness, 67
Public funds (allocation), budgetary
process, 60–61
Public overseers, 79
Public scrutiny, combination.
See Entrepreneurial money/
public scrutiny
Public trust, 61. *See also* Nonprofit
institutions
Public welfare, giving (increase),
284
Purchasing power parity, 243

R
Rader, P., 252
RAND Corporation, 201
Rationale manager, role. *See* Philanthropy
Raymond, S., 35, 252
Recipients, 25–26. *See also* IBM recipients
   capacity, 266
Redundant post secondary school
   foundations, annual income
   level, 201
Regulatory consciousness, 67
Reinsdorf, M.C., 5
Relationship resources, 150
Relationships, importance, 11–13
Religious groups, bequests, 224
Religious leadership, 38
Reporting systems, integrity, 73
Research philanthropy, problem, 215
Research-based universities, 200
Resource. *See* Central resources;
   Relationship resources
   distribution, 174
   flow. *See* Total resource flow
   accounting, 184
   poverty orientation/
   developing-nation orientation, 226
Results-based accountability, 52
Revenue
   inflation, 91
   sources. *See* Licensing; Nonprofits
   strategies, 127–128
Risk and Insurance Management Society
   (RIMS), 109
Robert Wood Johnson Foundation, 173,
   184
Rockefeller, John D. (quote), 28, 259
Rockefeller Foundation, 27–28
Rogers, Will, 65
Ruhm, Christopher, 35

S
Sachs, Jeffrey, 273
Saint-Exupery, Antoine (quote), 26
Salamon, Lester, 10
Salamon, L.M., 90, 248
Salvadoran American Health Foundation,
   239
Salvadoran Foundation for Health and
   Social Development, 239
Salvation Army, sales, 127
Samuelson, Paul A., 55
Schervish, Paul G., 141

Scholarship grants, usage, 194–198
Schumell, Donna Gardner, 154
Schwab, assets, 17
Schweitzer, Albert, 206k
Securities and Exchange Commission
   (SEC), 78
Selabe, Mullah Amirjan, 287
Seley, J.E., 49, 57
Self-governing processes, 71–75
Self-reliance, creation, 26
September 11 (2001)
   impact. *See* Philanthropy
   near-term difficulties, 219
   philanthropy sources, 280
   reflections, 279–280
Service
   providers. *See* For-profit service
   providers
   provision, cost-containing element,
   156
   revenues, 63
Shakespeare, William (quote), 13, 93, 106
Shapely, Peter, 154
Shaw, George Bernard (quote), 176
SIC. *See* Standard Industrial Classification
Sierra Club, 127
Signatory organization, 93
Silverman, L., 90
Similar organizations
   comparison, 109
   proviso, 106–107
Skepticism, creation, 80
Small businesses
   establishments, 47
   mergers, 48
   termination, rate, 48
   trends, comparison. *See* Nonprofits
Small nonprofits, dominance, 48
Small-scale innovation, 9
Smith, Adam (quote), 107
Smith, Craig, 268
Social benefit. *See* Private social benefit
Social enterprise, 128
Social goods, 73
Social services, decentralization/
   privatization, 95
Social value, production, 84
Social Welfare Research Institute
   (Boston University), 141
Socially responsible investment fund, 18
Societal benefit organizations, giving
   (increase), 284

Societal commons, 92
    citizen commitment, 231
Societal dilemmas, grantmakers (impact),
    37
Societal problems, 28
    individual initiative/behavior, impact,
        66
    resolution, 1
    resources, targeting, 39
    scrutiny, 80
Societal service, erosion, 231
Society, risk-takers, 53
Sokolowski, 248
Sommerfeld, M., 207
Spitama, Zarathushtra, 289
Sponsoring organization, 147
Standard Industrial Classification (SIC)
    subcodes, 270
State budgetary deficits, 121–124
State deficits, philanthropy ranking,
    122
State household income, corporate
    presence, 262
Steuerle, Eugene, 57
Stewardship
    importance, 83–85
    privilege/obligation, 83–85
Stockholders
    existence. See Nonprofits
    influence. See Private stockholders
Stone, A., 49
Strom, S., 57, 94, 99, 260, 290
Student aid grant, average, 197
Succession planning, 73
Sustainability, 26
Sympathy, importance, 253–257
Synergos Institute, 239

T
Taft Group. See Prospector's Choice
Tax income, forgoing, 22
Tax policy. See Corporate giving
Tax-exempt 501(c)(3) charities, 101
    income, 101
Tax-exempt organizations, IRS study,
    131–132
Tax-free status, privilege, 69
Teachers, wage gap, 34
Teachers Insurance Annuity Association
    and College Retirement Equities
    Fund (TIAA/CREF)
    nonprofit status, loss, 17–18
    ranking, 112
    tax-exempt status, 111
Teaching facilities, 164
Teaching hospitals
    sale, 180
    specialty services, percentage, 180
Telecommunications companies, 271
Thoreau, Henry David (quote), 226
Thrift institutions, annualized return on
    capital, 19
Thucydides (quote), 168
TIAA/CREF. See Teachers Insurance
    Annuity Association and College
    Retirement Equities Fund
Toepler, S., 248
Total funding, percentage, 169
Total net resource flow, change, 225
Total resource flow, 149
Trotter, Wilfred Batten Lewis (quote), 69
Trueblood, David, 139
Tulane University, hospital sale, 180
Turner, Ted, 226

U
Udall, Steward L. (quote), 68
Ueda, Dwight, 109
Undergraduate education
    (room/board/tuition), average, 192
Underground Railroad, 42
Underutilization, 23
Union of International Associations, 230,
    232
United Health Group, 252
United States
    diversity, creation. See Philanthropic
        opportunity/risk
    philanthropic comparisons.
        See Canada/United States
University foundations, 199–201
    Guidestar sampling, 200
    management, 16–17
University of Florida Foundation, 17, 201
University of Pennsylvania, 85, 108
University of South Alabama, University
    of South Alabama Foundation
    (feud), 18
University of Virginia, 200
Unrestricted grants, 118
Untruth, consequences, 80
Urban Institute, The, 103
Urban Institute Center on Nonprofits and
    Philanthropy, The, 115

U.S. Agency for International
  Development (USAID), 228
money, allocation, 10
U.S. Bureau of the Census, 10, 49,
  162, 228, 264, 290.
  See also Income tabulations
estimates, 287–288
U.S. corporations, contribution reporting,
  274
U.S. Department of Commerce, 226
  Bureau of Economic Analysis, 3
  estimates, 234
U.S. Department of Education, 189, 193,
  198, 201
U.S. Department of Health and Human
  Services, 60
U.S. Department of Justice, 78
U.S. Department of Labor. *See* Bureau
  of Labor Statistics
U.S. economy
  health, percentage, 160
  productivity, 102
U.S. educational enrollment, 188
U.S. elderly population, growth
  (age group), 161
U.S. Foreign Assistance Act of 1974, 231
U.S. General Accounting Office (GAO),
  136, 138
U.S. giving. *See* International affairs
U.S. Health Care Financing
  Administration, 162
U.S. healthcare expenditures, distribution,
  174
U.S. hospitals
  bond trends, 164
  margins, decrease, 164
U.S. immigrants, remittances, 226
U.S. Library of Congress, 62
  Trust Fund, 60
U.S. merchandise trade, inflation-adjusted
  value, 217
U.S. Office of Personnel Management,
  138
U.S. population, immigrants (percentage),
  288
U.S. resource transfers. *See* Developing
  countries
U.S. Small Business Administration, 49
U.S. tax-exempt organization types, 113

U.S. volunteer behavior, 119
U.S.-level compensation, reduction, 57
USA Group, Sallie Mae (merger), 15
USA Group Foundation, 15

V
Vanguard, assets, 17
Venture philanthropy
  impact-oriented extent, 30
  scalability, 29
  usage, 25–31
Venture Philanthropy Partners, 129
Verhovek, Sam Howe, 31
Voluntary support. *See* Higher education
Volunteer Center of Calgary, 289
Volunteers/volunteering/voluntarism,
  119–120, 169, 224
  behavior. *See* U.S. volunteer behavior
  increase, 283–284
  time, value, 101

W
Wall Street
  Blue Period, 55
  importance, 63–66
Washington, George (quote), 291
Wasow, Bernard, 143
Webb, N.J., 90
WebMD Foundation, 267
Weisbrod, B., 129
Wharton School of Business, 85, 108
Williams, D.J., 182
Winter, G., 198
W.K. Kellogg Foundation, 51
Wojciech, S., 248
Wolpert, J., 49, 57
World Bank, The, 120, 132, 133, 219, 276
  health measures, 183
  money, allocation, 10
World Health Organization, 252, 273, 277
  health measures, 183
World Wide Web, household connection,
  7
WorldCom, reality, 92
Worth.com study, 142

Z
Zakat, 288–289
Zellner, W., 49